River Cottage everyday

Photography by Simon Wheeler *Drawings by Mariko Jesse*

BLOOMSBURY

LONDON · NEW DELHI · NEW YORK · SYDNEY

For Marie, for every day

Hugh Fearnley-Whittingstall is an award-winning writer, broadcaster and food campaigner with an uncompromising commitment to seasonal, ethically produced food. He has been presenting programmes for Channel Four for over fifteen years, and this is the sixth River Cottage book he has written. His previous work includes *The River Cottage Cookbook*, for which he won the Glenfiddich Trophy, *The River Cottage Meat Book* and *The River Cottage Fish Book*, both of which won the André Simon Award, and *The River Cottage Family Cookbook*, which was the Guild of Food Writers Cookery Book of the Year. He writes a weekly recipe column for the *Guardian*. Hugh and his family live in Devon, a stone's throw away from River Cottage HQ, where Hugh and his team teach and host events that celebrate their enthusiasm for local, seasonal produce.

First published in Great Britain 2009

This paperback edition published 2013

Text © 2009 by Hugh Fearnley-Whittingstall
Photography © 2009 by Simon Wheeler
Additional photography © 2009 by Marie Derôme (pages 25, 330–1, 354)
Illustrations © 2009 by Mariko Jesse

The moral right of the author has been asserted

Bloomsbury Publishing Plc, 50 Bedford Square, London WC1B 3DP

A CIP catalogue record for this book is available from the British Library

ISBN 978 1 4088 0433 9

10 9 8 7 6 5 4 3 2 1

Project editor: Janet Illsley
Copy editor: Jane Middleton
Design: Lawrence Morton
Photography: Simon Wheeler
Illustrations: Mariko Jesse (www.marikojesse.com)

The text of this book is set in Avant Garde Gothic and Serifa
Printed and bound in Italy by Graphicom

www.bloomsbury.com/rivercottage
www.rivercottage.net

contents

introduction

Good food prepared from fresh ingredients – ideally seasonal and locally sourced – can and should be at the heart of every happy, healthy family kitchen. Yes, I genuinely believe that cooking from scratch (or with your own leftovers) is a possibility for everybody, pretty much every day. I realise, when so many of us are always in a hurry, and when easy access to fresh, local ingredients is not a universal privilege, that that's a controversial position. But I stand by my conviction, and I've written this book to show you how I think it can be done.

It often seems that we are something of a divided nation when it comes to food. A crude way of describing the divide is that we fall into two broad categories: those who care about food and those who don't. I have been accused at times of writing only for the first group or, to put it another way, of preaching largely to the converted. I can see why some would say that. I propose a degree of involvement with food – knowing and caring where it comes from, perhaps even growing some of it, or gathering some from wild places – that to many seems patently absurd. To some, I am 'that weirdo who eats anything'. Of course, to me, eating nettles, rabbits and suchlike makes perfect sense. It's completely normal. But it has been quite a journey for me to discover and embrace that kind of normality.

As a child, I was one of the fussiest eaters you can imagine. If it didn't come out of a Birds Eye packet and get fried up and served with ketchup, then I really wasn't that interested. So I have no qualms imagining that others can make journeys with food – even journeys they haven't yet imagined possible for themselves. In the twenty-odd years since I first became involved in the food business, I have seen entrenched attitudes to food, on the part of both stubborn individuals and monolithic institutions, shift massively. I've witnessed burgeoning excitement, enlightenment even, as more and more people get involved in cooking real food from fresh ingredients.

I've seen people's lives and family dynamics transformed by the discovery of good food and by a change of approach to acquiring and preparing food.

If you have watched any of the television programmes I've made over the last few years, you'll know I've spent a lot of time trying to persuade various people to change their way of shopping and cooking and to become more engaged with real fresh food. For the most part, I feel I've succeeded, at least to some degree. The individuals and families I've been growing and cooking food with are now, at the very least, a little more sceptical of ready meals, factory-farmed produce and anonymous, pre-packaged fare. Most of them have developed a determination to cook more with fresh ingredients and to make food a bigger part of their interaction with family and friends. But perhaps the most important thing is that all of them, I think it's safe to say, have had a good time. They've discovered how to cook ingredients they'd shied away from and how to get more out of foods they thought 'boring', and realised that some truly delicious meals can be thrown together from scratch in very little time at all.

The food media can only do so much to engage public interest in these issues. Luckily there are all kinds of other catalysts that bring about a change for good in people's relationship with food, and many of them can't be marshalled or predicted: a meal at a friend's house; a great dish encountered on holiday; a child coming home with something they've cooked at school; an unexpected gift of a fruit bush or veg plant. These can all kickstart a new and exciting future with food – one that turns out to be more accessible than you might have imagined. Buying your food becomes less of a chore, more of a pleasure, an adventure even, as you steer your trolley away from the ready-meals aisle and over towards fresh produce. Or perhaps start heading for the nearest farm shop rather than the supermarket. Suddenly it seems that your friends have discovered cooking too – though perhaps it's just that you are hearing the food-related content of their chatter when previously you were filtering it out.

That's why I think the 'us and them' view of our food culture is unduly simplistic. I see not two firmly entrenched camps who can never meet but rather a continuum, with those who are already thoroughly involved with the story of their food at one end and those who are entirely dependent on anonymous, industrially produced food, the origins of which are largely unknown to them, at the other. Everyone, and every household, has a place on this continuum. I see the main challenge of my work as helping people move along it in the direction

of more engagement with real fresh food, away from dependence on the industrial food machine. I believe it's a worthwhile enterprise for one simple reason: I'm convinced that a greater engagement with the source of their food makes people happier.

This book is my latest attempt to contribute to that happiness – by writing about the kind of food I eat at home, every day. I describe how bread, meat, fish, fruit and veg are dealt with in our house, how we juggle breakfast for three hungry school kids and how we sort out weekday lunches for two working parents. I reveal why so many of the meals we eat (including some of our absolute favourites) are made from leftovers. I try to show you how to put vegetables and fruit at the forefront of your family cooking, while eking out the most from precious foods such as meat and fish. I suggest ways to make entertaining at home less daunting, less expensive and altogether more fun. And I offer up the recipes I love to cook for my family – and those that, when I'm really lucky, they cook for me.

I make no prior assumptions about where you shop, what you may or may not know about growing vegetables or keeping livestock, whether you can tell the difference between a swede and a turnip, or know what to do with a belly of pork and a breast of lamb. Instead, I show you easy and confidence-inspiring ways with cuts of meat, types of fish and other ingredients you may not have tried before. And I offer you fresh approaches that I hope will breathe new life into familiar staples, such as rice, spuds, beans and your daily bread.

Above all, I intend to tempt you irresistibly towards a better life with food, with a whole raft of recipes that I think you will love. I hope some of them will become your absolute favourites, and the favourites of your dear friends and beloved family. I hope the dishes you like best will infiltrate and influence your cooking, giving you increased confidence and fresh ideas. In short, I hope that before long, cooking simple and delicious food from the best seasonal ingredients becomes second nature and first priority for you, not just once in a while, but every day.

A few of my favourite things

It's a truism that the quality and nature of your ingredients make all the difference to a finished dish, and I'd expect any cook worth their salt to choose the freshest, finest raw materials they can lay their hands on. However, there are a few staples to which personal preferences (or outright prejudice) also apply. The following basic store-cupboard ingredients appear time and time again in my recipes, so I feel they merit a little extra explanation – and, since I feel pretty strongly about their provenance, a little recommendation, too.

OIL

An entire book could be written about oils – I'm sure there must be several – but let me cut to the chase and tell you what you'll find in my kitchen. My general rule is to opt for organic and unrefined oils (the refining process can involve heating, the addition of solvents and even bleaching). Cold-pressed oil is also good because, while heating the seed or fruit increases the yield of oil, it affects the flavour and nutritional value, too. On the other hand, for deep- and shallow-frying you do need an oil that can be heated to a high temperature, and that usually (not quite always) means a refined oil of some kind.

Rapeseed oil Many British farmers are now producing this wonderful culinary oil, and I use a lot of it. Terrifically versatile, it has an incredible golden-yellow colour and a gentle, nutty flavour. Rapeseed oil is mild enough to use in mayonnaise but has enough character to contribute to a dressing, or to add flavour when trickled on to bread or soup. In addition, it's stable enough at high temperatures to be used for frying or roasting – though perhaps not prolonged deep-frying. I like R-Oil (www.r-oil.co.uk), produced in Gloucestershire, and The Seed Company Oil (www.theseedcompany.co.uk), which is produced in Dorset, and you may well be able to find a good one produced locally to you.

Olive oil I use quite a bit of olive oil but I don't worship it. I no longer use it much for frying or roasting; rapeseed oil has supplanted it as the first oil I reach for. I'm much more likely to use it for dressings and for general trickling, and even then only if it's that distinctive olive oil flavour I'm after. That might be in a classic vinaigrette or salsa verde, on sliced tomatoes or perhaps stirred into pesto. But these days it's always a conscious decision to reach for the olive oil, rather than an automatic one.

That means I'm happy to pay a bit more for a good organic extra virgin olive oil (extra virgin means the oil has a low acidity level and is guaranteed unrefined). I've been using a lovely organic oil from Clearspring recently (www.clearspring.co.uk; tel: 020 8749 1781), and it does all I ask of it. I don't dabble at the super-expensive end of 'luxury' olive oils – although once in a while, when someone gives me an exquisitely peppery, richly flavoured olive oil (usually Tuscan), I am reminded what all the fuss is about.

Sunflower oil This is a very lightly flavoured oil with a high burn point, which makes it ideal for general frying, including deep-frying. This is one case where I definitely wouldn't choose an unrefined oil, as the flavour would be too strong and it would most likely be adversely affected by the heat, but I do usually opt for organic and/ or Fairtrade. I like Clearspring's organic sunflower frying oil (see olive oil, above, for contact details). After using for deep-frying, sunflower oil can be recycled, by straining through a coffee filter or cotton cloth (when completely cold) and re-bottling. Don't leave it sitting round in the saucepan or deep-fat fryer, or it will go stale and impart a rancid flavour to the next batch of fried goodies. Groundnut oil is a good substitute for sunflower where a neutral frying oil is needed.

Hempseed oil Hemp oil is the Marmite of the culinary oils: you'll love or hate its pungent, grassy, throaty flavour. I love it. Its intensity means it compares to the very best olive oils, and makes a great trickling and dipping oil. It's full of goodness – loaded with omega fatty acids, which arguably give it the best nutritional profile of any raw culinary oil. It can be grown in the UK, and I particularly like Good Oil, produced by Braham & Murray (www.goodwebsite.co.uk), which I use on my breakfast toast and in a number of pestos.

VINEGAR

Vinegar (literally *vin aigre*, or 'sour wine') is a crucial part of my cooking repertoire, as indispensable as lemon juice when it comes to balancing flavours. I use it almost every day, mostly in dressings and mayonnaise but also when roasting vegetables, in sauces or marinades, or to deglaze the pan after frying meat. English cider vinegar is the type I turn to most, because it is fruity and robust but not overpowering (white wine vinegar is a perfectly good alternative, if that's what you happen to have in the cupboard). One of my favourite brands is Aspall (www.aspall.co.uk; tel: 01728 860510); their organic cider vinegar is pretty much a permanent fixture at home and in the River Cottage kitchen. I should make special mention of Aspall's English apple balsamic vinegar too, which is an aged blend of cider vinegar and concentrated apple juice. Dark, thick, rich and complex, it makes an excellent alternative to traditional Italian balsamic vinegars, which can be a little melodramatic and over-oaked for my taste.

FLOUR

I like my flour stoneground if possible, as traditional stone grinding involves less heat than modern steel-rolling techniques, thereby preserving more of the grain's goodness. Wholemeal is more likely to be stoneground than white.

Different flours vary enormously, not only in quality but in their colour, consistency and the way they absorb liquid. When you're making bread, pastry or batters, you should feel confident in adjusting the quantity of flour or liquid to reach the consistency you think is right. Note also that wholemeal flour tends to absorb more water than white, so you might need to increase the fluid content if you're converting a recipe from white to brown.

White and wholemeal flour (general purpose) If I need plain white flour, then I favour one that's produced from organically grown wheat. Doves Farm (www.dovesfarm.co.uk; tel: 01488 684880) and Marriage's (www.marriagesmillers.co.uk; tel: 01245 354455) are both trusty, widely available organic brands; Doves Farm also makes a gluten-free flour. However, I'm increasingly turning to wholemeal flour in order to make our everyday meals more wholesome – I like its toasty, wheaty flavour, too.

I've found there are few traditional 'white' recipes that can't be adapted to contain at least some wholemeal flour – a half-and-half blend of white and wholemeal is often very successful. I use a fine-milled organic wholemeal flour (such as Doves Farm's Fine Wholemeal or Marriage's Light Brown) for pastry, batters and the like. Both companies also make a self-raising version of these flours, which works well for cakes, muffins and drop scones. I'll happily knock out a Victoria sponge using this type of flour: the result is very nearly as light and fluffy as you get with white flour but with a lovely, nutty flavour that I actually prefer.

Strong flour This is what you should use for most bread recipes. It is milled from a particular type of wheat that is high in gluten, the substance that helps bread form the correct stretchy texture. Again, Doves Farm and Marriage's (see white and wholemeal flour, above) are good sources.

Spelt flour A grain I'm very fond of, spelt is an ancient type of wheat with a distinctive nutty flavour. Since it's being grown organically in the West Country by Sharpham Park, I also see it very much as a local ingredient. It differs from conventional wheat flours in that it contains a more delicate kind of gluten, which some people find more digestible. Wholegrain spelt flour makes very good bread, and can also be used in cakes and even pastry – or use the refined 'white' spelt if you fancy something lighter. These and other spelt products – including pearled spelt, an alternative to pearl barley – are available online from Sharpham Park (www.sharphampark.com).

SALT

Top-quality sea salt – sweet, flaky and fresh tasting – is an essential part of my everyday cooking. It differs from rock salt in that it's harvested from the open sea by traditional evaporation techniques rather than being pumped out of the ground. Fewer of its natural minerals are stripped away and fewer unnatural things, such as anti-caking agents, added. It also tastes much better – do a comparative tasting and I think you'll agree. Maldon Sea Salt is a kitchen classic of long standing but I also really like the newly available Cornish Sea Salt (www.cornishseasalt.co.uk; tel: 0845 337 5277).

There are times when a fine-grained salt is more appropriate than a coarse, flaky one – when seasoning a delicate cake batter, for instance. In addition, if you need to use salt in large quantities – when mixing up a cure for pork chops, say – using top-notch flaky salt would be rather extravagant. In these circumstances, I still opt for sea salt but a fine-grained type – you'll find it at any good deli or health-food shop.

PEPPER AND OTHER SPICES

Spices remain exotic ingredients – precious, fragrant substances that must be imported from regions of the world more lush and tropical than our own. These days, it's easy to find excellent examples, grown in a way that's respectful to the environment – and traded in a way that's respectful to the grower, too. Fairtrade and organic spices are available in many supermarkets and delis but it's online that you'll find the greatest variety – try www.steenbergs.co.uk.

Black pepper is so ubiquitous that most of us don't give it a second thought, but try a few different varieties and you might be surprised at the way their flavour and heat vary. Wynad peppers, for instance, are fragrant and warm, while Penja berries are incredibly hot. A specialist such as www.thespiceshop.co.uk is the place to go for pepper perusal.

Wherever your spices come from, certain rules apply: once ground, they lose their flavour and fragrance surprisingly fast. If you can buy whole spices and grind them yourself, you'll get much more bang for your buck. Find the time to dry-roast them gently in a frying pan before pounding them in a pestle and mortar and the results will be even more pleasing.

DRIED FRUIT

Sultanas, raisins, prunes, figs and dried apricots are store-cupboard essentials in my book (and in my kitchen). Foreign in origin they may be, but they are key to all sorts of British dishes, sweet and savoury. I choose organic where I can and also, as with many imported foods, Fairtrade if it's available – which, for dried fruit, it often is.

Many dried fruits – raisins, sultanas and currants in particular – have vegetable oil added to stop them sticking together. I see this as a pretty benign additive but one I'm less sanguine about is sulphur dioxide (E220) – used to preserve a fresh, bright colour. You're most likely to find it in dried apricots: if they're bright orange, you'll know sulphur has been used. This chemical also halts the natural oxidation process in the fruit, which is why sulphured apricots taste less rich, complex and toffeeish than the unsulphured variety. They've got a bit of a sherbety 'fizz' to them, which some people like. But I'm afraid it's the E220 you're tasting there. I prefer the natural, mellow, caramel flavour of organic, non-sulphured fruit.

Dried fruit in general, and apricots, prunes and figs in particular, are much more luscious, soft and juicy than they used to be. However, if you find yourself with a dry, tough batch, soaking the fruit in liquid (water, tea, freshly squeezed orange juice or a hefty slosh of alcohol) – particularly if it's hot – will soon plump it up.

I get most of my organic dried fruit from my local health-food shop, Ganesha, in Axminster, but I also like the Crazy Jack organic brand (www.crazyjack.co.uk), which is widely available in supermarkets.

BREAD

You'll see from the Daily Bread chapter just how passionately I feel about the importance of good bread. A robust, well-flavoured, crusty loaf brings so much more to a meal than a cotton-woolly, flabby bit of sliced white. I am now a total convert to sourdough, and I use it not only for my daily toast, sandwiches and general meal-accompanying needs, but also for breadcrumbs, croûtons and various other stale bread applications.

I realise that not everyone has access to good sourdough (though you can easily make your own – see page 66), and also that not everyone loves its tangy flavour and hearty texture. But I would nevertheless urge you to seek out a source of good bread – bread that does not dissolve on the tongue and go stale in 12 hours but that has flavour, texture and longevity – not just for these recipes but for every time you need a slice or two. You can find some good bread in supermarkets but it's the exception rather than the rule, because most supermarket bread is made using modern, industrial methods and ingredients. An artisan baker's is a far better bet, or a health-food shop, a farmers' market or farm shop.

STOCK

A good savoury broth, home-cooked from meat bones, herbs and aromatic vegetables, is a precious thing in the kitchen (see the recipes on pages 192 and 196). But I know it's unrealistic to expect everyone to have a pot of stock on the go at all times. I certainly don't. When I need stock instantly, I have various options. The ten-minute vegetable stock (on page 266) is an excellent solution to the no-stock situation (as long as you've got a carrot, an onion and a bay leaf available, you're in business – a couple of sticks of celery would be ideal, too).

Failing that, or if I'm really in need of a meatier brew, ready-made fresh liquid stocks, like Joubère's excellent organic chicken stock (www.joubere.co.uk; tel: 01293 649700), are the best replacement for home-made. Like all 'fresh' stocks, the best place to keep them for more than a day or two is in the freezer. But I am no stranger to the stock cube – Kallo Organic being the one I use most frequently. Kallo does a yeast-free vegetable stock, which is the first I reach for if I'm knocking up a soup, super-quick. Be aware, though, that cubes, pastes, granules and other concentrated, ready-made forms of stock are usually quite salty, so you'll need to adjust the seasoning of your dish accordingly.

CHEESE

I'm not about to tell you which cheeses you should eat – though I can give my opinion that you rarely need to look outside the British Isles or, often, outside your own county, for a good cheese, whether you want something hard, soft, semi-soft, mild, strong, blue, mould-ripened etc. However, I would like to let you in on what I personally find to be indispensable when it comes to cheese for cooking, as opposed to just sitting down and eating.

Instead of Parmesan I tend to use a hard, matured goat's cheese. Capriano, made by Woolsery in Dorset (www.woolserycheese.co.uk; tel: 01300 341991) has the same salty, granular texture and exquisite seasoning potential as Parmesan. Woolsery also produces soft, fresh goat's cheeses that are ideal for making cheesecakes (see page 44) or for mixing with herbs and other seasonings.

Ticklemore goat's cheese and Cornish Yarg are two semi-hard cheeses that I like to slice and crumble over salads (like the one on page 294). Ticklemore produces a Cheddar-style cheese, too.

If I cook with Cheddar or a similar hard cheese, then it's really got to be a mature one, otherwise the flavour just doesn't carry. But you don't always need one that's tangy to the point of making your eyes water. One of my favourites is Westcombe, made near Shepton Mallet in Somerset.

Blue cheese frequently finds its way into my cooking. I tend to forego the pungency of Stilton in favour of something a little sweeter and creamier, such as Dorset Blue Vinny. I'm also a massive fan of the wonderful Harbourne Blue goat's cheese.

All the cheeses mentioned above are available online from West Country cheese specialists, www.thecheeseshed.com.

OTHER STORE-CUPBOARD ESSENTIALS

It's a sad and sorry day when a scan of my larder doesn't show up at least some of these tried and tested standbys:

Organic tinned tomatoes and passata
Combined with nothing more than garlic, chilli and seasonings, these can turn no-supper into Yo, Supper! They can also be an alternative to stock in a soup or curry and are generally indispensable. Tinned tomatoes are chunky, of course, whereas passata is a smooth, sieved purée.

Dried pasta
We all have our own preferences when it comes to pasta shapes but one of my favourites is risoni, also known as orzo, which is available from delis. Shaped like fat grains of rice, it has a wonderful texture and is particularly good in soups and for soaking up sauces. I often make a 'risoniotto' (much quicker than a proper risotto) by simmering risoni in stock and adding sautéed onions and a few leftovers – cold fish or meat, grated cheese, wilted greens, etc.

Dried and tinned pulses
We eat lentils – usually nutty little Puy lentils – at least once a week. They are quick to cook (no soaking), absorb sauces and dressings deliciously and are packed with protein. I also keep chickpeas to hand, plus white beans such as cannellini. I prefer to use dried ones, soaking and cooking them from scratch, but I'd be lying if I said I always have time to do this, so I keep some organic tinned ones (usually the Suma or Essential brands) as well.

making breakfast

I've called this chapter 'Making Breakfast' to emphasise a point.

The great British breakfast is in danger of becoming moribund, suffocating under a tower block of cereal boxes or being sidelined altogether by those branded bars you're supposed to pick up at the newsagent's/service station with your morning paper (I remember when Alpen was a muesli, not a chocolate bar).

Now I'm not about to overwhelm you with recipes for a grand, heart-stopping Edwardian breakfast of devilled kidneys and kedgeree followed by a sideboard of cold meats and pickles. And I hesitate to trot out the mantra that breakfast is *the* most important meal of the day because it's such a tired cliché that it almost seems to provoke the protest of skipping it altogether. I'd rather combine cherished tradition with some sound modern nutritional knowledge and say that breakfast is simply an unmissable opportunity to start the day well.

Of course, not everyone has the same appetite for breakfast, or indeed feels the same way about breakfast from one day to the next. What is required is a modest but effective breakfast repertoire that covers the needs of the whole family on a daily basis, and also allows for special-occasion or weekend breakfasts when everyone has a little more time. And that's what I'm aiming to provide here.

On weekdays at home, we like to factor in just a little more time for breakfast than I suspect may be made available in many family households. Whilst we're still juggling with the usual chaotic rigmarole of unfinished homework, misplaced footie boots and attempts to shirk morning hygiene rituals, we try to make sure there's always time to make porridge or pancakes, or a soft-boiled egg with toast soldiers, as well as to squeeze some juice from a few oranges (or, in the autumn, from our own apples).

One of the best ways to make this work is to get the children involved from an early age. Easy breakfast dishes are the perfect nursery slopes for young cooks, and a little coaching of junior members of the household so they can do their bit at breakfast soon becomes a great asset to the whole family. Show them how to prepare their own favourite breakfast dish and before long they can take responsibility, once in a while, for dishing it up for the rest of the gang too.

Oscar, ten, can now knock out pancakes from scratch for the whole family, in about half an hour flat (well, they are pancakes). That's just as well, because we probably have pancakes for breakfast at least once a week. Chloe, twelve, makes wonderful porridge, and can fix anyone an egg or two just about any way they like it. Freddy's only six but he's very good at doing tomato toast and oily toast (see page 54), sometimes without getting either tomato or oil on his school shirt.

One strategy for taking the heat and rush out of weekday family breakfasts is to do a little basic prep the night before. Nothing too strenuous. But if you knock up a pancake batter and stick it in the fridge, then the job of the designated flipper the next morning is plain sailing. Similarly, pre-soaked porridge using pinhead oatmeal (see page 37) practically makes itself in the morning. And a ready-made fruit compote (see pages 339–44) chilling overnight in the fridge is at least half a breakfast waiting to happen.

On a Saturday or Sunday morning I love a pair of eggs on toast or a nice pile of creamy scrambled eggs with mushrooms or smoked salmon, but I'm pretty much a fruit and grains man during the week. Having said that, I certainly won't say no to a pancake or two, and if we've got a good fruit compote/salad on the go – perhaps rhubarb or apple in the colder months or macerated berries in the summer – I'll often have it with some yoghurt, and maybe a sprinkling of muesli or wheat flakes on top of that.

Fads for smoothies and the like come and go in our house; currently it's strawberry season, and I'm on an almost daily dose of strawberry and mint smoothie (page 28).

And so you can see that some form of fruit pops up on our breakfast table more days than not, which is clearly a good thing and should satisfy the phantom nutritionist whispering in our ear. But it's also life-affirming in a subtler way. A handful of summer berries for breakfast, or a tangy, crunchy autumn apple, a sweet juicy winter pear, or a bowl of tart poached or baked spring rhubarb, means that you head out of the house not just knowing what day of the week it is, but also what time of the year it is. Call me seasonally sentimental, but I think that counts for a lot.

Talking of heading out of the house, there's no getting away from the rushed start-to-the-day, and resulting missed breakfast syndrome, in some households. But that doesn't make the corner shop or the station buffet the right place to sort out the missing calories. A peanut butter and banana sandwich, plus an apple, is a genuinely delicious and actually pretty well-balanced portable breakfast. And the honey and peanut butter booster bars on page 39 will beat any branded so-called breakfast bar every time.

Although first thing in the morning is not the obvious time to be thinking of leftovers, in our house breakfast certainly begs, borrows and steals from other meals (and other chapters in this book). Our breakfast toast is usually made from our home-made sourdough loaf (page 66) and if it's second- or even third-day bread then it's none the worse (and quite possibly all-the-better) for that. The same goes for eggy bread – that lovely, substantial breakfast dish where pancakes and toast collide. And if ever an oversight leaves us breadless at breakfast, I'll soon be raiding the larder for oatcakes, home made (see page 87) or otherwise.

Personally I really like something a little sweet and a little sharp on the morning palate – but not too greedy or cloying. So any leftover apple or rhubarb crumble (see page 358) will make an appearance and usually disappear before any other options have even been discussed. Granted, it's more likely to get a dollop of yoghurt than custard or cream. Unless of course, there's some leftover custard or cream… By the same token, I wouldn't actually bake a sponge or fruit cake for breakfast, but if a home-made cake happens to be knocking around, I wouldn't hesitate to put it on the table as an option, though I might insist on some fresh fruit as a virtuous counterbalance.

If breakfast at the Fearnleys is starting to sound a bit lawless and outré, then I'm fine with that; because, so often, for so many, it's become the meal most hidebound by convention and tradition. But why is that? Perhaps it's because breakfast was the first of all our mealtimes to fall victim to industrialised food production and the seductive pressures of convenience consumerism. I understand that the box of cereal is a time-saving device that few modern families, including mine, would wish to abandon altogether. But do those multinational corporations who manufacture such products actually have to own our breakfast? Of course not!

So let's reclaim breakfast as an actual meal, and not just a calorie delivery system. Let's find things to savour and share that don't just fill us up, but make us feel good. And if we must squabble at breakfast time (it's in the DNA of most families, isn't it?) then let's cross spoons over the last strawberry or pancake, and not just scrabble for the plastic toy at the bottom of the cereal box. Then we can tackle the adventure of the day ahead with something good and wholesome and home made inside us. You can call it breakfast, or you can call it love.

Seasonal smoothies

I'm sure I'm not the only parent who gives thanks for the advent of the smoothie – an irresistible and fun way to funnel fresh fruit into otherwise reluctant children. Smoothies can be great for fruit-shy adults too, packing a satisfyingly high dose of goodness into a single glass.

The following recipes are mere guides; you can, and should, tailor-make your smoothie to suit your taste and mood – and, of course, your fruit bowl. Be led by what is seasonally available, add lemon juice to reduce sweetness, yoghurt for more creaminess or oats to make your smoothie a thickie – whatever floats your boat.

The best way to ensure your smoothies are nice and cool is to chill the ingredients beforehand. Alternatively, add two or three crushed ice cubes, though they will slightly dilute the fruit.

SPRING
Rhubarb and orange smoothie

Serves 2

2–3 rhubarb stalks, about 175g, cut into 2cm lengths

Finely grated zest and juice of 2 oranges

3–4 teaspoons honey

3–4 tablespoons plain yoghurt

Put the rhubarb in a pan with the orange zest and juice, honey and 2 tablespoons of water. Stir over a low heat until the honey dissolves. Cover the pan and stew the rhubarb very gently for about 8 minutes, until it softens. Add a little water if it starts to look dry. Switch off the heat and leave to cool completely. (You can, of course, prepare the rhubarb a day ahead and keep it chilled overnight.)

Put the rhubarb mixture in a blender with the yoghurt and whiz until smooth. Taste and add a little more honey, if you like. Pour into 2 glasses and drink straight away.

SUMMER
Strawberry and mint smoothie

Serves 2

300g ripe strawberries, hulled

4 tablespoons plain yoghurt

2 teaspoons finely chopped mint

1–2 teaspoons honey or sugar

Whiz the whole lot in a blender and serve straight away.

SUMMER
Peach Melba smoothie

Serves 2

2 handfuls of raspberries

2 large ripe peaches or nectarines, peeled, stoned and quartered

A small glass of freshly squeezed orange or apple juice

1–2 tablespoons honey

1 teaspoon vanilla extract

Put everything in a blender and whiz together until smooth. Serve immediately.

VARIATION
Apricot and raspberry smoothie
Use 4 ripe apricots in place of the peaches.

LATE SUMMER/AUTUMN

Dan's breakfast juice

This concoction from River Cottage baker Dan Stevens sounds weird, but tastes great. You do need a proper juicer to make it.

Serves 2

1 apple
1 pear
1 banana
1 carrot
2 celery stalks
½ beetroot, peeled
2cm piece of fresh ginger, peeled
2 or 3 sprigs of parsley

Ideally, chill all the ingredients in the fridge for an hour or two before you juice them.

Simply switch on your juicer and feed all the ingredients through. For a richer, thicker drink, don't juice the banana but place it in a blender, pour the other juiced fruit and veg over, then whiz.

Serve straight away and feel the goodness flow through you.

AUTUMN

Pear and cinnamon smoothie

Serves 2

2 very ripe pears
250g plain yoghurt
1½ tablespoons maple syrup or honey
1 teaspoon ground cinnamon, plus a little extra for sprinkling
1 teaspoon lemon juice
1 teaspoon grated fresh ginger

Peel, halve and core the pears and cut into chunks. Put into a blender with all the rest of the ingredients and whiz until smooth.

Pour into 2 glasses and serve with a little more cinnamon on top, if you like.

WINTER

Banana and oat thickie

Serves 2

2 ripe bananas
300ml ice-cold milk (or half milk and half yoghurt)
2 tablespoons porridge oats (not jumbo ones)
2 ice cubes

Put all the ingredients in a blender and whiz until smooth.

Honey-baked rhubarb

Rhubarb, I confess, is one of my very favourite fruits (though to be accurate, it's actually a vegetable with an identity crisis). I never tire of finding new ways to enjoy it. This sweet and fragrant breakfast compote is a fairly recent discovery and I absolutely love it.

Try it on eggy bread (page 47) or perfect pancakes (page 43), or spooned on to your customised muesli (page 34) or thick yoghurt. Alternatively, serve with vanilla ice cream for a pretty pud.

From January till early April, you can buy elegant, slender stems of indoor-grown 'forced' rhubarb. This gradually gives way to the thicker, darker, more robust outdoor-grown crop. Either will work in this recipe.

Serves 6

1kg rhubarb, cut into 5–10cm lengths

Juice and finely grated zest of 1 orange

4 tablespoons runny honey

Put the rhubarb in an ovenproof dish large enough to hold it in a single layer, then scatter over the orange zest and pour in the juice. Trickle over the honey and gently mix the whole lot together.

Cover loosely with foil and bake in an oven preheated to 150°C/ Gas Mark 2 for 45 minutes–1 hour, until the rhubarb is tender, giving it a gentle stir halfway through. The pieces of rhubarb should keep their shape rather than cook to a mush.

Leave to cool before serving. Sealed in a container, with the syrupy juices from the tray, this can be kept for a week or so in the fridge.

Two (or more) fruit salad

There's no syrup or juice here, no maceration is required, and sugar is an optional extra. It's really just a plate of fruit. The key thing is that you've taken the trouble to peel and slice or otherwise prepare it (a squeeze of lemon or lime juice is, for instance, a wonderful way to dress a ripe banana, and give it a bit of attitude). Children can eat this with their fingers or a fork.

1 banana per person, peeled and sliced

Plus 1 (or more) of the following per person:

A few strawberries, hulled, large ones halved or quartered

A few raspberries

A couple of plums or greengages, stoned and quartered

1 small or ½ large apple or pear, cored and sliced

A lemon wedge

1–2 teaspoons caster sugar (optional)

Arrange the prepared fruit on a plate. Squeeze a little lemon juice over the fruit (mainly on the banana). Sprinkle a scant amount of caster sugar on the tarter fruits, if you like, and serve at once.

Muesli with apple, orange and yoghurt

If you've never eaten muesli the Swiss way – soaked in freshly squeezed orange juice and dished up with grated apple and yoghurt – then you've never really given it a chance. It makes a much more exciting breakfast than muesli with just a slosh of milk. The recipe you see here is merely a guide to compiling a dry muesli mix based on your own preferences. Don't like sunflower seeds? Leave them out. No dried apricots in the cupboard? Use raisins or prunes. The idea is to customise it to suit yourself and your family.

The dried mixture will keep well for several weeks in an airtight jar, so you can put together a nourishing breakfast in minutes. Unsulphured apricots are my favourite dried fruit for muesli – they have slightly more sharpness than your average raisin. And my favourite nuts are almonds.

Makes about 12 servings

200g porridge oats

150g mixed dried fruit of your choice, such as raisins, sultanas, dried apricots, dates, prunes

100g nuts of your choice, lightly toasted if you have time

100g wheat flakes (optional)

3–4 tablespoons seeds, such as pumpkin, sunflower, sesame or flax (optional)

To serve (for 1):

1 crisp eating apple

Juice of 1–2 oranges (or a little milk, if you prefer)

Sugar or honey

Plain yoghurt

To make the muesli, put the oats in a bowl. Roughly chop larger dried fruits, such as apricots, dates and prunes. Leave the nuts whole, or chop them roughly if you prefer. Add the fruit and nuts to the oats, together with the wheat flakes and seeds if using, and stir to combine. Tip into an airtight container, seal and store in a cool, dark place until required.

For a serving of muesli, put about 50g of the muesli mix into a bowl. Coarsely grate or finely chop the apple (including the skin) and add this to the muesli. Squeeze the orange(s) and add the juice to the bowl (or use milk, if you like). Stir to blend everything evenly and leave to soak for about 10 minutes.

Finally, sprinkle over just a little sugar or trickle over some honey, add a good dollop of yoghurt and serve.

Quick porridge

It took a while for me to warm to this classic breakfast, after the experience of lumpy, cement-like porridge at school. In fact it was the Wallace porridge (see below) that converted me. Now I'd say there is no finer start to the day.

You can scale this up to serve as many people as you like. Just stick to the ratio of one part oats to two and a half parts water and/or milk (by volume).

Serves 2–3

120g porridge oats
700ml water or milk (or half and half)
A pinch of sea salt

To serve:
Milk, cream, honey, sugar, golden syrup, maple syrup or jam
Bananas, apples or raisins (optional)
A pinch of ground cinnamon (optional)

Tip the oats into a pan, stir in the water and/or milk and the salt and bring to the boil over a medium heat. Cook briskly for 3 minutes, stirring constantly (jumbo oats will take twice as long). If it's getting too thick, add a dash of hot water.

Serve the porridge with a little milk or cream and your choice of sweetener: honey, demerara, soft brown or white sugar, golden or maple syrup, or jam. Feel free to crank it up with sliced bananas, apple slices (gently fried in butter, if you like), raisins and/or a pinch of cinnamon.

VARIATION
Wallace porridge
So called because my friend Andrew Wallace showed me how to make it, this traditional Scottish approach to porridge uses coarse pinhead oatmeal rather than flat rolled oats, for a nuttier, grainier finish, which I love. It needs overnight soaking, and takes a bit longer to cook.

For 4 people, tip 250g pinhead oatmeal into a pan, pour in 900ml cold water and leave overnight. In the morning, add a good pinch of salt and stir gently over a medium heat until it begins to bubble and gloop like hot mud. Turn the heat down low and cook, stirring occasionally, for about 8 minutes, until the porridge is cooked through and creamy. If it is a little thick, a dash of boiling water from the kettle will loosen it. Serve with your choice of milk, cream, honey, jam, syrup or sugar.

Honey and peanut butter booster bars

These jam-packed near relatives of the flapjack are my antidote to the devil's work – those big-brand 'energy' bars that fester among the chocolate on every motorway service-station counter masquerading as a late breakfast. I wouldn't call these a substitute for breakfast and I wouldn't make outlandish health claims for them either. But the fruity, oaty, nutty, seedy elements will certainly ensure a hefty dose of natural goodness. Far more importantly, they taste delicious. Stick a couple in your lunchbox – one for elevenses, one for tea.

Makes 16

125g unsalted butter

150g soft brown sugar or light muscovado sugar

125g no-sugar-added crunchy peanut butter

75g honey, plus a little more to finish

Finely grated zest of 1 orange

Finely grated zest of 1 lemon

200g porridge oats (not jumbo)

150g dried fruit, such as raisins, sultanas and chopped apricots, prunes or dates, either singly or in combination

150g mixed seeds, such as pumpkin, sunflower, poppy, linseed and sesame

Grease and line a baking tin, about 20cm square.

Put the butter, sugar, peanut butter, honey and grated citrus zests in a deep saucepan over a very low heat. Leave until melted, stirring from time to time.

Stir the oats, dried fruit and three-quarters of the seeds into the melted butter mixture until thoroughly combined. Spread the mixture out evenly in the baking tin, smoothing the top as you go.

Scatter the remaining seeds over the surface and trickle with a little more honey. Place in an oven preheated to 160°C/Gas Mark 3 and bake for about 30 minutes, until golden in the centre and golden brown at the edges.

Leave to cool completely in the tin (be patient – it cuts much better when cold), then turn out and cut into squares with a sharp knife. These bars will keep for 5–7 days in an airtight tin.

VARIATION
Banana booster bars

Replace the peanut butter with 1 medium ripe banana (about 175g), mashed. Stir it in after all the other ingredients have been combined.

Wholemeal drop scones

Once you start eating these, warm and fluffy from the pan, it's hard to stop. They're great for weekend breakfasts, but just as good for afternoon tea. The kids love to help me with them, waiting for the bubbles to appear in the hot batter and judging the perfect moment to flip them over in the pan.

If you can't get hold of self-raising wholemeal flour (see page 15), use plain fine wholemeal flour with 2 teaspoons of baking powder added.

Makes 20–30

250g self-raising wholemeal flour

A pinch of baking powder

A pinch of sea salt

25g caster sugar

2 medium eggs

About 275ml milk

50g butter, melted

A little sunflower oil

To serve:

Butter

Caster sugar

A pinch of ground cinnamon (optional)

Jam, honey or macerated fruit, see page 336 (optional)

Sift the flour, baking powder and salt into a large bowl and stir in the sugar. Make a well in the centre and break in the eggs. Pour in about half the milk. Whisk, gently at first, and then as you start to get a thick paste, add more milk and the melted butter. Beat until you get a creamy batter a little thicker than double cream – you might not need all the milk.

Put a large, heavy-based frying pan or a flat griddle over a medium-high heat. Add a few drops of oil and rub with a thick wad of kitchen paper to oil the pan very lightly. Pour (or 'drop') a scant tablespoon of batter into the pan – to get a disc about the size of a digestive biscuit; you should be able to fit 4 or 5 in the pan.

After about a minute, little bubbles will start to appear on the surface of the drop scones. As soon as they cover the surface, flip the scones over with a spatula – be warned, the first batch may stick. Cook the other side for 40–60 seconds or so, then transfer the drop scones to a warm plate and cover them with a clean tea towel so they stay soft – or hand them over to those waiting eagerly to get stuck in.

Cook the remaining drop scones in the same way, adjusting the heat level if they start browning too quickly and re-oiling the pan with kitchen paper as necessary.

To serve, top with a little butter and sprinkle with some sugar, and a fine dusting of cinnamon, if you like. Or serve buttered and spread with jam, honey or macerated fruit. Eat quickly, while still hot.

VARIATIONS

Sultana and lemon drop scones

Add a little grated lemon zest to the batter and an extra 10g sugar. Sprinkle some sultanas or raisins on to the scones as they cook.

Savoury drop scones

Omit the sugar. Add about 50g grated Cheddar and a twist of black pepper to the batter, and maybe a couple of finely diced cooked bacon rashers. Very good as a quick supper with baked beans.

Perfect pancakes

Thin, crêpe-style pancakes have a bit of a reputation for being tricky, but I think that's because a lot of us only make them once a year. Confidence is the most important ingredient: the more you make, the better they'll be. They're great, quick breakfast fare and in our house we have them at least once a week. I like to eat them with a light dusting of sugar and a squeeze of lemon juice, but we also top them with sliced banana and honey, with fridge jam (page 50), or sometimes with a slosh of maple syrup.

The 30-minute rest is important (without it, your pancakes may be a bit wet). If we are thinking ahead, we often make the batter the night before and leave it in the fridge overnight. It won't keep for more than 48 hours though; i.e. two breakfasts in a row, tops.

Makes about 16

250g plain white or fine wholemeal flour
A pinch of sea salt
2 medium eggs, lightly beaten
About 600ml whole milk
A little sunflower oil

To serve:
Caster sugar and a squeeze of lemon juice (or see suggestions above)

Sift the flour and salt into a bowl and make a well in the centre. Pour in the eggs, add about 50ml of the milk and start to whisk, gradually incorporating the flour into the wet ingredients in the centre. When you have a thick batter forming in the middle, add a bit more milk and whisk in a bit more flour. Keep going in this way until all the milk has been added, all the flour is incorporated, and you have a smooth batter, about the consistency of single cream. One of the mistakes people make with pancakes is to leave the batter too thick. So if your batter is still more double than single cream, whisk in a little more milk. You can also make the batter by whizzing everything up in a food processor. Either way, let it rest for at least 30 minutes, then check the consistency again. If it's thickened up a bit, add a dash more milk to bring it back to the right consistency.

To cook the pancakes, heat a non-stick frying pan or crêpe pan, around 20cm in diameter, over a medium heat. When it's hot, swirl 1 tablespoon of oil around the pan, then tip out the excess. Add a small ladleful (around 50ml) of batter – just enough to coat the base of the pan – and swirl it around quickly until it covers the base. Cook for a minute or so, until lightly coloured underneath, then flip over and cook for a minute more. Depending on the pan, you may need to loosen the edges of the pancake with a palette knife before you flip.

Almost without exception, the first pancake will be a bit rubbish. Don't worry, this is normal; the next one will be much better. Dole them out as you make them, so they can be eaten hot – sprinkled with caster sugar and lemon juice.

Baked breakfast cheesecake

I know the idea of cheesecake for breakfast sounds odd, but this simple recipe is a great way to start the day, especially if you serve it with some fresh berries or a fruit compote. It is incredibly easy to throw together as there's no biscuit base, and you can get it on the table in little more than half an hour.

Besides making a luxurious weekend breakfast or brunch, it is also a delicious pudding. Until recently, I thickened the cheese mixture with a little semolina or flour, but I tried using oatmeal instead and the result was so successful that I now usually do it this way.

If using salted goat's cheese, don't add salt to the recipe.

Serves 10

650g curd cheese or cream cheese, or soft, very mild goat's cheese (preferably unsalted)

75g unsalted butter, melted and cooled slightly

3 tablespoons fine or medium oatmeal, semolina or wholemeal flour

A good pinch of sea salt

100g caster sugar

2 medium eggs, lightly beaten

Finely grated zest of 2 small oranges, plus 1 tablespoon juice

3 tablespoons raisins (optional)

To serve:

Fresh fruit or fruit compote (see pages 339–44)

Yoghurt or soured cream (optional)

Generously butter a 23cm springform cake tin.

Beat the cheese with a wooden spoon until smooth, then add the melted butter, oatmeal, semolina or flour, salt, sugar, eggs and orange zest and juice, and mix well (feel free to whiz the ingredients in a food processor). Fold in the raisins, if using.

Spoon the mixture into the cake tin and place in an oven preheated to 170°C/Gas Mark 3. Bake for about 25 minutes, until just set, with a slight wobble in the centre.

Serve hot, warm or at room temperature with some fresh fruit or fruit compote, and, if you like, yoghurt or soured cream.

Eggy bread with apples

More elegantly known as French toast, fried, egg-soaked bread – like pancakes – is a wholesome way for kids to start their day, especially if it is topped with fried apple slices. You could substitute pears for the apples, cooked in exactly the same way, or simply top the eggy bread with fridge jam (page 50), or macerated fruit (see page 336).

Serves 4

4 medium eggs

2 tablespoons milk

About 2 tablespoons caster sugar

4 thick slices of slightly stale white bread, crusts removed

Butter and sunflower oil for frying

½ teaspoon ground cinnamon (optional)

For the apples:

15g unsalted butter

A trickle of sunflower oil

2 crisp eating apples, peeled (or not, as you like), cored and cut into thin wedges

2 teaspoons caster or soft brown sugar (optional)

Beat the eggs together thoroughly with the milk and 1 tablespoon of the sugar, then pour into a shallow dish. Add the bread slices and submerge them in the egg, turning to coat them well. Let them soak, turning occasionally, for at least 10 minutes, or up to half an hour. Ideally, the bread should absorb almost all the egg – but it never quite does!

While the bread is soaking, cook the apples. Heat the butter and oil in a frying pan. Add the apple slices and cook over a medium heat, turning them occasionally, for 5–10 minutes, until soft and lightly golden. Add a little sugar towards the end, if you like, to create a buttery syrup in the pan. Scoop the apples out and keep them warm.

You can fry the bread in the same pan as the apples – but if you've added sugar you'll have to give it a quick clean. Heat the pan over a medium heat and add a little more butter and another dash of oil. Lay the eggy bread in the pan (cook it in 2 batches, if necessary) and trickle any leftover egg on top. Fry for 2–3 minutes, until the base is golden brown, then flip over and cook for 2–3 minutes more. Transfer to warm plates.

Scatter the remaining sugar over the bread (combining it first with a pinch of cinnamon, if you like), pile the warm apples and any syrupy juices on top and serve.

VARIATIONS

- Serve cinnamon-sprinkled eggy bread with roasted plums (see page 352), or with honey-baked rhubarb (page 30).

- Instead of sprinkling your eggy bread with sugar, trickle over some maple syrup and top with blueberries or raspberries.

- Serve plain, unsugared eggy bread with bacon or grilled kippers.

Home-made yoghurt

We use yoghurt all the time at River Cottage – in fruity fools and ice cream, in breads and cakes, and swirled into soups, stews and curries. We mix it with goat's cheese and herbs to make near-instant dips, and with toasted spices to spoon into bowls of soup (see page 274). But it is also, of course, an ideal breakfast food, wonderful with a spoonful of fridge jam (page 50) stirred in, or a trickle of golden honey on top. Pair it with fresh, dried or stewed fruit, or muesli (page 34) and it makes an even more satisfying start to the day.

Making your own yoghurt can save you money, and it also gives you complete control over what goes into it (organic or even unpasteurised milk, if you choose, and no preservatives). You just need some live yoghurt to start you off, a cooking thermometer and a warm bowl in a warm place or, easier still, a Thermos. The milk powder isn't essential either, though it will help to thicken the yoghurt. Make sure you don't eat all your first batch – keep a little back to make your next lot.

Makes 500g

500ml whole milk
25g dried milk powder
3 tablespoons live, plain whole-milk yoghurt

Pour the milk into a saucepan and whisk in the dried milk powder. Put the pan over a medium heat, stand a cooking thermometer in it and stir gently, watching the thermometer carefully, until the temperature reaches 46°C.

Take the saucepan off the heat and pour the milk into a warmed mixing bowl. Check the temperature hasn't gone beyond 46°C. If it has, stir the milk until the temperature drops back. Whisk in the live yoghurt. The bacteria within it will start to work on the fresh milk, converting it into yoghurt.

Cover the bowl with a lid or some cling film, wrap it in a towel and put it somewhere warm – in an airing cupboard or above a radiator are good places. Alternatively, you can pour the mixture into a warmed, wide-mouthed Thermos flask and seal.

Check the yoghurt after 6–8 hours, or leave it overnight. If it's still runny, leave it wrapped up in the warm for another 1–2 hours. When it has thickened and looks set, pour it into a clean container, seal and refrigerate. Home-made yoghurt isn't as thick as commercial varieties. If you'd like a thicker finish, you can strain the yoghurt through a muslin-lined sieve over a bowl in the fridge for a few hours.

Fridge jam

I invented what I call 'fridge jam' as a sort of halfway house between a full-blown preserve and a fresh fruit sauce. With only two-thirds the sugar of a standard jam, it has a softer, looser set and a sharper flavour. It's very versatile. You can still serve it on toast, of course, but at home we mostly have it for breakfast with pancakes or on yoghurt. It's outstanding with rice pudding, too. Make it with strawberries, raspberries or gooseberries, or try my favourite morello cherry jam (see below).

Makes about 2kg

1.5kg strawberries, raspberries or gooseberries

Juice of 1 lemon

1kg jam sugar with pectin

Sterilise some jam jars or other suitable containers by washing them in hot, soapy water and drying in a very low oven (or put them through a dishwasher cycle).

Divide the fruit in half, putting the smaller berries in one bowl, the larger ones in another (if the small ones are quite big, halve them). Roughly crush the large ones with a potato masher (or by hand), then add the uncrushed berries, lemon juice and sugar. Stir to combine, then leave for an hour to draw out the juices.

Transfer the mixture to a preserving pan, or a wide, heavy-based pan that is deep enough for the jam to bubble away safely. Bring it quickly to a rolling boil, stirring a few times to make sure all the sugar dissolves, then boil hard for exactly 5 minutes, skimming off any foam from the surface. Take off the heat and leave to cool for 5 minutes (this helps to keep the whole fruit suspended in the jam).

Pot the hot jam in the warm jars or other vessels and seal tightly. Label jars when cool. Unopened and stored in a cool, dry place, the jam will keep in jars for up to a year. But once opened, store in the fridge and use within 3 weeks.

VARIATION
Morello cherry fridge jam

Substitute 1.5kg morello cherries for the strawberries. I like to leave the stones in, as they lend a special flavour, but you may prefer to remove them using an olive/cherry stoner (tie the stones up in a square of muslin and add it to the jam while you boil it up).

Put the cherries in a preserving pan with 100ml water (no lemon juice) and bring slowly to the boil, stirring often, until the juices run. Simmer gently for about 10 minutes, until the cherries are soft. Add 1kg preserving sugar (sour cherries have good levels of pectin, so there is no need for sugar with added pectin), stir until dissolved, then bring to the boil and boil hard for 5 minutes. Pot as above.

Nut butters

Making your own nut butter is so simple and quick, and you can adapt the recipe to your own taste. Try toasting the nuts for a few minutes in a hot oven or leave them raw, or experiment with different nuts, in any combination. Cashew nut butter is my favourite, but almonds, hazelnuts and, of course, peanuts all work well.

Home-made nut butter is very good spread thickly on freshly baked bread and topped with your favourite jam. You could also spread it on oatcakes (page 87) or digestives (page 88), or roll it into balls and dip them in melted dark chocolate for a deliciously indulgent treat. It plays a starring role in our favourite 'late-for-school' sandwich, too – thick sourdough bread, nut butter and sliced banana.

Makes 200g

200g nuts (unroasted and unsalted), such as cashews, almonds, hazelnuts and/or peanuts

3–4 tablespoons rapeseed or sunflower oil

1–2 teaspoons runny honey

½ teaspoon flaky sea salt

Put the nuts in a food processor and pulse until quite fine. Add a tablespoon or two of the oil and process until you have a creamy paste, then add the honey and salt. Add a few more nuts just at the end of processing if you'd like a crunchy nut butter. Store in the fridge in an airtight container, where it will keep for up to 2 weeks.

VARIATION
Nut and seed butters

To any of your favourite nut butters, add 50g sunflower, sesame or pumpkin seeds, or a combination, at the end of processing to give extra texture and crunch.

Tomato toast

If you have ever had breakfast in Barcelona, there's every chance you were offered *pa amb tomàquet*. That's tomato toast to you and me. I can think of few things more delicious in high summer, when tomatoes are at their fleshy, sunny, flavoursome best. If you grow your own, it's an absolute must.

The messy, pulpy tomato-grating is fun for grown-ups and kids – this is one occasion when you're certainly permitted to play with your food.

Serves 2

2 thick slices of robust bread (sourdough, page 66, is ideal)

1 garlic clove, halved (optional)

2 ripe, juicy, large tomatoes, halved

2 tablespoons fruity extra virgin olive oil

Sea salt

Toast or grill the bread. If you don't mind a bit of garlic in the morning, rub the cut garlic clove gently over one side. Next, rub on the tomatoes, grating and squishing the cut side messily against the rough surface of the toast and squirting out the pulp as you go. Discard the skins. Trickle over the olive oil, sprinkle on a pinch of sea salt and eat immediately.

VARIATION
Oily toast

This is a delicious alternative to hot buttered toast. My kids absolutely love it for breakfast. Rub your hot toast with garlic if you like (we don't in the morning, but do if we're having the toast with soup or salad for supper). Then simply trickle the toast fairly generously with a good, tasty unrefined oil – we rotate hempseed, rapeseed and olive oil, and sometimes use a combination. Finish with a sprinkling of sea salt.

Big mushrooms on toast

Big, dark-gilled mushrooms, oozing garlicky, buttery juices, make a very easy cooked breakfast or brunch. This is a dish I particularly like to make in autumn, with horse or field mushrooms I've gathered myself, but any large, flat mushroom will do. With a salad on the side, this would make a light supper, too – or a simple starter for four.

Serves 2

4 large, flat, open-capped mushrooms

About 30g unsalted butter

1 fat garlic clove, finely chopped

A large sprig of thyme or lemon thyme

2 thick slices of bread (sourdough, page 66, and soda bread, page 72, are particularly good)

½ lemon

Sea salt and freshly ground black pepper

Put the mushrooms in a lightly buttered ovenproof dish big enough to hold them in a single layer. Cut the butter into little nuggets and dot them over the top of the mushrooms. Scatter over the chopped garlic, then strip the leaves from the thyme and scatter these over too. Season generously with salt and pepper.

Place in an oven preheated to 190°C/Gas Mark 5 and bake for about 15 minutes, until the mushrooms are tender and overflowing with garlicky, buttery juice. Meanwhile, toast the bread.

Put the toast on 2 warm plates, top with the mushrooms and trickle over any juices left in the dish. Finish with a generous squeeze of lemon juice and serve straight away.

Smoked salmon and scrambled eggs on toast

Salty, smoky salmon combined with rich, creamy scrambled eggs is one of the great brunch/weekend-breakfast dishes – and a pretty mean supper any day of the week. You may well have your own preferred method for scrambling eggs, but I include mine for those who are not yet set in their ways. As with any simple dish, the quality of the ingredients is everything. Use organically farmed salmon, and the freshest free-range eggs you can find.

Serves 2

About 100g sliced smoked salmon

4 medium eggs

20g butter, plus a little more for the toast

2 slices of good bread

Fine sea salt and freshly ground black pepper

Unwrap the salmon and lay the slices on a plate so they come to room temperature while you cook the eggs.

Break the eggs into a bowl. Add a good pinch of salt and a twist of pepper and whisk with a fork. Place a small, non-stick saucepan over a low heat and melt half the butter in it. When the butter begins to bubble, pour in the eggs and start stirring with a wooden spoon. Put the bread on to toast now.

As the mixture gets hotter, the eggs will start to thicken into soft lumps. This takes a few minutes – don't rush it by turning up the heat. Keep stirring gently, scraping the bottom and sides of the pan to move any setting egg back into the more yielding middle. As you approach the degree of runniness you like, remove from the heat, stir for another 10 seconds or so, then add the remaining butter, which will, with a final quick stir, help stop the eggs cooking any further.

Quickly butter the toast, lay a couple of slices of smoked salmon on each piece and pile the eggs on top. Serve straight away.

VARIATIONS

Scrambled eggs with ham

Instead of smoked salmon, use ham (sliced from a proper ham) at room temperature. Serve on the toast, under the scrambled eggs, as above.

Scrambled eggs with smoked pollack/haddock

In place of the salmon, use 250–300g smoked pollack or haddock fillet lightly poached in enough milk just to cover, with a bay leaf and a few peppercorns added (bring to a simmer, take off the heat and let the fish cook in the residual heat for a few minutes, then drain). Break the fish into large flakes, removing the skin and any bones. Gently stir into your scrambled eggs for the last minute or so of cooking.

Many home cooks, some professional chefs and at least one

semi-professional home cook (that's me) have culinary blind spots – areas of kitchen endeavour where they rarely attempt to tread. For some it may be pastry, for others fish, and for others perhaps long, slow cooking of meat, as in braises, stews and pot roasts. For me, until a few years ago, it was bread making.

Reasons for neglecting a certain set of cookery skills vary with the individual: some 'fess up to a lack of confidence, or plead restricted opportunity, others may even belittle the speciality in question as simply not worth bothering with. Sometimes it's hard to put your finger on it. It's just a strange, almost imperceptible creeping feeling that the gastronomic pursuit in question is not 'your bag'. This, of course, becomes a self-fulfilling prophecy, as the longer you go without breaking through, the more it seems to be part of the definition of what kind of cook you are, or aren't.

Rarely, if ever, is it because one doesn't enjoy the food in question. I love bread and always have done. But I somehow never cast myself as a baker. And the more I didn't bake bread, the more I began to think of myself as a non-bread-baking kind of cook. Then I moved into a house with a fabulous wood-burning bread oven in its ancient inglenook fireplace. I could hardly not try it out. In fact, what better way of reviving it than for our daughter Chloe's tenth birthday party, when we decided to fire up the dormant beast and bash out pizzas, kneaded, shaped and topped by a gang of frighteningly noisy young girls.

Apart from the sheer joy of the occasion, the pizzas we all put together weren't half bad. In fact, putting aside the fact that they were formed into some rather unconventional shapes (many could perhaps best be described as 'protozoan'), they were absolutely delicious. By the end of the day, I had taken the opportunity to knock out a couple of loaves too, pretty much following the instructions on the back of one of the packets of organic flour we had inevitably over-invested in for our pizza-making bonanza. They were also more than respectable. Lovely, in fact. And in one fell swoop my bread-baking jinx was busted.

Now we've moved house again, and we miss our inglenook-with-ancient-bread-oven like an old friend left behind. But we have a new friend, as we have installed a wood-burning range. It's easy to fire it up to get the top oven to a piping 250°C or more – ideal for bread and pizzas. (Incidentally, as long as you can get your oven to a temperature of 220°C/Gas Mark 7, you will be able to bake great

bread and pizza; if it's any less than that, in all honesty you will struggle.) We now have regular family pizza sessions – they make a fine alternative to a big Sunday roast dinner when you have friends over at the weekend. Personally I never tire of dabbling with the pizza theme, my current enthusiasm being for tomato-less types of 'pizza bianca'. The less-is-more concept is taken to its logical conclusion with the 'plain pizza' flatbread on page 85 (though I have to say, in my house the younger pizza makers are still deeply committed to the more-is-more approach…).

Latterly it is my wife, Marie, who has really been bitten by the bread-making bug. Rather than starting from scratch every time with bought yeast, she tends and nurtures a sourdough 'starter' (a fermenting batter of flour and water that contains natural airborne yeasts – see page 66) that we acquired from River Cottage baker Dan Stevens. She bakes an outstanding loaf from this just about every other day – often daily at weekends and during the holidays. If she's busy or away, I step in once in a while to start or finish a batch of dough, or bake off a risen loaf that's too impatient to await her return. And it is this very soothing, almost daily rhythmic ritual that has finally weaned us, as a family, off bought bread. I can't tell you how satisfying it is – it's right up there with growing your own veg – and I would urge you to give it a go.

I'm not going to pretend that baking bread is a complete doddle, however. Traditional, yeast-leavened bread is made by a time-honoured and time-consuming process, the rudiments of which need to be respected. My point is that they don't need to be feared. Just get stuck in, as I did, and there is every chance you will make delicious bread – and every chance you will greatly enjoy both the bread and the making of it. I hardly need to mention that, for both taste and goodness, the home-baked loaf has factory-made, supermarket-sold bread roundly thrashed every time. And with a little commitment and understanding, your own efforts can easily compete with the best artisan loaves, at a fraction of their (often eyebrow-raising) price.

Can it be done instantly? No. But it can readily be fitted round a busy working day, or week, and become a steady and even relaxing part of your routine. Techniques can be adapted to your timetable – and there's no shame whatever in using a mixer with a dough hook to do the kneading (we do it all the time). Even if you don't go all out for the sourdough starter as a nurtured 'family pet' (it needs 'feeding' regularly with flour and water), you'll find the overnight 'sponge' method, borrowed from the sourdough technique, can be applied to recipes using fresh or dried yeast (see page 70). So… mix before bed. Knead in the morning. Put somewhere cool (the fridge) for a long, slow rise. Knock back at the end of the working day and knead again. Shape your loaf, leave it for a quicker, warmer rise for a couple of hours (we use the airing cupboard), then bake. Your freshly baked loaf, started 36 hours previously, is ready for breakfast. Each little intervention takes only a matter of minutes. And you've hardly noticed the effort.

If you want to acquire a bread-baking habit (or perhaps just improve one), this chapter will show you the way. But besides yeast-risen doughs, there is much pleasure (and time) to be gained from more instantly gratifying forms of baking. Making soda bread, for example, is a great shortcut to wholesome and delicious home-made bread. It's really just a giant scone. And once you've got the knack, then adapting the basic recipe by adding seeds, dried fruit or even cheese and onion is not just acceptable, it's inevitable.

The American take on yeastless breads is dominated by cornbread – in many ways similar to soda bread, except that the principal flour is milled from corn (i.e. maize). It's taken a while for cornbreads to catch on in the UK but they are a beloved staple of American café culture, and when you start to play around with them you'll see why. They are falling-off-a-log easy but hugely rewarding.

'Breads' can be even simpler – though less obviously bread-like. Take the oatcake. We may class it these days as a kind of biscuit to be eaten with cheese, but it is really a very basic form of flatbread. Thinking of it this way can only help to emphasise its versatility. I'm just as likely to eat an oatcake for breakfast with marmalade, or for a quick lunch with a chunk of pâté, or alongside my suppertime soup, as I am with a hunk of Cheddar and a dab of chutney. Flatbreads in the more traditional sense don't get much easier, more primitive or more instant than the recipe on page 78, yet when you produce a batch of these, the chances are you'll feel very pleased with yourself as you serve up a stack with a pile of home-made hummus, or offer them to your guests to tear up and dunk into a soup or stew. This kind of unleavened bread has been around for millennia but it's just as relevant to the way we cook today as it ever was.

Sourdough loaf

Bread is, of course, a staple, something most of us eat every day, so it's a crying shame that much of it is so poor – pappy, tasteless and limp, laced with additives and completely lacking in character. Baking your own gives you the opportunity to eat really great bread every day – and to have access to wonderful toast and breadcrumbs too. Even stale home-made bread is a benefit, with myriad satisfying uses. In short, I urge you to become the baker of your own daily bread. It does require a certain amount of time and commitment, but I promise you, the rewards are phenomenal.

I could offer you a standard simple white bread recipe – the kind you'll find on the back of your bag of bread flour – but I want to go one better. Since I've been baking bread at home, I've discovered that you get a vastly superior flavour and texture in a hand-made loaf if it's leavened with wild yeasts, and if those yeasts have been allowed time to develop their personalities. I don't want to get too technical but, in a nutshell, the more time yeast spends feeding on flour, the more its secretions of alcohol and various acids build up and develop flavour. The truth is, slow-risen bread tastes better.

The bread we make at home now is almost invariably sourdough. It all began, as sourdoughs do, with what is aptly known as a 'starter' – a gently fermenting batter of flour and water in which natural airborne yeasts have settled and got to work. We acquired ours from Dan Stevens, my River Cottage baking chef, and you may be able to get hold of one too (from a friendly baker, or a friend who bakes). We're eternally grateful to Dan, who showed us the way with sourdough and helped make it, literally, our daily bread.

But you can also 'grow your own' starter from scratch. It may take several days – even a week or two – to get going, but once established, all it needs is regular feeds of flour to keep it frothing happily away. When we want to bake a loaf (which we do, on average, every other day), we take a portion of the starter and combine it with fresh flour and water to make a 'sponge'. This we leave overnight to ferment and develop flavour. The next morning we combine the sponge with more flour and some salt to make our dough proper, which we knead, rise, shape, prove and bake.

That may sound like a long-winded process but I promise you that, while it does take time, it does not take a great deal of effort. Your interventions are relatively brief – the yeasts do their work over several hours – but the baker doesn't do any more hands-on work than the baker of a conventional loaf. If you're still sceptical, all I can do is ask you to take a leap of faith. Try this method and you will produce bread with more flavour and texture than any loaf you've baked at home before. We love it!

For the starter:

About 100g strong bread flour (at least 50 per cent wholegrain flour, such as wholemeal, spelt or wholegrain rye), plus up to 1kg bread flour to 'feed' the starter

Making the starter

In a large bowl, mix the flour for the starter with enough warm water to make a batter roughly the consistency of thick paint. Beat it well to incorporate some air, then cover with a lid or cling film and leave somewhere fairly warm. A warm kitchen is fine, or a coolish airing cupboard. Check it every few hours until you can see that fermentation has begun – signalled by the appearance of bubbles on the surface and a smell of... well, of fermentation (it can actually smell quite unpleasant and acrid at this stage but don't worry, it will mellow as it matures). The time it takes for your starter to begin fermenting can vary hugely – it could be a few hours or a few days. But make your starter with wholegrain flour (which offers more for the yeast to get its teeth into), keep it warm and draught free and you should be rewarded with the first signs of life within 24 hours.

Your starter now needs regular feeding. Begin by whisking in another 100g or so of fresh flour and enough water to retain that thick batter consistency. You can switch to using cool water and to keeping the starter at normal room temperature – though nowhere too cold or draughty. Leave it again, then, 24 hours or so later, scoop out and discard half the starter and stir in another 100g flour and some more water. Repeat this discard-and-feed routine every day, maintaining the sloppy consistency and keeping your starter at room temperature, and after 7–10 days you should have something that smells good – sweet, fruity, yeasty, almost boozy – having lost any harsh, acrid edge. By this stage, it should be actively enticing you into baking with it. But don't be tempted to bake a loaf until it's been on the go for at least a week.

If you're going to bake bread every day or two, maintain your starter in this way, keeping it at room temperature, feeding it daily, and taking some of it out whenever you want to create a sponge (see right). However, if you want to keep it for longer between bakings, you can simply add enough flour (but no water) to turn it from a batter into a stiff dough, then it won't need another feed for 4 days or so. You'll just need to add more water when you come to make the sponge. Alternatively, you can lull your starter into dormancy by cooling it down – it will keep for a week in the fridge without needing to be fed. You'll then need to bring it back to room temperature and probably give it a fresh feed to get it bubbling and active again. Combine these two approaches – keep your starter as a stiff dough in the fridge – and you can leave it for 2 weeks before it will need your attention again. If you know you won't be baking for a while, you can even freeze the starter; it will reactivate on thawing.

Making the loaf

Makes 1 medium loaf

For the sponge:
About 100ml active starter
250g strong flour (white, wholemeal or a mixture)

For each loaf:
300g strong bread flour (white, wholemeal or a mixture)
1 tablespoon rapeseed or olive oil (optional)
10g fine sea salt

The night before you want to bake your loaf, create the sponge: take about 100ml of the active starter and combine it with 250g flour and 275ml warm water in a large bowl. Mix well with your hands, then cover with cling film and leave overnight. In the morning it should be clearly fermenting – thick, sticky and bubbly.

To make the dough, add the 300g flour to the sponge, along with the oil, if you're using it (it will make the bread a touch softer and silkier, but is not essential), and the salt (which is essential). Squish it all together with your hands. You should have a fairly sticky dough. If it seems tight and firm, add a dash more warm water. If it's unmanageably loose, add more flour, but do leave it fairly wet – you'll get better bread that way.

Turn the dough out on to a lightly floured work surface and knead until smooth and silky. This takes about 10 minutes, but it can vary according to your own style and level of confidence. To knead, place the fingertips of one hand in the middle of the ball of dough, then use the heel of your other hand to push the dough away from you in a long stretch. Fold the dough back on itself, then repeat the manoeuvre. Keep going, stretching and folding, giving the dough a quarter turn every few stretches, until it is silky and smooth. Alternatively, use the dough hook on your mixer!

Put the dough in a lightly oiled bowl and turn it to coat with the oil. Cover with lightly oiled cling film, or put the bowl into a large plastic bag, and leave to rise. Don't expect it to whoosh up to twice its original size in an hour, as a conventional loaf does. Sourdough rises slowly and sedately. The best thing is to knead it in the morning, then simply leave it all day – perhaps while you're out at work – in a fairly cool, draught-free place until it has more or less doubled in size and feels springy if you push your finger gently into it; alternatively, you could knead it in the evening and then leave it to rise overnight.

Knock back (deflate) the risen dough by punching it down with your knuckles on a lightly floured surface. You now need to prove the dough (i.e. give it a second rising). You are also going to be forming it into the shape it will be for baking. If you have a proper baker's proving basket, use this, first dusting it generously with flour. Alternatively, rig up your own proving basket by lining a medium-sized, fairly shallow-sided bowl with a clean tea towel, then dusting it with flour. Place your round of dough inside, cover again with oiled cling film or a clean plastic bag and leave to rise, in a warm place this time, for 1½–3 hours, or until roughly doubled in size. Then the dough is ready to bake.

Preheat the oven to 250°C/Gas Mark 10 (or at least to 230°C/Gas Mark 8, if that's your top limit). If possible, have ready a clean gardener's spray bottle full of water – you'll be using this to create a steamy atmosphere in the oven, which helps the bread to rise and develop a good crust. (You can achieve the same effect with a roasting tin of boiling water placed on the bottom of the oven just before you put the loaf in, but the spray bottle is easier – and much more fun.)

About 5 minutes before you want to put the loaf in the oven, place a baking sheet in it to heat up. Then take the hot baking sheet from the oven, dust it with flour and carefully tip the risen dough out of the proving basket/bowl, upside down, on to the baking sheet; it will now be the right way up. If you like you can slash the top of the loaf a few times with a very sharp serrated knife, or snip it with a pair of scissors, to give a pattern to the crust.

Put the loaf into the hot oven and give it a few squirts from the spray bottle over and around it. After 15 minutes, reduce the heat to 200°C/Gas Mark 6, give the oven another spray, and bake for a further 25–30 minutes, until the well-browned loaf vibrates and sounds hollow when you tap its base. Leave to cool for at least 20 minutes before you plunge in with the bread knife – it's okay to slice it warm, but not piping hot.

An alternative and very satisfying way to bake your sourdough loaf is by placing the dough directly on the floor of the oven – but you can only do this in a cast-iron range cooker. Tip the proved dough carefully on to a well-floured, lip-less baking sheet or, better still, a pizza shovel, and slide it on to the floor of the oven. We do this every time, and it gives a lovely toasty, chewy, nearly-but-not-quite-burned base to the loaf.

VARIATION
Cheaty yeasty sponge loaf

If you don't have a starter on the go, you can still take advantage of the overnight sponge method to produce bread with better than average flavour and texture. Combine 250g strong flour with 5g fast-action yeast, then beat in 325ml warm water to form a thick batter (alternatively, dissolve 10g fresh yeast or 5g ordinary dried yeast in the water, then beat it into the flour). Cover with cling film and leave overnight to ferment. The next morning, add another 250g flour and 10g fine sea salt, then knead as above. Leave to rise for an hour or two in a warm place, until doubled in size, then knock back, shape, rise again and bake as above.

Classic soda bread

I frequently turn to soda bread when the breadbin is bare. If there's nothing for lunch or to serve with soup for supper, it's a quick and simple answer – and sustaining, too. This classic recipe lends itself to endless tweaking and variation. Slot it into your repertoire and you'll never regret it.

Cultured buttermilk, which reacts with the bicarbonate of soda to make the bread rise, is pretty widely available these days. However, if you can't find it, live whole-milk yoghurt makes a great alternative.

Makes 1 medium loaf

500g plain white flour
2 teaspoons bicarbonate of soda
1 teaspoon fine sea salt
About 400ml buttermilk or live yoghurt
A little milk, if necessary

Sift the flour and bicarbonate of soda into a large mixing bowl and stir in the salt. Make a well in the centre and pour in the buttermilk, stirring as you go. If necessary, add a tablespoon or two of milk to bring the mixture together; it should form a soft dough, just this side of sticky. Tip it out on to a lightly floured work surface and knead lightly for about a minute, just long enough to pull it together into a loose ball but no longer – you need to get it into the oven while the bicarb is still doing its stuff. You're not looking for the kind of smooth, elastic dough you'd get with a yeast-based bread.

Put the round of dough on a lightly floured baking sheet and dust generously with flour. Mark a deep cross in it with a sharp, serrated knife, cutting about two-thirds of the way through the loaf. Put it in an oven preheated to 200°C/Gas Mark 6 and bake for 40–45 minutes, until the loaf sounds hollow when tapped underneath.

Cool on a wire rack if you like a crunchy crust, or wrap in a clean tea towel if you prefer a soft crust. Soda bread is best eaten while still warm, spread with salty butter and/or a dollop of your favourite jam. But if you have some left over the next day, it makes great toast.

VARIATION
Six-seed soda bread
Mix together 2 tablespoons each of sunflower, pumpkin, sesame, poppy and linseeds, plus 1 teaspoon of fennel seeds; set aside. Follow the main recipe but use half white flour and half wholemeal flour. Add all but 1 tablespoon of the seeds to the dry ingredients before proceeding as above. After cutting a cross in the top of the loaf, brush it with a little buttermilk or ordinary milk and sprinkle with the remaining seeds. Bake at 200°C/Gas Mark 6 for 40–45 minutes.

Parsnip and thyme bread

Dan Stevens, our baker at River Cottage, created this, inspired by Delia Smith's oatmeal and potato bread. It's a really lovely type of soda bread and, like all soda loaves, is great if you want to whip up some bread quickly to go with soup. It has a light, scone-like texture and, when it's warm from the oven, it's difficult not to devour the whole thing in minutes, spread thickly with butter.

Makes 1 small loaf

1 tablespoon rapeseed or sunflower oil

1 large onion, sliced

175g self-raising flour

½ teaspoon sea salt

1 teaspoon thyme leaves

50g Parmesan, matured hard goat's cheese or strong Cheddar, finely grated

175g grated parsnip

1 medium egg, lightly beaten

2–3 tablespoons whole milk

Freshly ground black pepper

Heat the oil in a frying pan, add the onion and cook gently for about 10 minutes, stirring occasionally, until soft and lightly coloured. Remove from the heat and cool slightly.

In a large bowl, mix together the flour, salt, thyme, cheese, grated parsnip and some pepper. Add the onion, followed by the egg and 2 tablespoons of milk, then mix to form a soft dough, adding the extra milk if needed. Don't overwork the dough; just bring it together with a little light kneading. Shape into a round and place on an oiled baking sheet.

Bake in an oven preheated to 180°C/Gas Mark 4 for 40–45 minutes, until the loaf is golden and makes a hollow sound when tapped on the bottom.

Leave to cool for a few minutes on a wire rack, then slice and serve while still warm.

Cornbread

This is another of those simple, quick, yeast-free breads that can be put together in next to no time. It's not bread at all really, more a sort of savoury cake, and I absolutely love it.

The plain version is delicious with bacon for breakfast, or as an accompaniment to hearty, beany stews or soups. However, if you add a few extra tasty ingredients (see suggestions below), it becomes almost a meal in itself and you don't need much with it except maybe some scrambled eggs or salad.

Makes 12 pieces

125g cornmeal or fine polenta (or use half fine and half coarse polenta for a crunchier texture)

125g plain white flour

2 teaspoons baking powder

1 teaspoon fine sea salt

½ teaspoon bicarbonate of soda

2 medium eggs

1 tablespoon runny honey or soft brown sugar

150g buttermilk (or plain whole-milk yoghurt)

150ml whole milk

25g unsalted butter, melted

Grease a 23cm square baking tin, about 4cm deep.

In a large bowl, mix together the cornmeal, flour, baking powder, salt and bicarbonate of soda. Make a well in the middle.

Whisk together the eggs, honey or sugar, buttermilk or yoghurt, milk and melted butter. Pour into the well in the dry ingredients and stir until everything is just combined. Don't overmix; a few lumps in the batter are fine. You need to get it into the oven as quickly as possible once the bicarbonate of soda and buttermilk start reacting.

Pour the batter into the baking tin and place in an oven preheated to 220°C/Gas Mark 7. Bake for about 20 minutes, until the cornbread is golden and has shrunk slightly from the sides of the tin. Place the tin on a wire rack to cool for a few minutes before cutting the bread into squares. Serve warm.

VARIATIONS

Cornbread lends itself to customisation. You might want to try adding fried bacon bits, fried diced chorizo, chopped olives, mushrooms (fried with a little garlic and well seasoned), and chopped herbs, such as coriander and chives.

Cheddar, chilli, sweetcorn and spring onion cornbread

Gently sweat 6 sliced spring onions and ¼–1 deseeded and finely chopped green or red chilli in a tablespoon of rapeseed or olive oil until soft but not coloured. Combine with 50g cooked sweetcorn (fresh or tinned). Make the cornbread as above, stirring 50g grated strong Cheddar cheese into the dry ingredients and adding the sweetcorn mixture with the wet ingredients.

Flatbreads

I love these wonderful, soft but slightly charred, yeast-free breads (also known as soft tortillas). I could eat a whole pile of them, hot from the pan, just trickled with oil and sprinkled with salt. However, they are incredibly versatile and the ideal partner to everything from hummus (pages 124–9) to a bulghur wheat salad such as tabula kisir (page 117). They are also ideal for wrapping burgers, sausages, kebabs and other barbecued meat or veg, and for mopping up a good wet curry or stew.

Makes 8

250g plain flour
1 teaspoon fine sea salt
1 tablespoon rapeseed, olive or sunflower oil

Sift the flour into a large bowl and add the salt. Add the oil to 150ml warm water, then pour this liquid into the flour in a thin stream, stirring well with a wooden spoon or your hands to form a slightly sticky dough. Turn the dough out on to a lightly floured work surface and knead for about 5 minutes, until it feels smooth and plump, sprinkling on a little more flour only if the dough feels very sticky. Cover the ball of dough with the upturned mixing bowl and let it rest for at least 15 minutes.

When you're ready to cook and eat the flatbreads, roll the dough into a sausage shape and divide it into 8 pieces. Roll each piece into a ball. Flour the work surface and rolling pin, then roll out each ball of dough into a round 2–3mm thick, using plenty of flour as the dough is liable to stick.

Place a heavy-based non-stick frying pan – or a cast-iron griddle – over a high heat and when it's good and hot, turn the heat down a bit. Have ready a plate lined with a clean tea towel so you can put your cooked flatbreads on it to keep them warm and soft.

Shake off any excess flour and carefully lay a flatbread in the hot pan. Let it sit for a minute or two, until the dough looks 'set' on top and is starting to lift away from the pan. Look at the underside and, if you can see dark brown patches forming, flip it over with a spatula or tongs. Cook the second side for 30–45 seconds. Wrap the cooked flatbread in the tea towel while you cook the others. If the flatbreads are colouring too quickly, lower the heat a bit.

Serve the flatbreads while still soft and warm. Once cold, they won't be quite the same. But they can be recycled by tearing them into pieces, brushing with a little oil, then crisping them up in a hot oven (at 220°C/Gas Mark 7) to make dipping chips, or flat croûtons for soups and salads.

Focaccia

This soft, tasty bread, with its light, oily, salty crust, is eminently tearable and dippable. Put a freshly baked focaccia on the table, plus maybe some dukka (page 134) and a few sliced ripe tomatoes – perhaps a bottle of chilled rosé – and the scene is set for a very good evening.

Makes 12 pieces (to serve 4–6)

500g strong white flour
10g fine sea salt
5g dried or fast-action yeast
2 tablespoons rapeseed or olive oil

To finish:
Rapeseed or olive oil
Flaky sea salt
Leaves from 2 sprigs of rosemary, finely chopped

Put the flour and salt in a large bowl and mix together. If you're using ordinary dried yeast, dissolve it in 350ml warm water. If using fast-action yeast, add it straight to the flour. Add the yeast liquid or 350ml warm water to the flour and mix to a very rough, soft dough. Add the oil and squish it all in.

Scrape the dough out on to a lightly floured work surface. With lightly floured hands, knead until it is smooth and silky – anything between 5 and 15 minutes. As it's a very sticky dough, you'll need to keep dusting your hands with flour; it will become less sticky as you knead.

Shape the dough into a round, put it in a lightly oiled bowl, then cover with lightly oiled cling film or a clean tea towel and leave to rise until it has doubled in size; this will take about an hour. Knock back the dough and, if you have time, leave it to rise again in the same way. Meanwhile, lightly oil a shallow baking tin, about 25 x 35cm.

Press the dough out into a rough rectangle on a floured surface, then lift into the baking tin and press right into the corners. Cover with oiled cling film or a tea towel and leave to rise for about half an hour.

Once risen, use your fingertips to poke rows of deep dimples across the surface. Trickle the top generously with oil, then sprinkle with salt and rosemary. Bake in the oven preheated to its highest setting (at least 230°C/Gas Mark 8) for 15–20 minutes, turning it down after 10 minutes if the focaccia is browning too fast. Serve just warm, or let it cool completely.

VARIATIONS

Focaccia is a bit of a blank slate: you can make it your own by adding all manner of different flavourings. Here are a few ideas:

• Add some finely chopped rosemary and/or thyme, or dried chilli flakes to the flour at the start.

• Knead some chopped black or green olives and/or sun-dried tomatoes into the dough after the first rising.

• Push some thyme sprigs, sage leaves or strips of roasted pepper into the dough when you poke the dimples before baking.

Pizza

There's pizza and there's pizza. There are thick-based, soggy, drooping excuses-for-pizza, covered with a melange of oversalted, barely identifiable odds and sods. And then there's thin-based, crisp, slightly charred and smoky pizza, topped with choice titbits – salty ham, garlicky scraps of mushroom, crumblings of good cheese – ingredients that function almost as mere seasonings for the glorious bread base, which is, quietly, the real star. No prizes for guessing what I'm presenting you with here. Once you've kneaded this easy dough, cranked up your oven to its highest setting and baked your first proper pizza, you'll never look back.

The tomato sauce suggested overleaf is just one possibility – you could use instead a few spoonfuls of the sieved roasted tomatoes that go into the sauce on page 142. Then again, you could cook a sauce with skinned, diced fresh tomatoes when they're in season. However you do it, the important thing is not to use too much – you're after a thin covering, not a swamping, so that you can still see patches of pizza base showing through. Don't be afraid to forego the tomato sauce altogether, as I have for the pizza illustrated here – just trickle the dough generously with good olive oil flavoured with grated garlic before you apply the toppings.

Makes 4–5 pizzas (each serves 1 generously)

For the pizza dough:

250g plain white flour

250g strong white flour

10g fine sea salt

5g dried or fast-action yeast

2 tablespoons rapeseed or olive oil

Cornmeal, or fine polenta or semolina, for dusting (optional)

For the quick tomato sauce (optional):

2 tablespoons rapeseed or olive oil

1 garlic clove, finely sliced

2 x 400g tins of chopped tomatoes (or 1 tin plus a jar of passata)

A pinch of sugar

Sea salt and freshly ground black pepper

Toppings:

Scraps of air-dried or cooked ham, or crisp nuggets of cooked bacon or chorizo

An egg, broken on to the pizza just before baking

A handful of sliced mushrooms, sautéed in oil with garlic until dry

Cheese – strips of buffalo mozzarella, coarsely grated hard cheese or crumbled blue or goat's cheese

Coarsely chopped olives

Anchovies, rinsed and drained

Sardines in oil, drained and coarsely flaked

Capers

Roughly chopped rosemary or thyme

For adding after baking:

Shredded basil or rocket, or torn flat-leaf parsley, or thyme leaves

To make the dough, combine the flours and salt in a large bowl. If you're using ordinary dried yeast, dissolve it in 325ml warm water and leave for 10 minutes or so. If you're using fast-action yeast, mix it straight into the flour. Add the yeast liquid or 325ml warm water and oil to the flour, mix to form a rough dough, then turn out on to a lightly floured surface and knead for about 10 minutes, until silky and elastic (follow the kneading technique on page 69). Don't be tempted to add too much extra flour, even if the dough seems sticky – it will become less so as you knead.

Put the dough in a lightly oiled bowl, turning it so it gets a coating of oil, cover with cling film and leave to rise in a warm place until doubled in size; this will probably take at least an hour.

Meanwhile, make the tomato sauce, if using: heat the oil in a frying pan over a gentle heat. Add the garlic and let it sizzle very gently for a minute or so. As soon as it starts to turn golden, add the tomatoes. Let them bubble gently, stirring often, for 10–15 minutes, until you have a thick sauce. Transfer to a jug and purée with a stick blender (if you do it in the pan, the sauce will go everywhere), or just crush the chunks of tomato in the pan with a fork until you have a reasonably smooth sauce. Season to taste with salt, pepper and the sugar.

Preheat the oven to 250°C/Gas Mark 10, or as high as it will go, and put 2 baking sheets in it to heat up.

Punch the risen dough down with your hands to knock it back on a floured surface and cut it into 4 or 5 pieces. Use a rolling pin or your hands (or both), to roll and stretch each piece into a thin circle or square, or a strange, amoeba-type shape, whichever you prefer; it should be no more than 5mm thick – thinner if you can get away with it.

Carefully take one of your hot baking sheets from the oven, scatter it with a little flour or, even better, some cornmeal, polenta or semolina, and lay the pizza base on it. Thinly spread a little tomato sauce – a couple of dessertspoons should be enough – over the dough (or trickle with garlicky olive oil, see page 82). Now add the toppings of your choice and grind over some pepper. Bake for 10–12 minutes, until the base is crisp and golden brown at the edges.

While it is cooking, roll out the next piece of dough, and prepare the next pizza in the same way. Serve hot, in big slices, trickled with a little more oil.

VARIATIONS

Pizza bianca

This is pizza without tomato sauce. A tangle of soft, sweet onions top the dough, seasoned with thyme or oregano and enriched with a little mozzarella or crème fraîche – a lovely, simple meal.

Make the dough (see left). While it is rising, heat 4 tablespoons of olive or rapeseed oil in a large frying pan, add 1kg very finely sliced onions and a good pinch of salt and cook gently for 20–25 minutes, stirring occasionally, until the onions are soft and translucent. Spread them over the rolled-out dough, scatter over some thyme or chopped oregano, then add a few dollops of crème fraîche or some mozzarella, broken into small pieces. Grind over some pepper, drizzle with a little oil and bake (as left).

Plain pizza

This is an excellent type of flatbread. Simply roll out the pizza dough (as left) and bake it, absolutely unadorned, for about 8 minutes, until crisp and golden. Remove from the oven and trickle generously with your very best extra virgin oil. Scatter with flaky sea salt, grind over some pepper, then serve. It's delicious with dips as a starter or part of a mezze, and also makes a good partner to soups or salads.

Grissini

The pizza dough can also be used to make grissini (breadsticks) for nibbling and dipping. Just shape small sausages of the knocked-back dough into long, thin sticks. Leave them plain or brush lightly with oil and sprinkle with flaky sea salt, or seeds, spices or herbs of your choice. Transfer to an oiled baking sheet, leave to rise for half an hour, then bake at 220°C/Gas Mark 7 for 15–20 minutes.

Bill's Rona oatcakes

At the end of a long day's fishing and filming on the Isle of Rona in the Inner Hebrides, Bill Cowie, the island manager, made us a batch of these for tea. We devoured the lot, some with marmalade, some with honey, and some with cheese and home-made chutney. This is now my standard oatcake recipe.

Makes about 20

150g medium oatmeal

150g porridge oats (but not jumbo oats)

½ teaspoon fine sea salt

A few twists of freshly ground black pepper (optional)

A small handful of sunflower or other seeds (optional)

75ml extra virgin olive, rapeseed or hempseed oil

Mix all the dry ingredients together in a bowl and make a well in the centre. Pour the oil into the well, stir and then pour in just enough boiling water (about 150ml) to bind it into a firm dough. Work quickly and don't worry if you over-water a bit – you can remedy the situation by adding more oatmeal, if necessary.

Shape the dough into a ball and leave it to rest for a few minutes. Roll it out on a lightly floured surface, or between 2 sheets of baking parchment, until about 5mm thick. Cut out rounds with a 6cm biscuit cutter. You can re-roll the offcuts to make more oatcakes but the dough will become increasingly crumbly the more you work it.

Place the oatcakes on 2 lightly floured baking sheets and bake in an oven preheated to 180°C/Gas Mark 4 for 20 minutes. Turn the oatcakes over and bake for a further 10 minutes. Leave to cool on a wire rack.

The oatcakes will keep for up to a week in an airtight container.

Digestives

If you like digestives, you might think your
favourite brand is hard to improve on. But
once you've made your own, you'll never look back.
I give two options for the sugar quantity in the recipe
below: the less sweet biscuits are better suited to
pâtés and charcuterie, while the sweeter ones are
good with cheese, or naked and unadorned
with a cup of tea. If you like, make them with
half wholemeal and half spelt flour, or entirely
with spelt flour, to give a slightly nuttier taste.

Makes 35–40

**250g wholemeal flour,
or wholemeal spelt flour**

**250g unsalted butter,
cut into small cubes and
slightly softened**

250g medium oatmeal

**75g or 125g soft brown
sugar, depending on
how sweet you want
your biscuits**

2 teaspoons fine sea salt

**2 teaspoons baking
powder**

About 1 tablespoon milk

Pulse the flour and butter together in a food processor until the
mixture resembles fine breadcrumbs, or you can do this in a large
bowl by rubbing the butter and flour together with your fingertips.
Add the oatmeal, sugar, salt and baking powder and mix together
with your hands, adding a little milk a few drops at a time until
everything comes together into a slightly sticky dough.

Dust with more flour, then press into a disc about 25cm in diameter.
Wrap in cling film and chill for at least 30 minutes, to rest and firm up
a bit. The dough will keep well in the fridge for a few days. Remove
it from the fridge about an hour before you want to roll it out, as it
will become very hard.

Dust the dough with flour and roll it out carefully, dusting regularly
with more flour to stop it sticking, until it is about 3–4mm thick.
As it is quite sticky and brittle, you may find it easier to roll between
2 sheets of greaseproof paper or cling film, also dusted with flour.

Cut the biscuits out with a 6–7cm cutter and use a spatula to transfer
them to non-stick baking sheets (or ordinary baking sheets lined
with baking parchment). Place in an oven preheated to 180°C/Gas
Mark 4 and bake for up to 10 minutes, checking regularly after the
first 5 minutes. They should be golden brown around the edges and
lightly coloured on top.

Remove from the oven and leave the biscuits to cool and firm up on
the baking sheet for a few minutes before transferring them to a wire
rack to cool completely.

As Tina Turner might have sung, 'What's lunch got to do with it?'

The fact is that for most of us these days, during the week at least, lunch is an irrelevance. Not so much because we don't eat it – we still generally manage to shovel some kind of calorific concoction into our mouths between the hours of noon and 2pm. No, the problem is that we scarcely notice we're eating it. We devour our food on autopilot, barely savouring the taste and texture, as our brains continue to tick over the day's workload.

To me, this is clearly so wrong. That's why the message of this chapter is simple. If you want to improve the quality of your working day, then improve the quality of your daily lunch. For anyone who is any kind of a home cook, the best way to do that, without a doubt, is to pack a lunchbox.

The home-made packed lunch works on so many levels. It ensures that you always eat something you like for lunch, because you (or someone who loves you) have prepared it specially. It slots neatly into a thrifty approach to feeding the family, because more often than not it will largely be made up of (top-quality) leftovers. And it gives you more time to enjoy the break in the middle of your working day, as you don't have to queue round the block for the same old sandwich. (I've got nothing against the sandwich, by the way. Many of the recipes in this chapter can be happily adapted to go between two slices of bread – and the resulting lunch will knock the product of your average city sandwich bar into a cocked bowler.)

Freed from the need to fight your co-workers for access to second-rate fast food, you can concentrate on finding somewhere nice – the park, the roof – to enjoy your own tiptop Tupperware tuck (or someone nice to enjoy it with). And it certainly saves you money. Even a relatively gourmet lunchbox (spiced chicken couscous; mackerel fillet with Puy lentils and pesto; beetroot hummus and goat's cheese sandwich…) will cost you only a couple of quid if it's put together at home. And for around £15 a week, I reckon you can lunch like a king. So, the notion of the portable working lunch is central to the recipes that follow. All but a very few are suited to making the journey with you to your place of work.

I feel passionately about lunchboxes because I make one several times a week for my wife, who goes out to work (and of course I feel passionately about her). Most of these recipes, or close variations thereof, have featured on her lunchtime menu at one time or another and so, of course, have many other wholesome combinations that I've never written down and probably never will.

However, there is a set of guiding principles that produces well-balanced combinations – always delicious, if rarely ever quite the same twice. It initially involves scouring the fridge for significant leftovers. In our house, this search is most fruitful in the early part of the week, since weekend menus usually have leftovers for weekday lunches factored in.

The first tier of the scavenge is the search for protein: generally meat or fish, so there might be some shreds of cold roast chicken, lamb or pork. A little more exotically, there could be some leftovers from a more elaborate recipe – for example, sticky glazed spare ribs (page 210). Gosh, they're good cold.

Next comes a scan for leftover starch and/or grains or pulses. Some cold new potatoes? Cooked rice or pasta? Lentils, perhaps? If this draws a blank, there's still the option of cooking something quick from scratch while we have our breakfast. Puy lentils are ready after boiling for just 20 minutes or so, and cool very quickly if spread out on a plate. Couscous is practically instant. If time is tight and other options limited, you can always open a tin of chickpeas.

In summer, there may be time to pick a few handfuls of French beans from the garden and fling them into a pan of simmering water for 5 minutes, or wash and pack a little bunch of baby carrots or crisp radishes, or simply throw in a handful of cheery cherry tomatoes…

Having two or three primary ingredients in hand, it's time for a little creative thought. Nothing too taxing, you understand, you're just asking yourself the question, 'What can I add now to make this really nice?' A scattering of capers or cornichons, a little crumbled goat's cheese or good old grated Cheddar? Some seeds/nuts/dried fruit, perhaps? And it's always worth keeping some dukka (page 134) handy – it's a lunchbox winner.

The final touch is usually some kind of dressing. It might just be a glug of good oil and a squeeze of lemon, or a thoroughly shaken and emulsified mustardy vinaigrette (see page 97). It could be a blob of mayonnaise from a jar – and you might want to pimp that with some lemon juice, a smidgeon of crushed garlic and a good blob of mustard. Or you might want to go to another level of premeditation with one of the fresh pestos on page 132. These will keep for several days, and will instantly transform an otherwise bland combo of leftover meat/fish and grains/pulses into a really excellent lunch.

If you have the facilities to heat food at work, a whole separate raft of options opens up. Marie has a microwave at work and, unlike me, she's not afraid to use it. So if there's some leftover stew and some leftover mash, or the remains of a big, hearty soup (you'll find several of these in the Thrifty Meat chapter), then the job of sorting the lunchbox is done before it's begun. Sometimes a little customising is in order. If there's stew but no mash, or a soup that's full of lively veg but light on substance, some quickly cooked couscous, rice or pasta, or tinned pulses, can be incorporated. If you can organise some plain hot pasta at work, by way of microwave, kettle or conventional hob, then your lovingly home-made pesto can reassert itself in a more conventional role, simply tossed with a mound of hot buttered spaghetti (or noodles).

Even if there are no leftovers at all, a lovely lunchbox can still be composed from scratch if you have some reasonable resources to draw on. In the summer, the combination of store-cupboard plus the vegetable garden (or veg box), with perhaps some good cheese standing by, should provide the makings of any number of substantial and really quite sophisticated salads. That's where the seasonal slaws (pages 120–3) are coming from. If you have the foresight/organisational skills to do something about your lunch the evening before, a whole load of lovely salads that use cooked vegetables as a main ingredient can then enter the fray. The two most frequently occurring examples in our kitchen are beetroot and squash. If ever we're cooking (usually roasting) either vegetable as a side dish, we'll try to cook enough for a lunchbox outing in the days ahead.

You'll have grasped by now that cooking more of something in order to enjoy the leftovers as lunch pickings is second nature in my kitchen, and pretty fundamental to my family's approach to eating. So much so that sometimes we actually cook something solely in order to be able to use it as leftovers. That sounds a bit batty, I know, but having a bowl of cooked Puy lentils or couscous standing by in the fridge means you always have a quick lunch (or indeed a quick supper, come to that) in waiting. Even if all you mix it with is a few scraps of leftover roast lamb and a dab of that oh-so-useful pesto.

Clearly these guiding principles of lunchbox assembly need not always lead, literally, to a lunch in a box. My own weekday working lunch is similar to, but different from, Marie's. If I'm working from home, I usually raid the fridge/store-cupboard/garden in much the same way as I do for her lunchbox – only I don't have to be quite so disciplined (by which I mean tidy), as there's no need to pack it all away in a neat, portable parcel. I'm more likely to spread out the bounty of my raiding party on the kitchen table and pick and mix to my heart's content.

In fact, it's an extension of this process that very often gives us our most enjoyable family lunches at weekends. I'm talking about a generous smorgasbord of leftovers (cold cuts of meat or fish, often tossed with dressed pulses), just-pickeds (salad and/or crudités from the garden or greengrocer's), ready-to-eats (good home-made or locally made ham, pâté or salami) and one or two quick and easy things that have been knocked up specially. The latter might be one of my favourite hummi (on pages 124–9), a big bowl of one of the slaws (on pages 120–3) or, when we've got plenty of eggs, a large frittata (on pages 106–9).

I am more than happy to extend this lovely way of eating to accommodate even quite large numbers of guests – especially in summer, when most lunches will effectively be picnics at the table, either inside or out. Besides the recipes in this chapter, many of the ones in the Vegetables Galore chapter fit perfectly into this scheme.

Sitting down for a more traditional Sunday lunch of big roast, big stew or big baked fish, plus trimmings and more or less traditional accompanying vegetables, isn't something we do every weekend. But when we do, then no sooner is my plate clean than I'm eyeing up what's left of the meal, imagining the myriad ways in which they might enhance the lunches (and suppers) of the coming week.

Tomato, chipolata and new potato lunch(box) with mustardy vinaigrette

This is comfort food for work days: herby sausages, tangy tomatoes and potatoes, all lightly coated in a mustardy dressing. If this doesn't cheer you up at lunchtime, nothing will.

Serves 1

About 4 cold boiled new potatoes, cut into chunks if large

A handful of sweet, ripe cherry tomatoes, halved

2–3 cold cooked herby chipolata sausages

For the dressing:

1 teaspoon English (or other strong) mustard

1½ teaspoons cider vinegar or white wine vinegar

2 tablespoons rapeseed or extra virgin olive oil

A small pinch of sugar

Sea salt and freshly ground black pepper

To make the dressing, whisk all the ingredients together in a bowl, or shake them in a small screw-top jar to combine.

Put the potatoes and tomatoes in a bowl, trickle over most of the dressing and toss together. Transfer to your lunchbox. Place the chipolatas on top and trickle on the remaining dressing. Seal your lunchbox and don't forget to take a fork and napkin with you.

note If you think your lunchbox might leak, take the dressing in the screw-top jar you mixed it in and add it before eating.

Sardine niçoise lunch(box)

I am a great fan of the tinned sardine and never tire of thinking up new ways to use it. With some cold potatoes and crunchy French beans along for the ride, it makes a healthy and delicious summer lunch(box). Feel free to embellish with other classic salade niçoise components: hard-boiled eggs, olives, anchovies, capers etc. But even without them, this is a very decent lunch.

Serves 1

2–3 cold cooked potatoes

About 75g cold cooked French beans

2–3 tinned sardines, drained

1–2 tablespoons rapeseed or extra virgin olive oil

A lemon wedge

Sea salt and freshly ground black pepper

Slice the potatoes thickly and arrange in a layer in your lunchbox (or on a plate). Scatter the beans over the top, followed by some salt and pepper. Add the sardines, broken into rough chunks if you like. Trickle on the oil, tuck in the wedge of lemon for last-minute squeezing, and seal your lunchbox (or serve up).

Beef with mustardy lentils and mint

This works as a portable lunchbox, picnic dish, or as part of a cold-cuts lunch or buffet spread. Lentils are best served slightly warm or at room temperature, so you can prepare them ahead.

You can also make this with leftover roast pork or chicken, cooked sausages, or cold ox tongue or salt beef, leaving the salt out of the dressing if you are using cured meat.

Serves 4

200g Puy lentils

1 bay leaf

2 tablespoons rapeseed or olive oil

1 onion, finely chopped

1 celery stalk, finely chopped

About 200g cold roast beef, cut into strips or torn into rough shreds

2 tablespoons roughly chopped mint

For the dressing:

2 good teaspoons English mustard

2 teaspoons cider vinegar

3 tablespoons rapeseed or extra virgin olive oil

Sea salt and freshly ground black pepper

Put the lentils in a saucepan, cover with plenty of cold water and add the bay leaf. Bring to the boil, turn down to a simmer and cook for about 20 minutes, until the lentils are al dente. Keep an eye on them, and taste after about 15 minutes, as they can go from al dente to soft very quickly. Top up with more water if necessary during cooking.

Meanwhile, heat the oil in another pan, add the onion and celery and sweat gently for about 5 minutes, stirring occasionally, until softened but still with a bit of crunch. Remove from the heat and set aside.

When the lentils are done, drain them, remove the bay leaf and return the lentils to the warm pan. Whisk together all the dressing ingredients and tip into the warm lentils, along with the sautéed onion and celery. Stir well and leave to cool.

Toss the beef and mint into the lentils, taste and add some more seasoning if you like.

VARIATIONS

Beef with horseradishy lentils

If you have horseradish sauce left over along with your beef, use a couple of teaspoons of this in the dressing instead of the mustard.

Leftover mackerel lunchbox

For a fantastic lunch for two, use roughly half the quantity of lentils listed above and toss with 100–150g flaked cold cooked mackerel (or other cold, cooked fish), loads of roughly chopped parsley and a tablespoon of small capers, rinsed.

Chicken, French bean and almond salad

Another simple three-way-combo salad that makes an easy summer lunchbox, not to mention light supper. If you can get hold of plump, sweet Marcona almonds, it will be particularly special. You can, of course, substitute other nuts and seeds – cashew, pumpkin etc, and combinations thereof. There's a touch of honey in the dressing to bring out the sweetness of the nuts and beans – replace with a pinch of sugar, if you prefer.

Serves 2

About 200g French beans, trimmed

A good handful of blanched almonds

About 200g cold cooked chicken, torn into shreds

For the dressing:

¼–½ garlic clove, crushed

½ teaspoon Dijon mustard or other mild mustard

1 teaspoon cider vinegar or white wine vinegar

About ½ teaspoon honey

2 tablespoons rapeseed or extra virgin olive oil

Sea salt and freshly ground black pepper

Cook the French beans in a large pan of boiling salted water for 3–5 minutes, until just tender but still with a bit of bite. Drain, refresh immediately under cold running water and pat dry.

Scatter the almonds in a dry frying pan and toast over a medium heat for a few minutes, shaking the pan occasionally, until golden brown. Leave to cool.

Whisk all the ingredients for the dressing together in a bowl or shake in a screw-top jar to combine.

Put the beans, shredded chicken and almonds in a large bowl and toss together with your hands. Trickle over the dressing, toss well and serve. Or, if you want to make a lunchbox of this, transfer the undressed salad to a plastic box or other suitable lidded container and seal. Take the dressing with you separately in a small screw-top jar and add just before you tuck in.

Chicken with couscous, honey and cinnamon

Whilst I've got nothing against a good chicken sandwich, there are many more exciting things you can do with a few shreds of cold roast chicken. Couscous is a very useful medium for leftover meat, and this is one of my favourite ways to eat cold chicken. Take a tub of this with you to work, or serve up with crisp lettuce leaves as a quick supper.

Serves 2

75g blanched almonds

2 tablespoons rapeseed or olive oil

1 onion, finely chopped

1 garlic clove, chopped

1 teaspoon ground cinnamon

125g couscous

1 tablespoon runny honey

About 250ml boiling water, or chicken or vegetable stock

About 150g cold cooked chicken, cut into small pieces

1 small pickled lemon, pulp discarded and skin finely chopped (or the grated zest of ½ fresh lemon)

A good squeeze of lemon juice

1 tablespoon chopped parsley or mint

Sea salt and freshly ground black pepper

Put the almonds in a dry frying pan and toast over a medium heat for a few minutes, tossing occasionally, until golden brown. Leave to cool, then chop them very roughly.

Heat the oil in a small saucepan, add the onion, garlic and some salt and pepper and sweat gently for about 10 minutes, until softened. Add the cinnamon, then take off the heat and stir in the couscous.

Stir the honey into the boiling water or stock until dissolved, then pour over the couscous (it should just cover it) and put a tight-fitting lid on the pan. Leave for 10 minutes, until the couscous has swollen up and absorbed all the liquid. Fluff it up with a fork, transfer to a bowl and leave to cool.

Toss the chicken pieces, almonds, pickled lemon or zest, and the lemon juice into the couscous and season to taste.

Pack into a lunchbox, or pile into a serving dish for serving at the table. Either way, finish with a sprinkling of parsley or mint and a good grinding of black pepper.

VARIATION

Leftover lamb with couscous, lemon and mint

Prepare the couscous as above, leaving out the cinnamon and honey. Toss about 150g shredded cold roast lamb into the couscous, along with the grated zest and juice of 1 lemon and 2 tablespoons of chopped mint. You can keep the almonds or not, as you prefer, and/or add a couple of handfuls of chopped dried apricots, if you like.

Three frittatas

A frittata is simply a thick, chunky omelette made with some vegetables and usually a little cheese. Served warm, in wedges, it makes an excellent supper. Left to go cold, then sliced into chunks, it's robust enough to pack into a lunchbox or picnic basket. In fact, it's ideal prepare-ahead food.

Quite apart from this, frittata appeals to me because you can add almost anything you like to it: bacon or cooked sausage, flaked fish, any kind of cheese, peas or broad beans, asparagus, kale, spinach or broccoli, mushrooms, and so on. My only caveat is to avoid 'wet' ingredients such as tomatoes, which will stop the eggs setting properly.

Spinach, bacon and goat's cheese frittata

Serves 4

1 tablespoon rapeseed or sunflower oil

75g pancetta or bacon, cut into small cubes

4 shallots, thinly sliced

100g young leaf spinach

8 medium eggs

25g Parmesan, Cheddar or other hard cheese, finely grated

A grating or two of nutmeg

100g soft goat's cheese, crumbled into biggish chunks

Sea salt and freshly ground black pepper

Heat the oil in a 25cm non-stick ovenproof frying pan over a medium heat. Add the pancetta or bacon and sauté until golden, then remove with a slotted spoon; set aside. Add the shallots to the pan, lower the heat and cook gently for about 10 minutes, until soft but not coloured. Add the spinach and turn until just wilted, then take off the heat.

Lightly beat the eggs in a bowl, then stir in the pancetta or bacon, spinach and shallots, grated cheese, nutmeg and seasoning. Put the frying pan back over a low heat, pour in the egg mixture and cook gently, without stirring, letting the eggs set slowly from the base up. After about 5 minutes, give the pan a little shake: the bottom half of the frittata should be set, with a layer of wet egg still on top.

Dot the goat's cheese over the top, then place in an oven preheated to 180°C/Gas Mark 4 for 5–10 minutes until just set, or put the pan under a medium-hot grill, ideally not too close to the heat, for about 5 minutes. Let cool slightly (or completely) before slicing and serving.

Frittata niçoise

A French salad reinterpreted through the medium of an Italian omelette?
Why not? The proof is in the eating. Please only use sustainably sourced,
pole-and-line-caught tuna. Alternatively, you can make this with tinned
sardines, using the oil from the tin to fry the onions.

Serves 4

2 tablespoons rapeseed
or sunflower oil

About 6 spring onions,
sliced on the diagonal

1 garlic clove, finely
chopped

8 medium eggs

About 150g cold cooked
new potatoes, thickly
sliced

About 50g cold cooked
French beans, cut into
2cm lengths

About 100g tinned tuna,
drained and roughly
flaked

About 20 stoned black
or Kalamata olives in oil,
drained

Sea salt and freshly
ground black pepper

Heat the oil in a 25cm non-stick ovenproof frying pan over a medium
heat. Add the spring onions and garlic and cook gently for 3–4
minutes, until soft but not coloured, then remove from the heat.

Lightly beat the eggs in a large bowl, then stir in the potatoes, beans,
tuna and olives. Add the spring onions, season and mix well.

Return the frying pan to a low heat and tip in the egg mixture,
making sure the olives are evenly distributed. Cook gently, without
stirring, just letting the eggs set slowly from the base up. After about
5 minutes, give the pan a little shake: the bottom half of the frittata
should be set, with a layer of wet egg still on top.

Either place in an oven preheated to 180°C/Gas Mark 4 for 5–10
minutes until just set, or put the pan under a medium-hot grill,
ideally not too close to the heat, for about 5 minutes. Allow to cool
slightly (or completely) before slicing and serving.

Onion frittata

The classic Spanish tortilla is similar to an Italian frittata. You can turn this recipe into a tortilla by simply adding about 300g thickly sliced cold cooked waxy potatoes (such as Charlotte) to the beaten egg with the softened onions.

Serves 4

3 tablespoons rapeseed or sunflower oil

2 large onions, chopped

8 medium eggs

1–2 tablespoons finely chopped parsley

25g Parmesan, Cheddar or other hard cheese, finely grated

Sea salt and freshly ground black pepper

Heat the oil in a 25cm non-stick ovenproof frying pan over a medium heat. Stir in the onions and a sprinkling of salt, then lower the heat and cook for about 15 minutes, until the onions are very soft and translucent but not coloured.

Lightly beat the eggs in a bowl and then mix in the parsley and two-thirds of the cheese. Season with salt and pepper (remember the cheese is quite salty), then stir in the onions.

Put the frying pan back over a low heat, pour in the egg mixture and cook gently, without moving the ingredients about, just letting the eggs set slowly from the base up. After about 5 minutes, give the pan a little shake: the bottom half of the frittata should be set, with a good layer of wet egg still on top.

Sprinkle over the remaining cheese, then either place the frittata in an oven preheated to 180°C/Gas Mark 4 for 5–10 minutes until just set, or put the pan under a medium-hot grill, ideally not too close to the heat, for about 5 minutes. Allow to cool slightly (or completely) before slicing and serving.

Three savoury pasties

Inspired by the great original, the Cornish pasty, these are all filling, portable meals, neatly wrapped in their own edible packaging. If you don't have time to make the rough puff pastry, you could make shortcrust (see page 328), or use a good, ready-made, all-butter puff or flaky pastry. Eat the pasties hot from the oven, cold at your desk or in the park, or even – dare I say? – reheated (thoroughly) in the office microwave.

Chicken and leek pasties

Serves 4

For the rough puff pastry:
300g plain flour
A pinch of sea salt
150g chilled unsalted butter, cut into small cubes

For the filling:
25g butter
2–3 medium leeks (about 500g), trimmed and finely sliced
1 teaspoon roughly chopped thyme leaves
150ml double cream
1 teaspoon English mustard
About 400g boned chicken thigh and breast meat (or leftover cooked chicken), cut into thick slices
1 tablespoon rapeseed or olive oil (if using fresh chicken)
Sea salt and freshly ground black pepper

To finish:
1 medium egg, lightly beaten with 1 teaspoon milk, for glazing

To make the pastry, mix the flour with the salt, then add the cubed butter and toss until the pieces are coated with flour. Add just enough iced water (8–10 tablespoons) to bring the mixture together into a fairly firm dough.

Shape the dough into a rectangle with your hands and, on a well-floured surface, roll it out in one direction, away from you, so you end up with a rectangle about 1cm thick. Fold the far third towards you, then fold the nearest third over that (rather like folding a business letter), so that you now have a rectangle made up of 3 equal layers. Give the pastry a quarter-turn, then repeat the rolling, folding and turning process 5 more times. Wrap the pastry in cling film and rest it in the fridge for about 30 minutes, or up to an hour.

To make the filling, melt the butter in a frying pan, add the leeks and thyme, and sweat gently for 5–10 minutes, until the leeks are very tender. Stir in the cream and cook gently for 4–5 minutes to reduce and thicken. Stir in the mustard, season well and leave to cool.

If using fresh chicken, season well and fry in the oil in a frying pan over a medium-high heat until evenly browned.

Roll out the pastry on a lightly floured work surface to about 3mm thick. Using a plate or a cake tin as a template, cut out four 20cm circles; you may have to gather up the trimmings and re-roll them to get your fourth circle.

Spoon the leek mixture on to one half of each circle and pile the chicken on top. Brush the pastry edges with a little water, fold the other half of the pastry over the filling to form a half-moon shape and crimp well to seal.

Place on a lightly oiled baking sheet and brush the tops of the pasties with beaten egg. Bake in an oven preheated to 190°C/Gas Mark 5 for about 25 minutes, until the pastry is golden brown. Eat hot or cold.

Leftover stew pasties

Practically any stew will do for this, but particularly good are the oxtail stew with cinnamon and star anise (page 228), rabbit ragù (page 219) and the pot-roast pheasant with chorizo, butter beans and parsley (page 234). If you don't have enough stew left for the filling, you could also add some leftover cooked vegetables, such as diced potatoes or carrots or shredded greens, or a handful of cooked beans or other pulses.

Serves 4

1 quantity of rough puff pastry (see page 110)

For the filling:
About 450g cold leftover stew

To finish:
1 medium egg, lightly beaten with 1 teaspoon milk, for glazing

For the filling, drain off any excess juices from the stew so that the meat and veg are just lightly coated in gravy. Take any large chunks of meat or veg and chop them up roughly before stirring back together. Taste the stew and make sure it's seasoned to your liking. Leave to cool completely.

Roll out the pastry on a lightly floured work surface to about 3mm thick. Using a plate or a cake tin as a template, cut out four 20cm circles; you may have to gather up the trimmings and re-roll them to get your fourth circle.

Spoon the stew on to one half of each circle. Brush the pastry edges with water, fold the other half of the pastry over the filling to form a half-moon shape and crimp well to seal.

Place the pasties on a lightly oiled baking sheet and brush the tops with beaten egg. Bake in an oven preheated to 190°C/Gas Mark 5 for about 25 minutes, until the pastry is golden brown. Eat warm or cold.

Lentil and squash pasties

If you don't fancy making pastry, double the quantities and this makes a delicious filling for a meat-free, mash-topped vegetarian shepherd's pie.

Serves 4

1 quantity of rough puff pastry (see page 110)

For the filling:
1 tablespoon rapeseed or olive oil

1 small onion, finely chopped

1 small celery stalk, finely chopped

1 small carrot, finely chopped

1 garlic clove, finely chopped

100ml white wine (optional)

100g green or brown lentils

300ml stock (such as ten-minute vegetable stock, page 266)

1 bay leaf

A sprig of thyme (optional)

250g butternut or other squash, chopped into 1cm dice

2 teaspoons apple balsamic or other balsamic vinegar (see page 14)

2 teaspoons hot English mustard

Sea salt and freshly ground black pepper

To finish:
1 medium egg, lightly beaten with 1 teaspoon milk, for glazing

For the filling, heat the oil in a saucepan, add the onion, celery, carrot, garlic and some salt and pepper and cook gently for 10–15 minutes, until soft. Add the wine, if you're using it, and let it bubble away to nothing. Add the lentils and stock, season well, then add the bay leaf and thyme, if using. Stir well, cover and simmer gently for about 10 minutes.

Add the squash and simmer for another 20 minutes, or until both lentils and squash are tender. If the filling looks a bit wet, you can either drain off some of the liquid and/or take out a couple of spoonfuls of the lentils, mash them, then stir them back in to thicken the sauce. Stir in the balsamic vinegar and the mustard and check the seasoning. Leave to cool.

Roll out the pastry on a lightly floured work surface to about 3mm thick. Using a plate or a cake tin as a template, cut out four 20cm circles; you may have to gather up the trimmings and re-roll them to get your fourth circle.

Spoon the filling on to one half of each circle. Brush the pastry edges with a little water, fold the other half of the pastry over the filling to form a half-moon shape and crimp well to seal.

Place the shaped pasties on a lightly oiled baking sheet and brush the tops with beaten egg. Bake in an oven preheated to 190°C/ Gas Mark 5 for about 25 minutes, until the pastry is golden brown. Eat warm or cold.

Tartiflette toastie

Lunch doesn't get more comforting – or greedy, frankly – than this sumptuous version of cheese on toast, which is also a great way to use up leftovers. It's not something you can take to the office, granted, but it is just the sort of thing I like to rustle up for lunch when I'm at home. It's inspired by the Savoyarde dish, tartiflette, a rich baked combination of potatoes, cheese and bacon. Tartiflette is usually made with Reblochon but any semi-soft, washed-rind cheese works well – from Brie (not too ripe) to Irish Ardrahan – or try a semi-hard cheese, such as Cornish Yarg.

Serves 1

1 tablespoon rapeseed or olive oil

2 bacon rashers, or a slice of cold ham, cut into small strips

1 cold cooked potato (baked, boiled or even roasted), thickly sliced

1–2 tablespoons double cream or crème fraîche

1 large, thick slice of bread

3–4 thickish slices (about 30g) semi-soft or semi-hard cheese, or Cheddar (at a push)

Sea salt and freshly ground black pepper

A few crisp, bitter salad leaves, such as chicory, radicchio or frisée, to serve

Heat the oil in a small frying pan over a medium heat. If you are using bacon, add it to the pan and fry for a few minutes, until cooked. Add the potato and fry until it is heated through and starting to colour a little. If you're using ham, add this now and stir until well heated through.

Stir in the cream or crème fraîche and allow it to bubble and reduce for a couple of minutes. Remove from the heat and season to taste.

Toast the bread, pile the mixture on top, then cover with the sliced cheese and whack under a hot grill. As soon as the cheese is melted and bubbling, whip out from under the grill and transfer to a plate. Serve at once, with a few crisp, bitter leaves on the side.

Tabula kisir

This is a lovely herby, spicy bulghur wheat dish from Turkey, similar to tabbouleh. It's the piquant dressing that makes it special. Despite the lengthy list of ingredients, it is quick and easy to make. When my greenhouse tomatoes are in full swing, I often double the quantity of tomatoes, leaving out the peppers. And you can make a very respectable version using couscous instead of bulghur wheat.

Serves 4–6

200g bulghur wheat

50g walnuts

350g ripe tomatoes

3–4 spring onions, top green part discarded

1 red pepper, cored and deseeded

1 green pepper, cored and deseeded

5 tablespoons finely chopped flat-leaf parsley

4 tablespoons finely chopped mint

3 tablespoons finely chopped dill

For the dressing:

4 tablespoons lemon juice

1 tablespoon tomato purée (concentrated)

Pinch of dried chilli flakes

1 teaspoon ground cumin

1 teaspoon paprika

1 teaspoon sea salt

1 teaspoon freshly ground black pepper

5 tablespoons rapeseed or extra virgin olive oil

To serve:

Pitta bread and/or Little Gem or Cos lettuce

Place the bulghur wheat in a large bowl, pour over 200ml boiling water, stir, then cover and leave for 20 minutes. The bulghur should retain some bite at this stage.

Meanwhile, make the dressing. Mix together the lemon juice, tomato purée, dried chilli, cumin, paprika, salt and pepper, then whisk in the oil. Pour the dressing over the warm bulghur and stir well. Leave to cool completely.

Put the walnuts on a baking tray and toast in an oven preheated to 180°C/Gas Mark 4 for 5–7 minutes, until fragrant. Leave to cool and then chop roughly.

Meanwhile, core, deseed and dice the tomatoes. Slice the spring onions finely, and cut the peppers into dice.

Once the bulghur is cool, combine it with the tomatoes, peppers, spring onions, walnuts and herbs. Leave to stand for at least 20 minutes so the flavours can mingle, then taste and adjust the seasoning, adding more salt, pepper and/or chilli flakes if you like. Serve with pitta bread and/or lettuce leaves.

VARIATION

Courgette kisir

Omit the green and red peppers. Slice, season and quickly fry 400–500g small courgettes (follow the recipe for lemony courgettes on toast on page 263, if you like), then add them to the salad with the tomatoes. Very firm, fresh young courgettes can be added raw – chop into small dice rather than slice.

Egg tartare

This feisty little mixture is so named because it combines all the elements of a classic tartare sauce. However, I've jiggled the quantities so the eggs become the main event, deliciously bound together with all the other ingredients. It makes the best egg sandwich you could ever tuck into your lunchbox. Alternatively, served on a single slice of bread, it makes a lovely and surprisingly elegant starter.

Makes enough for 4 substantial sandwiches, or serves 4–6 as a starter

6 medium eggs, at room temperature

4 spring onions or 2 small shallots, finely chopped

3–4 gherkins (about 30g), finely diced

1 tablespoon capers, rinsed

2 tablespoons finely chopped parsley

1 tablespoon finely chopped dill (optional)

2–3 tablespoons mayonnaise (page 282)

A dab of Dijon mustard

2–3 dashes of Tabasco sauce (optional)

Sea salt and freshly ground black pepper

Slices of wholemeal, sourdough, rye or your favourite bread, to serve

First, boil the eggs. They should be what I call soft-hard-boiled – that is, the whites completely set but the yolks just a bit runny in the middle. I achieve this pretty reliably by putting them in a pan of hand-hot water, covering it and bringing it quickly to the boil, then boiling for exactly 4 minutes – 5 if they are extra large. Then I run the eggs under the cold tap and peel them as soon as they are cool enough to handle.

Roughly chop the eggs and mix with the spring onions or shallots, gherkins, capers, parsley and dill, if using.

In a small bowl, whisk together the mayonnaise, mustard and Tabasco, if using. Gently combine this mixture with the eggs and season with salt and pepper. Serve on wholemeal, sourdough or rye bread, as closed or open sandwiches.

Three seasonal slaws

I make crunchy slaws of grated roots and shredded cabbage throughout the year, using whatever vegetables are in season. You need to take your time slicing and grating everything finely, but once you've got a big bowlful in the fridge, you need only transfer a portion to a lunchbox (or plate), add a little cold meat, cooked egg, cheese or other protein-rich finishing touch, and you have a filling, wholesome lunch.

To make a complete meal of these slaws, accompany them with one of the following:

- A couple of oatcakes and some shredded cold chicken, ham, pork or lamb.
- A slice of pork pie.
- A chunk of blue cheese, crumbled over the top, plus some lightly toasted walnuts.
- A wedge of cold frittata (see pages 106–9).
- A wholemeal roll filled with soft, mild goat's cheese sprinkled with salt and pepper.

Summer slaw

Serves 4

8 fat radishes, trimmed

A few small summer carrots, scrubbed

1 large or 2 small fennel bulbs

½ small red onion

1 tablespoon finely snipped chives

4 small lettuce hearts, such as Little Gem (optional)

For the vinaigrette:

1 teaspoon English mustard

1 tablespoon cider vinegar or white wine vinegar

3 tablespoons rapeseed or olive oil

Sea salt, freshly ground black pepper and a pinch of sugar

Very finely slice the radishes and carrots, using a mandolin if you have one, and place in a large bowl. Trim the base and tops off the fennel bulbs and remove the tough outer layers. Quarter the bulbs, remove the cores, then slice very finely and add to the radishes. Chop the red onion very finely and add to the bowl, along with the chives if you're using them.

Make the dressing by whisking everything together, then adjust the seasoning to taste. Toss the vegetables with the dressing. Taste the slaw and adjust the seasoning, if necessary.

If you're serving this at home, make sure you let it sit for at least half an hour before eating. Cut the lettuce hearts into quarters, if using, and arrange them around the edge of a large bowl. Spoon the slaw into the middle and serve – try it with crumbled blue cheese on top or some cold meats on the side. For a lunchbox, pile the slaw into a suitable container with the lettuce and other savoury items.

VARIATION

For a creamier slaw, dress with mayonnaise rather than vinaigrette.

Two-root slaw

In this lovely winter salad, I've simply added carrot to what is essentially a fairly classic celeriac rémoulade. You could include a little shredded white cabbage, which would take you further from rémoulade and closer to a traditional coleslaw.

Serves 6

2–3 large carrots
½ celeriac (about 400g)

For the dressing:
4 tablespoons good mayonnaise (page 282)
2 teaspoons English mustard
Juice of ½ lemon, or a dash of cider vinegar
1 tablespoon caraway seeds, lightly toasted in a dry frying pan (optional)
Sea salt and freshly ground black pepper

Peel the carrots and celeriac and coarsely grate them into a bowl (or use a mandolin on the matchstick setting, if you have one).

Beat together all the ingredients for the dressing, pour them over the grated vegetables and stir to coat thoroughly.

Pack in your lunchbox or serve at home, allowing the flavours to develop for an hour or so beforehand. It's good with cold meats, especially ham and tongue, or after a stew or shepherd's pie.

VARIATION

For a lighter dressing, make a mustardy vinaigrette, such as the one on page 120.

Purple slaw

This is a favourite autumn lunch for me, and a great way to use red cabbage. It always looks vibrant and stunning.

Serves 6

400g red cabbage
200g lightly cooked beetroot (see page 294)
75g walnuts, toasted and roughly chopped
75g raisins

For the dressing:
2 tablespoons rapeseed or extra virgin olive oil
2 tablespoons walnut oil
1 tablespoon cider vinegar
1 teaspoon runny honey
Sea salt and freshly ground black pepper

Finely shred the red cabbage and place in a bowl. Coarsely grate the beetroot (or cut it into matchsticks on a mandolin) and add to the cabbage along with the walnuts and raisins.

Whisk together all the ingredients for the dressing, adding salt and pepper to taste. Stir the dressing into the salad.

Either transfer a portion to a lunchbox or serve the salad at the table, after resting it for at least half an hour. This slaw is particularly good with ham or cold beef.

Three hummuses

Or should that be hummi? Authentic hummus is, of course, made with chickpeas and tahini, but I love the idea of making thick, dippable purées with fresh vegetables too. These are a few of my favourites. For lunchboxes, they make delicious sandwich fillings, but don't discount the idea of a portable hummus dip. Pack in a tub and take along some simple crudités – celery, cucumber, broccoli, cauliflower, peppers etc – and pitta bread. Or have as part of a mezze lunchbox, with a few olives, some flatbreads (page 78) or pitta, and some ready-made falafel or cubes of halloumi cheese.

Very lemony hummus

You might like to try this hummus in a sandwich with sliced tomatoes and a smear of harissa paste, or with grated carrot and a few torn mint leaves. If you are short of time, instead of cooking dried chickpeas, you can use a tin, well drained and rinsed; add a little water to them for the initial puréeing.

Serves 4–6

125g dried chickpeas
1 bay leaf
Juice of 2 lemons
½–1 small garlic clove, crushed with a little salt
2–3 tablespoons tahini (sesame seed paste)
2–3 tablespoons rapeseed or extra virgin olive oil
A pinch of ground cumin (optional)
Sea salt and freshly ground black pepper

Rinse the chickpeas thoroughly, then place them in a large bowl with enough water to cover them well. Leave to soak for at least 12 hours, or overnight.

Drain the chickpeas and put them in a saucepan with the bay leaf and enough cold water to cover generously. Bring to the boil, then turn the heat right down and partially cover with a lid. Simmer gently for about 3 hours, until the chickpeas are really soft, skimming the surface and topping up with boiling water as necessary to keep the chickpeas covered. Add ½ teaspoon of salt near the end of cooking. Drain the chickpeas, reserving the liquid, and discard the bay leaf.

Put 3–4 tablespoons of the hot cooking liquid into a food processor or blender with half the chickpeas, 4 tablespoons of the lemon juice and the garlic. Whiz for a few seconds. Add the remaining chickpeas, 2 tablespoons of tahini and 2 tablespoons of oil, then whiz again until you have the consistency you like. Scrape into a bowl.

Season with salt and plenty of pepper. If you think it needs more oil, lemon juice or tahini, add a little at a time, beating well, until you're happy with the flavour. Top with a sprinkling of cumin, if you like.

VARIATION
Add 3 or 4 tablespoons of finely chopped flat-leaf parsley, chervil or chives – or all three – to create a lovely, green-flecked purée.

Beetroot and walnut hummus

This glorious purple concoction – a revelation for people who claim not to like beetroot, or walnuts come to that – is wonderful with crisp crudités, in a sandwich with goat's cheese, or scooped up with flatbreads (page 78).

Serves 4

50g walnuts

1 tablespoon cumin seeds

25g stale bread, crusts removed

200g cooked beetroot (not pickled), cut into cubes

1 tablespoon tahini (sesame seed paste)

1 large garlic clove, crushed

Juice of 1 lemon

Sea salt and freshly ground black pepper

A little olive or rapeseed oil (optional)

Put the walnuts on a baking tray and toast in an oven preheated to 180°C/Gas Mark 4 for 5–7 minutes, until fragrant. Leave to cool.

Warm a small frying pan over a medium heat. Add the cumin seeds and dry-fry them, shaking the pan almost constantly, until they start to darken and release their aroma – this should take less than a minute, so be careful not to burn them. Crush the seeds with a pestle and mortar or a spice grinder.

Break the bread into small chunks, put in a food processor or blender with the walnuts and blitz until fine. Add the beetroot, tahini, most of the garlic, a good pinch of the cumin, half the lemon juice, a little salt and a good grind of pepper, then blend to a thick paste.

Taste the mixture and adjust it by adding a little more cumin, garlic, lemon, salt and/or pepper, blending again until you are happy with it. Loosen with a dash of oil if you think it needs it. Refrigerate until required but bring back to room temperature to serve.

Broad bean hummus

Towards the end of the summer, when broad beans get fat and floury and a little bitter, I like to whiz them up into this hummus. As well as making a fine dip, it is a great lunchbox addition – pack with some Little Gem lettuce leaves, crumbled ricotta and flatbreads (page 78); or use to fill a bap or pitta bread, along with a slice of ham.

Serves 4

400g shelled broad beans (late-season larger beans are fine to use)

½–1 garlic clove, crushed with a little salt

About 3 tablespoons rapeseed or extra virgin olive oil

A generous squeeze of lemon juice

Sea salt and freshly ground black pepper

Put the broad beans in a pan, cover with water and bring to the boil. Lower the heat and simmer for 5–10 minutes (depending on age and size) until tender, then drain. Set aside to cool, then slip the beans out of their skins.

Put the skinned broad beans in a food processor or blender with the garlic, 3 tablespoons of oil, a good squeeze of lemon juice and some salt and pepper. Process to a thick, slightly coarse purée, adding more oil if it seems too thick and dry.

When you're happy with the texture, transfer the purée to a bowl. Taste and adjust the seasoning with more salt, pepper and lemon juice as needed.

Pestos

Traditionally, pesto is tossed with hot pasta or spooned on to classic Italian minestrone, but I'm much more likely to use it as part of my lunchtime repertoire. I love to add it to sandwiches made with cold roast meat, tomatoes and crisp salad leaves. In fact, if I've got some really good, fresh white bread, I'm happy to anoint it with a generous slick of pesto and nothing else. It's also very good as a dressing for lunchbox salads. You could even take some to work to augment hot soup or a plain baked potato from the office canteen.

Classic pesto is, of course, made with basil, pine nuts, garlic, Parmesan and olive oil – and lovely it is too, especially if you've grown the basil yourself and harvested it minutes before blitzing. But the basic notion of pesto – a nutty seed (or seedy nut) pulverised with herbs, hard cheese and richly flavoured oil, is ripe for experimentation and customisation. At River Cottage we've had a lot of fun, and a lot of success, inventing pesto variations. Parsley is my favourite pesto herb, since it is so abundant and easy to grow. Here are a few favourite pestos. They will keep in the fridge for several days, or longer if the surface of the pesto is covered with a thin layer of oil.

Parsley and pumpkin seed pesto

Makes 6–8 tablespoons

75g pumpkin seeds

1 garlic clove, roughly chopped

A large bunch of parsley (about 50g), leaves only

150–200ml rapeseed or extra virgin olive oil

50g Parmesan or matured hard goat's cheese, finely grated

Juice of ½ lemon

Sea salt and freshly ground black pepper

Put the pumpkin seeds and garlic in a food processor or blender and pulse until the seeds are in coarse grains. Add the parsley leaves and pulse briefly until finely chopped and blended with the seeds. Then, with the machine running, pour in the oil in a slow, steady stream until you have a fairly thick, nicely grainy paste.

Scrape the mixture into a bowl. Stir in the cheese, thin with a little more oil if you want, then taste and adjust the seasoning with salt, pepper and lemon juice.

VARIATIONS

Parsley and walnut pesto

Make as above, but with 75g lightly toasted walnuts instead of the pumpkin seeds.

Basil and pumpkin seed pesto

Simply replace the parsley with basil (or include both herbs).

Parsley, walnut and blue cheese pesto

Make as above, but use 75g lightly toasted walnuts instead of pumpkin seeds, and replace the suggested cheese with Dorset Blue Vinny, Harbourne Blue, Beenleigh Blue or another crumbly blue.

Brown bread, hemp oil and parsley pesto

Makes 6–8 tablespoons

60g coarse wholemeal or Granary breadcrumbs

A large bunch of parsley (about 50g), leaves only

1 small garlic clove, roughly chopped

150–200ml hempseed oil

50g Parmesan or matured hard goat's cheese, finely grated

Juice of ½ lemon

Sea salt and freshly ground black pepper

Toast the breadcrumbs in a small frying pan for a few minutes, until crisp and nutty, then leave to cool.

Put the parsley leaves and garlic in a food processor and pulse until finely chopped (or chop them by hand, if you prefer). Transfer to a bowl and stir in enough oil to create a thinnish paste. Stir in the cheese and breadcrumbs, thin with a little more oil if you want, then adjust the seasoning with salt, pepper and lemon juice.

The breadcrumbs give this pesto a coarse, chunky texture. It's absolutely delicious with jacket potatoes.

Use these pestos in the following ways:

- Spread thickly between slices of white bread, along with shreds of cold chicken, pork or beef and a few lettuce leaves.

- Combine in a sandwich with some of the broad bean hummus on page 129.

- Spread thinly over a flatbread (page 78) or tortilla and top with crumbled goat's cheese or thickly spread soft cheese. Add a little leftover ham or cooked bacon, if you have some, then finish with a few peppery salad leaves and roll up into a neat parcel.

- Toss with cooked white beans, such as cannellini (tinned or cooked at home from scratch), plus diced tomatoes and some cold cooked potatoes to make a substantial lunchbox salad.

- Mix with leftover peas and/or leeks, then combine roughly with some torn buffalo mozzarella and pack into a pitta bread.

- Cook 350–400g pasta shapes, drain and toss with one quantity of pesto while still hot. Leave to cool. Use this as the base for various portable salads, by adding cheese, cubes of ham or chicken, flakes of sardine, mackerel or cold leftover fish, roughly chopped hard-boiled egg, cooked pulses, or chopped cold roasted vegetables.

- Use a heaped tablespoon of pesto to replace the parsley and Parmesan in the onion frittata on page 109.

- Pesto thinned down with a little extra oil and lemon juice makes a good dressing for any of the slaws on pages 120–3, or the tabula kisir on page 117.

- To make pesto bread, slice a ciabatta or French stick diagonally at 3–4cm intervals, without cutting right through to the base. Spread any pesto thickly between the slices and trickle with a little oil. Place on a baking sheet, cover with foil and bake in an oven preheated to 190°C/Gas Mark 5 for 10 minutes, removing the foil for the last 3–4 minutes. Especially good for summer barbecues, and to serve with soups.

Dukka

This Egyptian blend of coarsely ground seeds, spices and nuts is traditionally used, with olive oil, as a dip for bread. Its fragrant flavours and pleasing crunch make it a great addition to salads (sprinkled on top) or dips (blend with a little oil and trickle over), too. You could also include it in a flatbread (page 78) wrap with hummus, toss it into a beany salad, or add it to a lunchbox tub of leftover roast veg and chunks of halloumi cheese. Dukka can be kept in an airtight container in a store-cupboard for a few weeks.

A handful of hazelnuts

½ tablespoon cumin seeds

1 tablespoon coriander seeds

2 tablespoons sesame seeds

½ teaspoon dried chilli flakes

½ teaspoon sea salt

A small handful of mint leaves, finely shredded

First, toast the hazelnuts. Spread them out on a baking sheet in a single layer and place in an oven preheated to 180°C/Gas Mark 4 for about 5 minutes, until they are lightly coloured and the skins are blistered and cracked. Wrap them in a clean tea towel for a minute and then rub them vigorously with the towel until the skins fall off.

Toast the cumin and coriander seeds in a small frying pan over a medium heat until they just begin to release their fragrance – barely a minute. Bash them with a pestle and mortar until broken up but not too fine. Put the sesame seeds into the pan and heat gently until just golden. Add the hazelnuts, sesame seeds, chilli flakes and salt to the spice mix and bash again until the nuts are broken up into small pieces. Stir in the mint and the dukka is ready to use.

The simplest and most fun way to eat it is with some delicious fresh white bread (ideally sourdough) and a little bowl of your best culinary oil: olive, rapeseed, pumpkin seed or walnut, for example. Tear off a small hunk of bread, dip it in the oil, then dip lightly in the dukka, so it picks up a dusting of the nutty, spicy seeds. This is delicious with a glass of chilled rosé.

Fish is an exceptionally good food, but increasingly a worrying one.

The main purpose of this chapter is to make sure that the fish you eat always tastes delicious. But before we get to that, I think it's vital to consider briefly the worrying aspects of choosing to make fish a regular part of our diet.

The demand for fish is unprecedented, as are the technologies and resources being applied to extract it from our oceans. At least a quarter of humanity – coastal dwellers around the globe – relies on it as its primary source of protein. Meanwhile, another quarter – the wealthy West – rates it so highly that it is prepared to spend almost without limit to see it brought to the table. The result of this pressure on fish stocks is as predictable as it is depressing: all over the globe, the most sought-after species are on the brink of collapse.

As it happens, the last book I wrote before this one was *The River Cottage Fish Book*, co-authored with my friend, Nick Fisher. In it we considered in some depth the complex issues of how our fisheries are run and the implications for various species both in the UK and across the world. Of course, I'd love you to get a copy, if you haven't already, and to bone up on the rather alarming story of what's happening to our fish and what you can do about it. But I realise that not everyone can become a fully informed fish conservationist in their spare time. Nevertheless, with a bit of steer on how to shop for fish responsibly, everyone who wants to enjoy fish can do so in the knowledge that their net contribution is to the solution rather than the problem.

So let us cut to the chase: the overarching question for the conscientious fish buyer is surely, 'What fish should I avoid at all costs?' My answer to that would be, firstly, don't buy any species that are known to be in ecological crisis and, secondly, try to avoid fish of any species caught using methods that harm the marine environment. There is a big overlap between these two considerations, but they are not quite the same thing. There is sustainably fished line-caught sea bass, for example, and unsustainably fished trawled sea bass. For this reason, lists of 'fish to avoid' will inevitably contain the odd qualification. But I think such lists are worthwhile, and I'm happy to offer my current 'blacklist' (see left). I apply it when buying fish to eat at home, and we apply it also to the fish we serve at River Cottage.

Now when it comes to lists, clearly it's a boon to fish lovers to have a few ticks as well as a bunch of black crosses. So I've also given a list of UK-landed fish that it's generally reckoned we could eat more of, in order to help alleviate some of the pressure on threatened species.

My fish-to-avoid list

1 Cod (unless certified by the Marine Conservation Society)
2 Haddock
3 Bass (unless line caught and tagged as such)
4 Hake
5 All sharks and huss (except dogfish)
6 Skates and rays
7 Bluefin tuna (and frankly, most other fresh tuna, though some tinned tuna is certified as sustainable)
8 Wild salmon
9 Wild halibut
10 Whitebait

My fish-to eat-more-of list

1 Mackerel (particularly line caught)

2 Pollack and coley/ saithe (particularly line caught)

3 Black bream (especially from the Southwest and Wales)

4 Cornish sardines

5 Gurnard (except when beam trawled)

6 Megrim and witch (two flatfish, members of the sole family)

7 Red and grey mullet

8 Pouting

9 Organically farmed salmon and trout

10 Garfish

My sustainable shellfish list

1 Brown crabs (also velvet and spider crabs)

2 Whelks

3 Mussels (especially rope grown)

4 Scallops (but only hand dived, not dredged)

5 Oysters (UK farmed)

6 Squid (especially British, jig caught)

And if you're on the look-out for guilt-free seafood, shellfish is often a better bet than fin-fish, provided the method of catching/gathering is not damaging to the marine or shore environment – or, if the shellfish is farmed, it's being done in a sustainable way. Below is a list of some to feel good about.

Incidentally, prawns, delicious as they may be, are increasingly hard to find from a sustainable source. Since many people can't resist them, it's perhaps worth mentioning that coldwater prawns caught in the North Atlantic (the standard 'shell-on' cooked prawn sold by many fishmongers) are certainly less environmentally heinous than trawled or farmed tropical prawns, commonly known as tiger prawns.

The good news is that you should be able to find most of the 'eat-more-of' and sustainable species without too much trouble. The only caveat is that the assessment of what is and isn't sustainable is under constant review – so that if you're reading this a year or more after the time of writing, the list of 'fish to eat more of' is likely to look rather different. The best way to keep up with the latest scientific and environmental thinking on fish stocks is to log on to www.fishonline.org, a website run by the Marine Conservation Society (MCS). It's very easy to use, as you just type in the name of the fish species in question for a brief assessment of its ecological status, plus a 1–5 rating, where 1 is the most sustainable and 5 gives the gravest cause for concern.

Besides favouring sustainable species over blacklisted fish, it's also helpful to know the method by which a fish has been caught. The most destructive fishing techniques are generally the least selective, and the ones that do permanent damage to the sea floor. Worst of the lot are beam trawling and dredging: both drag heavy gear along the bottom of the sea, which disturbs and destroys the soft corals and invertebrates that are the foundation of life on the seabed. 'Static bottom nets' are better because they are lowered and raised to and from the bottom without having much physical impact on the sea floor itself.

Line fishing is generally regarded as the most sustainable means of commercial fishing for two key reasons: firstly, the fish are usually alive when they reach the boat, meaning that untargeted species and undersized fish can be returned unharmed to the sea. Secondly, the hooks, lines and weights are generally fished clear of the bottom. Although there is some snagging, it is the hooks and lines that are inclined to break, rather than the marine features to which they have become attached.

FISH

So where should you go in search of top-quality sustainable fish? A well-stocked and busy fishmonger's shop is certainly a good place to find the best quality, but as far as sustainability goes you are likely to encounter a mixed bag. Very few fishmongers, if any, restrict themselves to the sale of sustainable species. However, some are more committed than others, and the best will always be prepared to tell you where a fish comes from and how it was caught (if he or she can answer neither of these questions, then I would suggest you go elsewhere).

If you are a regular customer, you can undoubtedly cultivate a somewhat privileged relationship with your fishmonger – and you shouldn't be in the least bit shy of doing so. Assuming you are in every week and he or she knows what you like – a nice whole gurnard or grey mullet, or some fat fillets of line-caught pollack or coley – then you'll be looked after. When you're on the hunt for something really special, a phone call a couple of days in advance will stand you in good stead when the fishmonger places his or her order or goes to market.

Things tend to be very different in supermarkets, where those serving at the wet-fish counter are rarely experts on the fish they are selling. On the other hand, some supermarkets are taking the issue of sustainability very seriously and have even banned certain species or rejected certain fishing methods. A few are also working closely with organisations like the Marine Stewardship Council to get major product lines such as fish fingers, smoked mackerel and tinned tuna certified as sustainable, or at least 'dolphin friendly'. I would urge you to look hard for signs of genuine commitment in the way fish is presented and labelled in supermarkets, and reward meaningful initiatives with a purchase – provided, of course, the fish in question is in tiptop condition.

And that brings me to the most important factor in choosing fish, at least from the point of view of your own pleasure: it should be spanking fresh. A really fresh fish has an aura about it that simply shouts, 'Buy me!' It is shiny and plump, in head as well as body. It looks as if, were you to drop it accidentally into the sea, it might just perk up and swim away. Its eye is bright and seems to be looking at you; its scales are glistening and sparkle with the light.

Ideally two further operations will confirm your suspicions that a fish either is or isn't in perfect nick. Ask to have a look at the gills: the pinker they are, the better. A little sticky red blood is not a bad sign, but a slimy, gummy, grey-brown mucus suggests time has marched on since the fish met its end – and you should march on too. Finally, if you are allowed to handle the fish on the slab, prod the thickest part of the flesh gently. It should be firm – if super-fresh, almost rock hard. If it gives to your finger and you leave a little dent behind, then walk on by…

Remember that your mission is to find the best possible fish available for the money you are prepared to spend. In fact, many of the fish on the fish-to-eat list are very good value, and definitely at the cheaper end of the fish spectrum. So don't get hung up on species. In the recipes that follow, there's plenty of flexibility. Even where a specific fish is named in the recipe title, alternatives are always given, and further alternatives could be found too.

Now, I know that cooking fish makes some otherwise highly competent home cooks just a little bit jumpy – particularly as they are nervous of committing the perceived arch-crime of fish cuisine – overcooking it. So the best general tip I have for you is this: a piece of fish is cooked as soon as it is hot – technically about 55°C. If the heat has reached the middle of the fish, or fillet, so that the outside is just too hot to touch, it's done, and you should cook it no longer. Furthermore, if the fish is hot, it will have changed colour – usually from some more or less translucent shade of white, buff or red/brown to an opaque version of the same. And it will 'flake', so that it comes away from both the next flake and the bone.

The various tests for doneness are based on these straightforward, dependable, observable events. You can take the temperature in the middle of your fish by inserting the tip of a knife, then touching it to your fingertip or lip: if it's hot, the fish is cooked. Similarly, slip a thin blade into the thickest part of the fillet/fish and check whether it is opaque/flaky in the middle/next to the bone.

Finally, here is one sure-fire therapy for anyone who is, for whatever reason, just not quite getting along with fish in their kitchen. Go fishing. Cook what you catch. Eat it with friends. You'll never look back, I promise.

Five ways with fish fillets

Each of the following simple treatments works well with fillets taken from all my favourite sustainable white fish – gurnard, grey mullet, bream, pollack, plaice, megrim and lemon sole.

Fried fish fillets with roasted tomato sauce

An ideal dish for late summer and early autumn, when I've usually got more home-grown tomatoes than I know what to do with. In fact, I often make up a really big batch of the sauce, without the sugar and vinegar, and freeze it for use in soups, stews and curries later in the year.

Serves 4

4 fish fillets (see above), ideally with the skin on

1–2 tablespoons sunflower oil

3–4 tablespoons plain flour

For the roasted tomato sauce:

1.5kg ripe, flavoursome tomatoes, such as fleshy plum tomatoes, halved

3 garlic cloves, finely chopped

A few sprigs of thyme (optional)

2 tablespoons rapeseed or olive oil

1 bay leaf

A little soft brown sugar

A little white wine vinegar or cider vinegar

Ground mace

Sea salt and freshly ground black pepper

First, make the tomato sauce. Lay the tomato halves, cut-side up, in a single layer on a large baking tray. Scatter over the garlic and the thyme, if using, trickle over the oil and season generously. Place in an oven preheated to 180°C/Gas Mark 4 and roast for an hour, or until the tomatoes are soft and starting to brown. Tip them into a large sieve and rub through with a wooden spoon; discard the skin and pips.

Measure the sieved tomato purée, then put it into a wide saucepan with the bay leaf. For every 500ml purée, add 1 heaped teaspoon of soft brown sugar, 1 tablespoon of vinegar and a pinch of mace. Bring to a simmer and cook gently, stirring often, until reduced by between a third and a half to form a thick, glossy sauce – not quite a ketchup, but quite saucy nonetheless. Season to taste and adjust the sugar/vinegar content too, if you like. Set aside while you cook the fish.

Pour the oil into a large frying pan and place over a medium heat. Put the flour on a plate and season it well. Lightly dust the fish fillets in the seasoned flour, shaking off the excess, then transfer to the pan, skin-side down. Sizzle gently for 4–5 minutes, until the skin is crisp, the edges lightly browned, and the flesh about two-thirds cooked through. Turn over and cook for 1–2 minutes longer.

Spoon the sauce on to warm serving plates, add the fried fish and serve with pasta, noodles or sautéed potatoes.

Breaded fish fillets with tomato salsa

Here's another variation on the fried-fish-with-tomatoes theme – the tomatoes are fresh and zesty this time, the fillets in a crisp crumb coating. However, you could easily swap the sauces, around – for this and the previous recipe. As an alternative to tomatoes, you could serve the fillets with caper mayonnaise (see page 152).

Serves 4

4 fish fillets (see page 142)

3–4 tablespoons plain flour

1 medium egg, lightly beaten

About 100g fine, fresh breadcrumbs (or half fresh, half dried)

A pinch of cayenne pepper or hot smoked paprika (optional)

1 teaspoon very finely chopped thyme (optional)

Sunflower or groundnut oil for frying

Sea salt and freshly ground black pepper

For the tomato salsa:

500g ripe, tasty tomatoes, diced

1 shallot or ½ small red onion, very finely diced

1–2 tablespoons tiny capers, rinsed (optional)

A small squeeze of lemon juice

2–3 tablespoons rapeseed or extra virgin olive oil

A tiny pinch of sugar

A few mint or parsley leaves, finely chopped

For the tomato salsa, combine the tomatoes, shallot or onion, and capers, if using, in a bowl. Whisk the lemon juice and oil together in a small jug, season well with salt and pepper and add the sugar. Add to the salsa with the chopped mint or parsley and toss lightly; set aside.

If you prefer your fish skin-free, use a sharp knife – ideally a filleting knife – to slice the fillets neatly off their skin (you could ask the fishmonger to do this when you buy them).

Put the flour on a plate and season it well. Pour the beaten egg into a shallow dish. Put the breadcrumbs on another plate and season them with a little salt and a pinch of cayenne or paprika, or the thyme leaves, if you like.

Dip each fillet first in the seasoned flour, shaking off the excess, then in the egg until lightly coated, and finally in the seasoned breadcrumbs, patting them on so they form an even layer all over.

Heat a layer of oil, 1.5–2cm deep, in a large frying pan over a medium-high heat. To test whether it is hot enough, throw in a few breadcrumbs; they should immediately 'fizz' and bubble vigorously in the oil.

Put the crumbed fillets into the pan (you might need to cook them in 2 batches). Fry for about 3 minutes (more like 2 minutes if you're using a flat fish), resisting the urge to move the fish until the breadcrumbs are crisp and crunchy underneath. Carefully turn the fillets over and cook for 2–3 minutes on the other side. Transfer to a plate lined with kitchen paper to drain.

Serve the fish immediately, with the tomato salsa. Some good bread and a leafy salad on the side wouldn't go amiss.

Fried fish fillets with herbs and lemon

This simple dish relies on a sort of deconstructed salsa verde – a mixture of fresh herbs, lemon and capers – which is thrown in with the frying fish to flavour it and create an instant, aromatic sauce. It is one of my favourite ways to cook white fish fillets, but it also works with fillets of trout and salmon, and the real 'oilies', such as mackerel and sardines/pilchards.

Serves 2

2 fish fillets (see
page 142)
A dash of sunflower
or groundnut oil
20g unsalted butter,
at room temperature
Sea salt and freshly
ground black pepper

For the herb mix:
1 small garlic clove
A small bunch of flat-leaf
parsley, leaves only
10–12 basil or mint
leaves
2 teaspoons capers,
rinsed and dried
Juice and finely grated
zest of 1 small lemon
A little rapeseed or
olive oil

Start with the herb mix: chop the garlic finely, then add the parsley, basil or mint, capers and lemon zest to the board and chop the whole lot together fairly finely. Scrape the mixture into a bowl, add the lemon juice, some salt and pepper and just enough oil to give a thick purée; set aside.

To cook the fish, heat a little sunflower or groundnut oil in a large frying pan over a medium heat. Season the fish fillets with salt and pepper. When the pan is hot, put the fish in, skin-side down, and fry for about 3 minutes, until crisp and well coloured underneath. Turn it over carefully and cook for another 1–2 minutes.

When the fish is just about done, add the butter and the herb mix. As the butter melts, stir it together with the herbs and spoon them over the fish in the pan – this last stage of cooking, with the herbs and butter going over the fish, should last only 30 seconds or so.

Transfer the fish to warm plates, spoon all the buttery, herby juices over and serve straight away – with a generous spoonful of creamy mash and perhaps a green salad to follow.

Roast fish fillets with roast potatoes

Though unconventional, this dish makes a lot of sense. Roasting potatoes to perfection takes a little effort – heating the oil in the roasting tin, parboiling the spuds, roughing them up a little – but when you get it spot on, you have something approaching the perfect chip, albeit rather chunkier in shape. And if you've got a tray of sizzling hot oil on the go in the oven, you also have an ideal medium for cooking a nice fat fillet of well-seasoned fish. Surely it makes sense to take advantage…

Serves 2

500g fairly floury potatoes (try Maris Piper, King Edward or Desiree), peeled and cut into smallish chunks

3–4 tablespoons sunflower, groundnut or rapeseed oil, or goose fat

About 500g fish fillets, such as 2 gurnard or bream fillets, 1 fat fillet of pollack, or 4 large mackerel fillets

A few bay leaves

Sea salt and freshly ground black pepper

Put the potatoes in a pan, cover with cold water and add a good pinch of salt. Bring to the boil, simmer for 8 minutes, then drain well and return to the empty pan to steam off for a few minutes.

Put the oil or fat in a large roasting tin and place in an oven preheated to 200°C/Gas Mark 6 until smoking hot. Meanwhile, generously season the potatoes in their pan, then rough them up: either hold the lid on and give the pan a little shake or use a sharp fork to scratch their surfaces.

When the oil is smoking hot, tip in the potatoes. Baste them well with the oil, then return the tin to the oven for 45 minutes, giving them a stir after about 30 minutes. By this stage, the potatoes should be almost done – i.e. have a golden crust all over but look as if they could still take a bit more crisping up. Create a space in the middle of the tin for the fish.

Add the fish to the tin, sprinkle it with salt and pepper, then tuck in the bay leaves. Return to the oven for 10–15 minutes, until the fish is just cooked. Serve at once, with pea purée (see page 156) or mushy squash (page 311) and, by all means, ketchup – or roasted tomato sauce (see page 142).

Foil-baked fish fillets with fennel, ginger and chilli

Baking fish scrunched up in a foil parcel with a handful of aromatics is an easy and delicious option. Fillets of gurnard, lemon sole, bream, mullet and line-caught bass all respond well to this treatment, as well as thick fillets of pollack. And it's not just fillets that benefit from the foil parcel approach. In fact, this is one of my favourite ways to cook small-to-medium whole fish (see variation).

Serves 2

2 tablespoons sunflower or groundnut oil

2 fennel bulbs, trimmed, quartered and sliced fairly finely (2–3mm)

2 garlic cloves, finely sliced

1 teaspoon grated or finely chopped fresh ginger

1 small red chilli, deseeded and finely sliced

2 large (150–200g) or 4 small (80–120g) fish fillets

Soy sauce

Sea salt and freshly ground black pepper

Heat half the oil in a pan, add the fennel and cook gently for a few minutes, until it starts to soften. Add the garlic, ginger and chilli and cook for a few minutes more, so everything starts to soften and release its flavour. Remove from the heat and set aside.

Take 2 pieces of strong kitchen foil, roughly 25cm square, and oil them well with the remaining oil. Pile the fennel mixture in a little mound in the middle of each one. Season the fish fillets generously and curl them around the fennel mixture – either 2 small fillets or one large per parcel. Sprinkle a little soy sauce and a good grinding of black pepper over each pile, then bring up the sides of the foil and scrunch them together tightly to form well-sealed but baggy parcels.

Place the parcels on a baking tray, transfer to an oven preheated to 190°C/Gas Mark 5 and bake for 15 minutes. Open up the steaming, fragrant parcels and pile the contents, including all the lovely juices, on to 2 warm plates. Serve with noodles, mash or rice and some wilted greens, such as spinach, pak choi or choi sum.

VARIATION

Whole fish baked in foil

Almost any small-to-medium fish will do, including trout, bream, bass, gurnard, large mackerel or flat fish such as plaice, lemon sole or megrim. You need a one- or two-person-sized fish, between 500g and 1kg. Get your fishmonger to gut and clean it for you.

Lay the fish on the well-oiled foil. Put a few bay leaves and lemon slices in the cavity and some more under the fish. Add extra herbs – parsley, fennel and/or thyme – if you like. Dot the fish with butter. Bring up the sides of the foil a little and pour in about half a glass of white wine and a squeeze of lemon juice. Season the fish generously. Scrunch the foil together to form a tightly sealed but baggy parcel. Bake at 190°C/Gas Mark 5. Allow 15–20 minutes for small flat fish; 20–25 minutes for 500–750g fish; 30–35 minutes for 750g–1kg fish.

'Dab in a bap'

This is a very quick lunch, and a great way to use dab. It's one of our less-appreciated, yet more sustainable, native fish, so we can enjoy it with a clear conscience. The recipe also works well with other flattie fillets, such as small fillets of lemon sole or plaice.

The caper mayonnaise is a kind of pared-down tartare sauce – miles better than anything you can buy in a jar. I serve it with all sorts of fried fish dishes.

Serves 1

2 fillets of dab or other flat fish, such as lemon sole or plaice, about 75g each, skinned if you prefer

A knob of butter, plus extra for the bap

1 tablespoon sunflower or groundnut oil

2 tablespoons plain flour

1 large, white floury bap

Lettuce leaves

A squeeze of lemon, a dash of Tabasco sauce and a squirt of ketchup (all optional), to serve

For the caper mayonnaise:

2 tablespoons good mayonnaise (page 282)

2 teaspoons capers, drained and finely chopped

1 tablespoon chopped parsley

Lemon juice (optional)

First, combine the mayonnaise, capers and parsley, adding a squeeze of lemon juice too, if you have any. Set aside while you cook the fish.

Heat the butter and oil in a non-stick frying pan over a medium heat. Put the flour on a plate and season it well. Dust the fish with the seasoned flour, shaking off the excess, and fry for about 2 minutes on each side (if you are leaving the skin on, fry it skin-side down first for about 3 minutes, then give it a minute on the other side to cook through).

Slice the bap in half and butter it generously. Lay a few lettuce leaves on the bottom half and put the fish on top, seasoning it further, if you like, with lemon juice and/or Tabasco. Dollop on the mayonnaise and/or a bit of ketchup if you prefer, then close the bap and eat right away, while the fish is still warm.

Roasted slashed fish with aromatic paste

This is a simple but impressive way of cooking a whole fish. Slashing the flesh lets the pungent flavourings penetrate, and also ensures that thick-bodied fish cook quickly and evenly. There's no end to the potential variations for the paste – see below for a couple of suggestions. For bigger fish, to feed more people, increase the quantities for the paste and extend the cooking time.

Serves 2–3

1 bream, bass, grey mullet or gurnard, about 1kg, gutted and descaled

A few bay leaves

1 tablespoon sunflower or rapeseed oil

For the aromatic paste:

2–3cm piece of fresh ginger, finely grated

2 fat garlic cloves, finely grated

½–1 small, hot red chilli, deseeded and finely chopped (optional)

1 small shallot, grated

1 star anise, pounded with a pestle and mortar

About 1 tablespoon soy sauce

Sea salt and freshly ground black pepper

First, make the paste: combine the ginger, garlic, chilli, shallot and star anise. Season with salt and pepper, then add just enough soy sauce to make a thick paste.

Lay the fish on a well-oiled baking sheet. Using a sharp knife, make 3 or 4 slashes, 1–2cm deep, in the thickest part of the fish, being careful not to go through to the bone. Turn and repeat on the other side. Using your fingers, rub the aromatic paste into the slashes, smearing the rest inside the cavity and over the top of the fish.

Tuck bay leaves into the slashes and cavity. Trickle a little oil over the fish, place in an oven preheated to 190°C/Gas Mark 5 and roast for 20–25 minutes, until the fish is just cooked through. Check by pushing a fine-bladed knife into the thickest part, between 2 slashes: the flesh should be opaque and just coming away from the backbone.

Bring the fish to the table in its roasting dish and ease large chunks of the flesh away from the bones with a knife and fork. Turn the fish over and remove the remaining flesh, then spoon any aromatic pan juices on to each portion. Serve with plain rice or noodles, and stir-fried greens flavoured with a little ginger, garlic and soy.

VARIATIONS

Herby paste

Mix 2 tablespoons of finely chopped parsley, 1 teaspoon each of finely chopped thyme and rosemary, 1 finely chopped garlic clove and the grated zest of ½ lemon with 1–2 tablespoons of rapeseed or olive oil to make a thick paste. Season with salt and pepper. Proceed as above.

Spicy paste

Heat 2 tablespoons of sunflower oil in a frying pan and fry 1 teaspoon of brown mustard seeds briefly until they start to pop. Add a finely chopped large shallot and cook until soft. Add a finely chopped garlic clove and a grated 2cm piece of fresh ginger, then take off the heat. Grind ½ teaspoon each of coriander and cumin seeds with a pinch of fennel seeds and a pinch of dried chilli flakes and stir into the shallot mix with ½ teaspoon of ground turmeric and some salt and pepper, adding more oil, if necessary, to make a thick paste. Proceed as above.

Scallops with pea purée and ham

I adore scallops, especially when partnered with some salty pork. I often cook them with little nuggets of Tupperware Mexican chorizo (page 206), frying them in the spicy red fat released by the meat. But they're also great with slivers of air-dried ham – lightly fried until crisp – or you could use thin rashers of streaky bacon.

I always buy diver-caught scallops. Dredging, the most common method of retrieving them, can have a disastrous effect on the seabed. In any case, diver-caught shellfish are invariably in better nick too, and less gritty.

The combination of scallops with a warm pea and mint purée was devised by the chef, Rowley Leigh, and has since become a classic. In the autumn you can achieve an equally delightful effect with a purée of squash – just substitute mushy squash (see page 311) for the pea purée.

Serves 4 as a starter

1 tablespoon sunflower or groundnut oil

4 large, paper-thin slices of air-dried ham (or 8 thin-cut streaky bacon rashers)

12 hand-dived scallops, cleaned

A little extra virgin olive or rapeseed oil, to serve

For the pea purée:

400g fresh or frozen peas or petits pois

1 tablespoon rapeseed or olive oil

1 small garlic clove, finely chopped

50g unsalted butter

Leaves from 1 large bunch of mint, chopped

Sea salt and freshly ground black pepper

First, make the pea purée: cook the peas in boiling salted water until tender, then drain, reserving the cooking water, and tip the peas into a blender or food processor. Put the oil and garlic in a small pan and allow to sizzle gently for barely a minute until the garlic just begins to colour. Quickly pour it into the blender with the peas. Add the butter, mint and a pinch each of salt and pepper. Blend to a purée, adding a little of the cooking liquid if necessary, to give a consistency similar to that of coarse hummus. Taste and adjust the seasoning; keep warm.

To cook the scallops, put a large, non-stick frying pan over a medium-high heat and add the oil. Tear the ham into large shreds and add to the pan, turning the pieces over in the oil as soon as they start to crisp up – this should take less than a minute. Transfer to a warm plate. Season the scallops, add them to the pan and cook for about a minute, until golden brown underneath. Turn them over and cook for a minute on the other side.

Immediately transfer the scallops to 4 warm plates, adding a few scraps of ham to each one. Put a good dollop of pea purée next to the scallops, trickle with a little extra virgin oil, plus the juices from the scallop pan, and grind over some pepper. Serve straight away.

Salt and pepper squid with quick sweet chilli dipping sauce

Just a little more elaborate – and piquant – than basic squid rings, this salty, spicy combination is a real winner.

Serves 4 as a starter

2 teaspoons Szechuan peppercorns

1 teaspoon black peppercorns

½ teaspoon dried chilli flakes (optional)

2 tablespoons sea salt

120g cornflour

About 1 litre sunflower or groundnut oil for deep-frying

500g squid, cleaned and cut into rings about 1cm thick, plus the tentacles, washed and dried but left intact

1 egg white, lightly beaten (optional)

For the sweet chilli dipping sauce:

3 tablespoons redcurrant or crab apple jelly

1 tablespoon cider vinegar

1 teaspoon soy sauce

1 red chilli, deseeded and very finely chopped

1 small garlic clove, very finely chopped

A few twists of black pepper

Toast all the peppercorns in a small, non-stick frying pan for a couple of minutes until they become fragrant (this is not essential, but it does enhance the taste). Remove from the heat and grind with the dried chilli flakes, if using, and the salt, using a pestle and mortar or a spice grinder, until well combined. Mix with the cornflour until evenly combined. This seasoning for the squid can be made in advance and kept in a jar.

To make the dipping sauce, simply combine all the ingredients in a small saucepan and stir over a low heat until the jelly has dissolved and you have a silky syrup. Bring to a simmer and allow to bubble gently for a few minutes. This will mellow the harshness of the garlic. Allow to cool and serve at room temperature. If the sauce re-sets to a jelly when cool, whisk in a splash of warm water.

To cook the squid, heat the oil to 180°C in a deep-fat fryer or a heavy, high-sided saucepan. If you don't have a cooking thermometer, test that it's hot enough by dropping a small piece of bread into the oil – it should bubble and fizz, turning golden brown in about a minute.

The squid rings should be slightly damp and sticky, but not dripping wet, for the seasoning mixture to coat them well. If they are too dry, you can massage them with a little beaten egg white. The easiest way to coat them is to place a few rings of squid in a sieve with a few tablespoons of the mixture, then shake the sieve until the squid is evenly coated and any excess seasoning has dropped through.

Fry the seasoned squid in the hot oil, a few pieces at a time, for about a minute, until just golden. Transfer to a tray lined with kitchen paper and continue to cook the rest. Serve straight away, with the sweet chilli dipping sauce.

Leek, celeriac and smoked pollack soup

This soup combines all the classic elements of a chowder: a milky base, potatoes and chunks of fish. Celeriac, which is a very fish-friendly root, adds another dimension. Smoked pollack, which we call 'smollack' at River Cottage, is a favourite ingredient of mine. Kippers will also work well, though they have a stronger, oilier flavour.

Serves 6

500g smoked pollack or kipper fillets

1 litre whole milk

1 bay leaf

A bunch of parsley, leaves chopped, stalks reserved

A large knob of butter

2 large leeks, finely sliced

300g potatoes, peeled and cut into roughly 5mm dice

300g celeriac, peeled and cut into roughly 5mm dice

1 tablespoon finely snipped chives

Sea salt and freshly ground black pepper

Put the smoked fish in a pan and add the milk, bay leaf and parsley stalks. Place over a low heat. As soon as the milk comes to a simmer, switch off the heat and cover the pan. The fish will carry on cooking in the hot milk. After about 5 minutes, it should be just cooked through; if not, leave it in the hot milk for a little longer, then drain in a sieve placed over a bowl, reserving the milk. Discard the bay leaf and parsley stalks.

Heat the butter in a large, heavy-based pan, add the leeks, cover and sweat for about 5 minutes. Stir in the potatoes and celeriac, then add the warm, fishy milk. Bring to a simmer and cook gently for about 10 minutes, until the vegetables are tender.

Meanwhile, flake the fish into smallish pieces, removing the skin and any bones.

Stir the fish back into the soup and season to taste, being generous with the pepper. Ladle into deep bowls, scatter over the chopped parsley and chives, then serve.

Thrifty fish soup with cheaty rouille

This is a pleasingly frugal recipe. You buy an inexpensive fresh fish, such as gurnard or grey mullet, get the fishmonger to fillet it for you, then use the head, skin and bones to make a flavourful stock. The broth is enhanced with a few herbs and vegetables, the fish flesh goes in at the end, and you can splash out on a bit of squid or a few scallops, if you like. The finishing touch is a swirl of garlicky, chilli-hot rouille, though I have to say, the soup is delicious even without it. And croûtons, made from leftover bread, add crunch.

Serves 4

1 medium, firm-fleshed fish, 750g–1kg, filleted and skinned, skin, head and bones saved

For the stock:
2 celery stalks, chopped
1 garlic clove, peeled
1 onion, roughly chopped
1 large carrot, sliced
A sprig of thyme
1 bay leaf
Stalks from a bunch of parsley, leaves reserved
A few black peppercorns
A splash of white wine

For the soup:
2 garlic cloves
1 large onion
2 celery stalks
2 leeks
500g floury potatoes
2 tablespoons rapeseed or olive oil
½ teaspoon fennel seeds, roughly crushed
100–200g cleaned squid, or 4–8 scallops (optional)
Leaves from the parsley bunch, finely chopped
Sea salt and freshly ground black pepper
Wholemeal croûtons, to serve

For the rouille (optional):
1 hot red chilli
1 quantity of mayonnaise (see page 282), made with 1 garlic clove

First, make a simple fish stock: put the fish head, skin and bones in a saucepan with all the ingredients for the stock. Add 1 litre of cold water and bring to a gentle simmer. Cook very gently for half an hour; do not allow it to boil hard, as this spoils the flavour. Strain the stock, discarding the fishy bits and vegetables.

For the soup, finely chop the garlic, onion, celery and leeks. Peel the potatoes and cut into 1cm cubes. Heat the oil in a large saucepan, add the fennel seeds, garlic, onion, celery and leeks, then cover and sweat for about 10 minutes, until soft. Add the potatoes and the stock and return to a gentle simmer. Cook for 15 minutes, or until the potatoes are tender.

Meanwhile, make the rouille, if you are serving it, by chopping the chilli very finely and mixing it with the garlic mayonnaise; set aside.

Now, slice the fish fillets into bite-sized pieces. If using squid, slice the pouches into rings; if using scallops, clean and slice horizontally in half. Add all the fish and any shellfish to the simmering broth. Cook for 2 minutes, until the fish is just done, then remove from the heat. Add the parsley and season to taste.

Serve the soup in warm bowls, topped with a few crisp croûtons and a good blob of rouille, if you like.

VARIATION
When fennel is in season, in summer and autumn, try using it instead of the leeks.

Mussels with cider, leeks and bacon

Mussels are the ultimate fast seafood, and their sweetness goes brilliantly with salty bacon. You could try this with white wine instead of cider, if you prefer.

Serves 2 as a main course, 4 as a starter

1kg mussels

A small knob of butter

1–2 tablespoons rapeseed, olive or sunflower oil

100g unsmoked streaky bacon or pancetta, chopped

1 large or 2 medium leeks, finely sliced

1 teaspoon thyme leaves

1 bay leaf

250ml medium-sweet cider

1 teaspoon wholegrain mustard

2–3 tablespoons double cream

Sea salt and freshly ground black pepper

Lots of chopped parsley, to serve

Scrub the mussels and remove the wiry little 'beards' that are attached to the shells. Discard any open mussels that don't close when given a sharp tap.

Place a large saucepan over a medium heat and add the butter and oil. When the butter is foaming, add the bacon or pancetta and cook for 4–5 minutes. Stir in the leek, thyme and bay leaf and cook for 2–3 minutes, until the leek softens a little.

Turn the heat up high, pour in the cider and bring to the boil. Stir in the mustard, then tip in the mussels and place a lid on the pan. Steam the mussels for 2–3 minutes, giving the pan a good shake once or twice. When the mussels have nearly all opened (discard any that remain firmly shut), stir in the cream.

Season with salt and pepper and serve in deep bowls, scattered with parsley and accompanied by plenty of bread – or, even better, home-cooked *frites* – to soak up the sauce.

Thai fish curry

This looks like a complicated recipe, but it isn't really. I like to make the paste in double or triple quantities and freeze some, so I can whip up a curry quickly. You can vary the fish and shellfish, adding strips of squid or thickly sliced scallops if you like, or increasing the proportion of white fish in relation to shellfish for a more economical dish.

Serves 4

2 tablespoons sunflower or groundnut oil

400ml tin of coconut milk

200ml fish stock or water

2 tablespoons Thai fish sauce (nam pla)

2 teaspoons sugar

125g French beans

100g spring onions

500g firm fish fillets, such as pollack, gurnard or grey mullet, skinned

300g fresh crabmeat – a mix of white and brown, or all white if you prefer

A handful of coriander, Thai basil or ordinary basil leaves, roughly torn

For the curry paste:

2–6 small green chillies, according to heat, deseeded if you like

3–4 small shallots or 1 small onion, chopped

100g fresh ginger, chopped

4 garlic cloves, peeled

2 tablespoons galangal paste (optional)

3 lemongrass stalks, tough outer layers removed, finely sliced

2 teaspoons ground coriander

2 tablespoons ground cumin

Juice and grated zest of 1 lime

4 kaffir lime leaves, chopped (optional)

1 teaspoon Thai shrimp paste

1 teaspoon sea salt

Put all the curry paste ingredients into a food processor or blender and whiz to a fairly smooth paste, adding a tablespoon of water to help it along if necessary.

Heat the oil in a heavy-based saucepan, then scrape in the curry paste. Fry over a low-medium heat for 3–4 minutes, stirring often, without letting it colour. Add the coconut milk, stock or water, fish sauce and sugar. Bring to a gentle simmer and cook, uncovered, for 20–25 minutes.

Meanwhile, cut the French beans into 2–3cm lengths and slice the spring onions on the diagonal. Add these to the curry sauce and cook for 5 minutes.

Cut the fish fillets into large bite-sized pieces. Add these to the pan, cover with a lid and simmer gently for 2–3 minutes, until the fish is just cooked. Stir in the crabmeat and heat through gently for another minute.

Serve in deep bowls, scattered with the coriander or basil and accompanied by boiled rice.

Hot-smoked trout pâté

I like to serve this with rye bread as a starter, or on toast as a canapé with drinks. It keeps quite well for a week or so in the fridge: just spoon it into a jar, pressing down carefully to ensure there are no pockets of air, then seal the top with a layer of clarified butter. The recipe works well with hot-smoked mackerel, too.

Serves 4 as a starter

300g hot-smoked trout (or mackerel or salmon) fillet, skinned

2–2½ teaspoons English mustard

1 heaped tablespoon crème fraîche

½ teaspoon caster sugar

1 tablespoon lemon juice, or to taste

1 teaspoon coarsely ground black pepper

2–3 tablespoons chopped dill or chives

½ teaspoon paprika (optional)

Put half the smoked fish into a food processor or blender with the mustard, crème fraîche, sugar and lemon juice and blend until smooth. Transfer to a bowl.

Break the remaining fish into flakes and stir it into the blended mixture with the pepper and dill or chives. Taste and add more lemon juice, if necessary. Ideally, leave to rest in a cool place for an hour or two before serving.

Serve the pâté with a dusting of paprika, if you like, and with buttered bread or toast. A scaled-down version of this, on small pieces of toast, makes a lovely canapé.

Crab cakes

Very simple and very, very crabby, these make a great starter served with a delicate side salad – but you can also eat them as a snack or canapé, dipping them into the garlicky mayo with your fingers.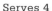

Serves 4

500g mixed white and brown crabmeat

Grated zest of 1 lemon

1 tablespoon finely chopped parsley and/or chives

1–2 tablespoons crème fraîche (optional)

4 tablespoons plain flour

1 medium egg, lightly beaten

50g slightly stale white breadcrumbs

A large knob of butter

4 tablespoons sunflower or groundnut oil

Sea salt and freshly ground black pepper

To serve:

1 quantity of mayonnaise (see page 282), made with 2 crushed garlic cloves (or more)

Lemon wedges

A few salad leaves and chives (optional)

Put the crabmeat into a bowl with the lemon zest, parsley and/or chives and plenty of seasoning. Mix together, adding a little crème fraîche if necessary to bind the mixture. Divide into 8 and shape each portion into a fat cake, about 2cm thick. Chill for about an hour.

Put the flour on a plate and season it well. Pour the egg into a shallow dish, then scatter the breadcrumbs on another plate. Take a crab cake and dip it into the flour, turning it over so that it is lightly coated on both sides, then dip it into the beaten egg and finally into the breadcrumbs. Set aside on a plate. Repeat with the rest of the crab cakes.

Heat the butter and oil in a large frying pan. When the butter starts to sizzle gently, add the crab cakes to the pan and fry over a medium heat for 3–4 minutes, until crisp and golden brown underneath. Turn them over and cook for another 2–3 minutes, checking from time to time that they're not colouring too quickly and adjusting the heat as necessary.

Serve immediately, with the mayonnaise and lemon wedges, along with a few salad leaves and chives if you like.

Kippers with crushed new potatoes

Kippers are an honourable
part of the proud fish-smoking
tradition we have in this country.
If you choose properly smoked
ones without dyes or artificial
flavourings, I think you'll find this
a wonderfully satisfying dish.

Serves 4

1kg new potatoes,
such as Jersey Royals,
scrubbed

4 double kipper fillets

A knob of butter

1–2 tablespoons
rapeseed or olive oil

2 tablespoons finely
chopped parsley and/
or chives

Lemon juice

Sea salt and freshly
ground black pepper

Boil the new potatoes in a pan of lightly salted water until tender.

Meanwhile, skin the kipper fillets, removing any pin bones, and cut
or tear the flesh into large bite-sized pieces. Heat the butter and oil in
a frying pan and fry the kipper pieces gently for a couple of minutes,
until cooked through. Take off the heat and stir in the herb(s).

When the potatoes are cooked, drain well and return them to the pan.
Using a potato masher or wooden spoon, crush them lightly to form
a rough, very chunky mash.

Combine the fish and any juices in the pan with the rough mash.
Season well with black pepper and lemon juice and serve, just warm,
with a crisp lettuce salad to follow or on the side.

Smoked fish and spinach omelette

Loosely based on the famous omelette Arnold Bennett, this is a fantastic way to use up leftover cooked fish. Smoked fish work best (smoked pollack is my favourite), though fresh salmon, mackerel, trout or almost any other fish would do. You could also make it with fresh fish if you poach the fish in the milk and strain off the milk before mixing it with the egg yolks. In all cases, the rich omelette allows you to make a little bit of fish go quite a long way. It makes a very decent lunch for two, or a nifty starter for four.

Serves 2 as a main course, 4 as a starter

200ml whole milk, or a mixture of double cream and whole milk

2 medium egg yolks

About 200g cold cooked smoked fish, such as mackerel, salmon, trout, pollack or kippers, broken into large flakes

50g unsalted butter

1 small onion, finely chopped

400g fresh spinach, tough stalks removed

4 medium eggs

50g mature Cheddar or Gruyère cheese, grated

Sea salt and freshly ground black pepper

Put the milk, or milk and cream, in a pan, bring to just below the boil, then remove from the heat. Lightly beat the egg yolks together in a bowl. Slowly pour on the hot milk, whisking constantly, to form a smooth custard. Stir in the flaked fish.

Heat half the butter in a frying pan, add the onion and a pinch of salt and fry gently for about 10 minutes, until soft. Meanwhile, cook the spinach in a large pan of boiling salted water for just a minute, until wilted. Drain, leave until cool enough to handle, then squeeze out the water with your hands. Chop coarsely. Stir the spinach and onion into the fish mixture and season with a few grinds of black pepper.

Lightly beat the 4 whole eggs together with a pinch each of salt and pepper. Heat the remaining butter in a 23–25cm non-stick frying pan over a medium heat. When it's foaming, pour in the beaten eggs. As they cook, gently move the set egg around a bit with a fork to allow the uncooked egg to run over the base of the pan. When the omelette is half-cooked – set on the base but still quite wet on top – take the pan off the heat.

Spoon the fish and spinach mixture over the omelette, scatter the grated cheese on top and put the whole thing under a preheated hot grill for a few minutes, until golden, bubbling and slightly puffed. Let the omelette cool for a couple of minutes, then slice it in the pan. Serve with some peppery salad leaves to cut its richness.

Curried fish pie

Few meals, indeed few things in life, are as comforting and reassuring as a fish pie, piping hot from the oven – and I've recently discovered that adding some gently sweated onion and a good whack of curry powder to my usual recipe produces a startlingly good result. You could, of course, leave out the curry-flavoured onion to make a classic fish pie, but I would urge you to give this one a go. If you don't fancy pastry, top the pie with mashed potato instead.

Serves 4–6

For the fish:
2 fillets (about 600g) of firm white fish, such as pollack or coley
200g smoked pollack or kippers
750ml whole milk
1 onion, roughly chopped
1 large carrot, roughly chopped
1 celery stalk, roughly chopped
1 bay leaf
A few peppercorns

For the pie:
75g unsalted butter
75g plain flour
1 tablespoon sunflower or groundnut oil
1 large onion, finely chopped
1 tablespoon fairly hot curry powder or curry paste (or try the spicy paste on page 154)
1–2 handfuls of cooked peeled prawns (optional)
1 tablespoon chopped coriander
250g puff pastry (either the rough puff pastry on page 110, or ready-made all-butter puff)
A little beaten egg for glazing
Sea salt and freshly ground black pepper

Put the fish fillets in a pan and add the milk, vegetables, bay leaf and peppercorns. Place over a low heat. As soon as the milk comes to a simmer, switch off the heat and cover the pan. The fish will carry on cooking in the hot milk. After about 5 minutes, it should be just cooked through; if not, leave it in the hot milk for a little longer, then drain in a sieve placed over a bowl, reserving the milk. Discard the vegetables, bay leaf and peppercorns.

Now make a béchamel sauce: melt the butter in a saucepan, add the flour and stir well to make a roux. Cook gently for a couple of minutes, stirring every few seconds, then gently whisk in a third of the fishy milk. Add another third of the milk, whisking all the time, and then the final third, so that you end up with a smooth, creamy sauce. Season with salt and pepper, turn the heat down low and cook very gently for 2 minutes.

Peel the skin off the fish, check for any bones and gently break the flesh into chunks.

Heat the oil in a saucepan, add the onion and cook gently for about 5 minutes, until translucent and soft. Stir in the curry powder or paste and cook for another 5 minutes or so. Add the curry-flavoured onion to the béchamel, then stir in the flaked fish, the prawns, if using, and the coriander. Taste the sauce and add more salt, pepper or curry powder/paste if you think it needs it.

Roll out the pastry on a lightly floured work surface and cut it to fit the top of the dish. Put the filling into the dish. Dampen the rim of the dish, lift the pastry over the filling and press down the pastry edges to seal. Brush with a little beaten egg and place in an oven preheated to 200°C/Gas Mark 6. Bake for about 30 minutes, until the pastry is golden and puffed and the fishy sauce is bubbling underneath. Serve with buttered peas or greens.

thrifty meat

Meat is the most precious of foods, I've said it before and I'll say it

again. It has its special status by virtue of being the flesh of animals, which must be killed in order to provide it. I won't reprise the several hundred pages I spent exploring this theme in *The River Cottage Meat Book*, but I will summarise thus: to my mind, in order to feel good about meat, we have to feel good, or at the very least okay, about how the animals who provided it have lived and died. My preferred way to do that is to raise the animals myself. But it can also be done simply by buying meat from trustworthy sources that you know place a vital emphasis on the importance of good animal husbandry.

More on sourcing meat shortly, but first let's consider some of the practicalities of cooking this great food. Strange as it may seem, cooking meat has an ethical dimension too. And the exciting thing is that it dovetails very nicely with the economic considerations – at least it does to my way of thinking. That's because if we want to do the right thing by the animals we've raised for food, then instead of wasting their meat we should put all of it to the best possible use. That means learning to make delicious meals from the less obvious types of meat – or 'secondary cuts' (as opposed to prime cuts).

These pieces of meat tend to be tougher, comprising harder-working muscles with more sinew and sometimes more fat and bone too. This is one of the reasons they are cheaper. The other, related, reason is the assumption many people make that getting the best from this kind of meat is going to be hard work. But don't panic. Because it isn't. You don't have to be a butcher, or an anatomist, or a Michelin-starred chef. You just have to know what to ask for and what to do with it. Dishes made from these cuts are usually both straightforward and forgiving. It's your cooker, not you, that does most of the work.

What makes it worthwhile is that the very features that render this meat more affordable – a tougher grain and a bit more skin and bone – mean that, given the right treatment, it is absolutely rammed with flavour. That treatment is usually the long, slow application of a gentle heat, either from the oven or beneath the slowly simmering stewpot. But sometimes the barbecue, grill or frying pan will also come into play.

As it happens, making the best of these cuts of meat is one of my great passions – and the principal focus of this chapter. I'm not planning to overwhelm you with a comprehensive list of obscure body parts. I'm just going to concentrate on a few that are easy to acquire, straightforward to prepare and completely delicious to eat.

Here is a rough summary of the cuts I think it pays to be familiar with, and which will be the main ingredients for the recipes that follow:

Beef: brisket, oxtail, shin, topside, mince
Pork: shoulder, belly, spare ribs, ham hocks, mince
Lamb: shoulder, breast, scrag end (or neck chops), mince
Chicken: whole ones, sometimes jointed
Game: pheasants, wild rabbits, whole or jointed
Venison: shoulder, mince
Offal: pig's liver, chicken livers and lamb's hearts

If you are not accustomed to cooking these cuts of meat, you could use the list above as a way of opening up new avenues in your meat cookery. Choose a cut from the list that you haven't cooked before and ask for it next time you're at the butcher's (or try to find it at the supermarket). Have a go at one of the recipes and, if you like the results, peruse other cookbooks to find more dishes using that ingredient. It may soon become a trusted friend. Then move on to another unfamiliar cut of meat. Before you know it, your repertoire will be expanding at a rate of knots.

So where should you go to buy your meat? Call me old-fashioned, but how about your local butcher's? A good butcher really can provide all the meat you'll ever want. If you're lucky enough to have one near you, then you really should support him (or her) with your custom. It's having enough regulars like you that will keep them in business, and keep the quality of their offering high.

The best butchers source their meat locally and actually visit the farms they source from. They can usually tell you which farm any given piece of meat has come from and what breed of sheep, cow or pig is being raised there. They offer free-range pork and chicken, stock game in season and make not only their own sausages but a few specialities – pork pies, perhaps, or faggots. They may even cure their own bacon, and cure and bake their own hams. They may or may not sell organic meat as a matter of course, but they should be able to get hold of it if you ask nicely. Most of all, though, they should be talkers: always ready to tell you about the meat on offer, happy to cut it this way or that, as it suits you, perhaps even ready to suggest a recipe or two…

Unfortunately, just because the word butcher appears above the shop door, you cannot take it for granted that these ideal standards will be upheld. The brutal truth is that a second-rate butcher's is really no better a place to buy your meat than the supermarket, and quite possibly worse. If little or no information is offered about the origin of the meat, and moreover the staff show a marked reluctance to engage in conversation on that matter, then I would say you are entitled to assume the worst. Such shops – and sadly they are not a rarity on our high streets these days – are not really butchers' at all. They are clearing houses for cheap meat. It's not hard to identify such an emporium and, having done so, you should avoid it.

If you are not blessed with a good local butcher, then perhaps you have access to a good farmers' market or farm shop. Either can be an excellent place to find meat of the highest quality. Usually the meat will be pre-packed in some way, as the hoops you need to jump through to have a full butchery counter in your farm shop, or to be allowed to cut and wrap meat on a market stall, are considerable and prohibitive. My preference is for meat that has been tray-wrapped rather than vacuum-packed, as the latter method tends to draw blood from the meat, then bind it back to the surface in a kind of 'blood marinade'. It's not terminal, but if you do buy meat like this it's worth freeing it from its pack as soon as you get it home. Wipe it dry and let it breathe a bit, keeping it on a plate or tray in the fridge either wrapped in greaseproof paper or covered with a cotton cloth.

In the best farm shops the staff should know as much about the origins of the meat they are selling as any good butcher – and some or occasionally all of the meat may, of course, be from the farm on which the shop is sited. At a farmers' market, anyone selling meat should be able to answer *all* your questions about their product. That's because, if they are playing by the rules, they should be a family member or employee of the farm on which the meat was raised. To me that's the ultimate transparency, and the best possible reason to support your local farmers' market – not just for meat but for all truly local produce.

Having said that, I understand that many people find it irresistibly convenient to buy meat at the supermarket. Now it's no secret that I have a few opinions on the way our major retailers deal with our farmers, and on the consequences of that for the welfare of our farm animals. You've perhaps noticed that I've been particularly exercised about chickens. They may provide our favourite meat but, on the evidence of how the vast majority are treated, you'd be forced to conclude that they are one of the least cared-for creatures on the planet. The same is true of pork, and pigs.

In fairness to the supermarkets, I should point out that many of them are now selling good-quality meat reared to high welfare standards, including excellent free-range and organic chickens and pork from outdoor-reared pigs. The problem is that such meat is usually marketed as a premium brand, and therefore perceived by many as a luxury item. If I were to buy meat from the supermarket, I would choose only products that gave me sufficient assurance about both the welfare of the animals and the quality of the meat – organic or free-range poultry, organic pork and grass-fed, well-aged beef. If that means favouring only the premium brands, then so be it. If enough supermarket shoppers express their concerns about meat quality and animal welfare by shopping in this way, supermarkets will improve the extent of their 'ethical meat' offering, and will eventually raise their standards across the board. I know this is the case because it is already happening in a genuine and encouraging way in the world of chickens.

Finally, don't overlook the internet as a means of buying meat. Some of the best meat reared in the UK is now sold online. Farms that do business in this way tend to have a 'unique selling point' – which they will emphasise in the marketing of their product. It might be that their meat is organic, or from specialised or rare breeds, or both. Although this kind of meat tends to be expensive, by cutting out the middleman and selling direct, farmers can manage to keep online prices quite keen, especially if you buy in bulk. Many farms that sell meat online do a whole- or half-lamb box, and similar 'mixed cut' packages for pork and beef.

I wholeheartedly approve of this way of selling meat, as it encourages a holistic approach to the carcass. You'll need a freezer, of course, to help manage the meat. By 'managing', I mean making sure you don't accumulate a pile of 'difficult cuts' – breasts of lamb, knuckles of pork – lurking in the darker corners. And that's where I'm delighted to offer my help. I promised they wouldn't be difficult, and here are the recipes to prove I'm as good as my word.

Lamb chops with garlic, thyme and capers

This is such a good way to serve up lamb chops. They are packed with fantastic flavours and the pan juices make a delicious gravy.

Serves 4

1 large or 2 medium heads of garlic

A little rapeseed or sunflower oil

4 lamb loin chops or chump chops, or 8 neck end cutlets

2 tablespoons capers, rinsed

A good handful of thyme sprigs

A few sprigs of rosemary

A small glass of white wine or strong cider

Sea salt and freshly ground black pepper

Set the oven at 220°C/Gas Mark 7 and put an ovenproof dish in it to heat up. Release all the cloves from the head of garlic but do not peel them. Just squash them a little with the flat of a knife to help release their flavour.

Heat a little oil in a large frying pan, add the garlic cloves and fry for a few minutes over a medium heat. Add the chops and brown them lightly on both sides, seasoning as you go. Transfer to the preheated dish. Remove the garlic cloves from the frying pan too, and scatter them over the chops with the capers and the sprigs of thyme and rosemary, tucking some underneath as well.

Return the pan to the heat and pour in the wine or cider. Let the liquid bubble away, stirring to deglaze the pan, until it has reduced by half. Tip the contents of the pan over the chops, along with a small glass of water. Season well and return the dish to the oven.

Roast for 15–20 minutes, until the meat is cooked through, the fattier edges of the chops are crisping nicely and the garlic cloves are sweet and tender. Serve with some kind of creamy mash (see pages 308–11) and steamed cabbage or greens.

Overnight home-cured bacon chops

Curing meat is not the sole preserve of the experts. There are simple, small-scale curing methods that any cook can use to excellent effect. This is one of them: a fail-safe technique for curing pork overnight that will introduce you to the simple principles of the process – i.e. using salt not merely to preserve but also to intensify the flavour of the meat.

Once you've familiarised yourself with the cure recipe and the method, you're only a step away from creating your own home-cured bacon (see variation), which can be used wherever bacon is called for in sauces, soups and stews.

Serves 4

4 large pork chops
2 tablespoons sunflower or groundnut oil

For the cure:
50g fine sea salt
25g caster sugar or soft brown sugar
3 bay leaves, finely shredded
12–16 juniper berries, crushed
1 teaspoon freshly ground black pepper

Combine all the ingredients for the cure and put them into a plastic container or ceramic dish (a metal one is liable to react with the cure). Add the pork chops and rub the cure lightly all over the meat with your fingers.

Cover the container and leave in a cool place (a cool larder or fridge) overnight or for at least 12 hours, or 24 hours for extra-large or thick-cut pork chops, but no longer. Turn the chops once or twice, if you remember. Then rinse them well and pat dry. That's it: your pork is now cured, your chops are now bacon. They can be used immediately, but will keep in a sealed container in the fridge for 5–6 days, and the flavour will improve all the time. They also freeze well.

To cook the chops, heat the oil in a large frying pan over a medium heat and fry them fairly gently for about 6 minutes per side, until cooked through. Or you can grill them, brushed lightly with oil. Season with pepper and serve with mashed potato or a mixed root mash (see page 308), and leeks and greens (page 300) or just greens.

VARIATION

Home-cured bacon belly

Instead of chops, use 1kg pork belly, off the bone but skin on. Cut into strips 3–4cm thick and cure in the same way, but this time for 48 hours, turning the meat over a few times. After rinsing, the bacon belly strips can be kept in the fridge for 5–6 days or frozen.

You'll struggle to turn this bacon into 'rashers' without a meat slicer, but – like pancetta – it's perfect for cutting into chunks or small dice and browning gently in a frying pan to add to sauces or stews. Or try scattering fried matchsticks over salads or scrambled eggs.

Pig's liver with sage and onions

It's essential that you use the freshest pig's liver you can get your hands on. Otherwise, this lovely dish asks little of the cook – it's very straightforward, and also works brilliantly with venison or lamb's liver.

Fried pig's liver, cut into little chunks and served on toast, makes a very tasty and quick canapé, too.

Serves 4

2–3 tablespoons sunflower oil, lard or goose fat

20–25 baby onions, halved

About 500g fresh pig's liver

4 tablespoons plain flour

1 teaspoon sea salt

1 teaspoon freshly ground black pepper

6–8 sage leaves

100ml aged cider vinegar or balsamic vinegar

Heat 2 tablespoons of the oil or fat in a large, heavy-based frying pan, add the onions and cook gently for about 20 minutes, stirring regularly, until they are caramelised on the outside and tender all the way through. Transfer to a warm dish while you prepare the liver. (Alternatively, you could roast the onions in the oven at 190°C/Gas Mark 5 for 30–40 minutes, turning them over every 10 minutes or so.)

Meanwhile, peel any membrane from the liver and trim out any tough ventricles. Using a sharp knife, cut the liver into slices about 1cm thick, or even thinner if you prefer.

Mix the flour with the salt and pepper. Dip the liver slices into the seasoned flour until well coated, then shake off the excess.

Pour the rest of the oil or fat into the frying pan, place over a high heat and, when very hot, add the liver slices along with the sage leaves. Cook for ¾–1½ minutes on each side, depending on the thickness and how you like your liver. Transfer to a warm plate while you quickly finish the dish.

Deglaze the pan by pouring in the vinegar and letting it bubble while you scrape up any tasty brown bits from the base of the pan. Simmer the liquid until it has reduced to a tablespoon or two. Return the caramelised onions and liver to the pan and spoon the juices over the liver. Serve with some creamy mash.

Devilled lamb's hearts

It's not just the traditional kidney that responds well to simple devilling. Livers and hearts are also delicious in this piquant but creamy sauce. If you want to make more of a meal of this, you could serve it with Puy lentils, cooked as for the recipe on page 101 and tossed with oil, salt, pepper and lemon juice.

Serves 2–3 as a lunch

4 lamb's hearts

1 small onion, roughly chopped

1 carrot, sliced

1 celery stalk, chopped

1 bay leaf

A sprig of thyme

A few black peppercorns

2–3 thick slices of good bread

A little butter

A little sunflower or groundnut oil

A small glass of dry sherry

1 tablespoon white wine vinegar or cider vinegar

1 teaspoon redcurrant jelly

A few good shakes of Worcestershire sauce

A good pinch of cayenne pepper

1 tablespoon English mustard

1 tablespoon double cream

2 tablespoons chopped parsley (optional)

Sea salt and freshly ground black pepper

Cut the lamb's hearts into quarters. Rinse them well under cold running water to remove any blood, then trim away the tough tubes from the top (don't worry about any little bits of white fat). Put them in a pan with the onion, carrot, celery, bay, thyme and peppercorns and pour on enough cold water just to cover. Bring to a simmer and cook very gently for 1½–2 hours, until completely tender. Take out the hearts and leave them to cool. Trim them again, if necessary, then slice thickly.

Put your bread in the toaster, or fry it in butter with a dash of oil until crisp. Keep it warm while you quickly devil the hearts.

Heat a dash of oil in a small frying pan over a high heat. Add the heart pieces, season with a pinch of salt and sizzle for just a minute to brown them, tossing them occasionally. Then add the sherry and let it bubble for a moment. Add the vinegar and redcurrant jelly and stir until the jelly dissolves. Add the Worcestershire sauce, cayenne pepper, mustard and plenty of black pepper. Let it all bubble down and reduce until thick and glossy – about 2–3 minutes if the heat is high enough.

Finally, add the cream and let it bubble for another minute or two, shaking the pan occasionally, until the sauce is reduced and nicely glossy again. Taste and add more salt or cayenne and black pepper, if you like.

If you've toasted the bread, butter it now. Pile the hearts on to the toast or fried bread, sprinkle with the parsley, if you're using it, and serve straight away – as it is, or accompanied by a green salad.

Spring chicken broth

If I buy a chicken for roasting, I always make stock from the carcass. One of my favourite ways to use it is in a simple soup, like this one. I cook three or four seasonal garden vegetables in the simmering stock, sometimes adding a handful of barley, rice or small pasta, and if there's any chicken meat left over from the roast that will go in too. No two chicken broths are ever quite the same: the ingredients change with the seasons and according to what I fancy. In summer, it could be sliced French beans, peas, spring onions and shredded spinach or chard; in autumn, perhaps beetroot, carrot and kohlrabi matchsticks, plus some shredded Savoy cabbage; in winter, diced potato, parsnip, carrot and celeriac or swede.

Serves 4–6

For the chicken stock:

1 cooked chicken carcass

Giblets from the chicken, if available (not the liver)

2 onions, roughly chopped

2 large carrots, roughly chopped

3–4 celery stalks, roughly chopped

A few leek tops, roughly chopped (optional)

A few black peppercorns

2 bay leaves

A sprig of thyme

A few parsley stalks (optional)

A glass of white wine (optional)

For the broth:

About 75g pearl barley or pearled spelt (optional)

1–1.5 litres chicken stock

About 150g baby carrots, scrubbed and halved

About 150g podded fresh (or frozen) peas

About 150g shelled broad beans

Leftover cold chicken (optional)

Sea salt and freshly ground black pepper

To make the stock, after you've picked every last scrap of meat off the carcass, break it up into fairly small pieces (or use tough kitchen scissors) and pack into a medium saucepan or stockpot, along with the giblets if you have them, plus any bits of skin or gristle or jellied juices left from your roast – anything that's not actually meat. Add all the chopped vegetables, peppercorns and herbs, plus the wine if using. Cram everything down with a wooden spoon, so you won't need too much water to cover it all – the stock will be that much tastier as a result.

Now pour on enough cold water just to cover the whole lot – you should need no more than 1.5 litres. Bring to a very gentle simmer, then cover and cook, just barely simmering, for at least 3 hours and up to 5 hours. Strain the stock through a colander and then through a muslin-lined sieve. Leave to cool completely, then store in the fridge. If there's a significant layer of fat on top, you can scrape it off once it's chilled.

If you're including the pearl barley or spelt in the broth, put them in a saucepan, cover with cold water and bring to the boil, then reduce the heat and simmer until tender – about 45 minutes for barley, 20–25 for spelt. Drain and set aside.

Bring the stock to a gentle simmer in a large saucepan. Add the barley or spelt, if using, and return to a simmer. Add the baby carrots and cook for 3–5 minutes, then add the peas and broad beans, as well as any cold chicken you have. Return to a simmer and cook for just 2–3 minutes more. Season the soup to taste, then ladle into warm soup plates and serve straight away.

Scotch broth salad

This substantial dish combines many of the lovely, earthy elements of a traditional Scotch broth – barley, lamb, greens and onions – but serves them up in a less wet and soupy format, somewhere between a warm salad and a risotto. Despite being an easy leftovers supper, it's a rather elegant dish, and I wouldn't hesitate to serve it as a starter at a dinner party. There's something about the nutty texture of the barley, robed in a rich dressing, that takes it to a different level.

Serves 3–4

150g pearl barley or pearled spelt

100g curly kale (2 good handfuls), washed, coarse stems removed, and roughly chopped

1 tablespoon rapeseed or olive oil

1 red onion, chopped

About 250g cooked lamb, shredded

A large handful of flat-leaf parsley, roughly chopped

For the dressing:

3 tablespoons rapeseed or olive oil

2 tablespoons cider vinegar or white wine vinegar

1 tablespoon crème fraîche

1 teaspoon soft light brown sugar

A few mint leaves, finely shredded (optional)

Sea salt and freshly ground black pepper

Put the pearl barley or spelt in a large saucepan, cover with cold water and bring to the boil. Cover and simmer gently until tender – about 45 minutes for barley, 20–25 minutes for spelt. Drain in a colander and set aside.

Blanch the kale in lightly salted boiling water for 2 minutes. Drain, refresh under cold running water and drain again.

Whisk together all the ingredients for the dressing and set aside.

Heat the oil in a small frying pan, add the onion and cook gently for about 10 minutes, until softened. Increase the heat slightly, add the lamb and cook for a few minutes until lightly browned. Add half the dressing and warm through.

Put the barley or spelt into a large bowl, add the kale and parsley, then tip in the lamb and onion mixture and stir to coat everything well. Check the seasoning, then serve, dotting and dabbing a little more dressing on each plateful.

Split pea and ham soup

This is a wonderfully thrifty sort of dish, using inexpensive ingredients to create a rich, filling, protein-packed soup. You can make it either with a ham bone, which is already cooked (most of the meat having been eaten), or a knuckle of bacon, which is cured but uncooked. Either will be available from a good butcher, but this is also a nice way to use the bone and leftover meat from a ham that you've cooked yourself.

Serves 6

1 cooked ham bone or uncooked bacon knuckle

A knob of butter

1 large onion, finely chopped

1 large carrot, finely chopped

1 celery stalk, finely chopped

2 bay leaves

300g yellow or green split peas, soaked in cold water overnight if possible

Sea salt and freshly ground black pepper

If you're using a ham bone, trim all the bits of meat off it, cover and set aside.

Melt the butter in a large saucepan. Add the onion, carrot and celery, cover and sweat gently, stirring regularly, for about 10 minutes, until soft. Add the ham bone or bacon knuckle to the pan with the bay leaves, split peas and 1.5 litres of water. Bring to the boil and skim off any scum that comes to the surface.

Reduce the heat to low and simmer gently, covering the pan loosely to allow for some evaporation. If you're using a cooked ham bone, you just need to simmer until the peas are completely soft – 45 minutes to an hour, perhaps less if they were pre-soaked. If you're using a bacon knuckle, the soup will need longer in order to render the bacon good and tender – aim for about 1½ hours.

Remove the bacon knuckle and set aside, if using; discard the ham bone and bay leaves. You can either use a blender to purée the soup or, for a coarser texture, just mush up the peas and vegetables roughly using a potato masher. Trim all the meat and skin off the bacon knuckle, if using, then cut into small pieces (skin and all, if you like), or cut up the ham from the bone that you set aside earlier.

Return about half of the meat to the soup, taste and season (the ham may have contributed all the salt you need). Heat through again and serve, topped with the rest of the meat and a grinding of pepper.

Bloody Mary burgers with horseradish dressing

These are exceptionally good burgers; I've never known them fail to please anyone. They are essentially a kind of seared steak tartare – with the spicy seasonings leaning more towards a Bloody Mary.

You can't use any old minced beef for them. Ideally, ask your butcher to mince some top rump or topside for you, on a medium (4–5mm) rather than a fine (2mm) setting. If you're shopping in the supermarket, go for minced steak rather than minced beef – preferably organic. The better the meat, the more you can be inclined to serve these burgers pretty rare.

As an alternative to the horseradish dressing, you could serve the burgers simply with hot mustard and mayonnaise.

Makes 4

1 tablespoon tomato purée (concentrated)

1½ teaspoons strong horseradish sauce

½ teaspoon celery seeds

4–8 dashes of Tabasco or other hot sauce, to taste

½ teaspoon Worcestershire sauce

½ teaspoon fine sea salt

600–750g minced topside (not too finely minced)

A little rapeseed or olive oil

Freshly ground black pepper

For the dressing:

2–3cm piece horseradish root, freshly grated

1 teaspoon cider vinegar

2 tablespoons crème fraîche

Sea salt and freshly ground black pepper

To serve:

4 good bread buns, ciabatta rolls or thick slices of baguette

A few Cos lettuce leaves

A few tomatoes, sliced

Ketchup (optional)

In a medium bowl, mix together the tomato purée, horseradish sauce, celery seeds, Tabasco, Worcestershire sauce, salt and a generous grinding of black pepper. Add the beef and mix thoroughly with your hands, making sure the seasonings are spread throughout the meat. Leave for at least an hour for the flavours to develop.

Meanwhile, make the horseradish dressing: mix all the ingredients together in a bowl, seasoning with salt and pepper to taste.

Break off a small piece of the beef mixture, the size of a walnut, and fry in a little oil until well cooked. Taste and adjust the seasonings if necessary.

Shape the meat into 4 patties about 2cm thick. Lightly brush each one with oil, then place on a barbecue over a high heat. It's hard to give exact cooking instructions due to variables such as the thickness of the burger, the heat of the grill and personal preference. For a medium-rare burger, you will probably need to grill for 3–4 minutes, then flip over and cook the other side for a couple of minutes. If you're cooking the burgers indoors, use a lightly oiled, heavy-based frying pan set over a medium-high heat. Leave the burgers to rest for a minute or two while you prepare the buns.

To serve, toast the buns or other bread lightly on the cut side, then top with the lettuce leaves and tomato slices. Add the burgers and smear with horseradish sauce, and a dollop of ketchup if you like. Top with the other half of the bread.

Good with chips, obviously, but if they're too much effort, warm up some good-quality plain salted crisps in the oven.

Venison and pork burgers with sautéed pears

Minced venison shoulder, combined with some pork to keep it succulent, makes a mean burger. If you have a mincer, choose the meat yourself and put it through the medium (4–5mm) plate. If you don't have one, you can ask your butcher to do the mincing for you. Good-quality minced venison is available by mail order from some online butchers or game dealers.

The fried pears sound unusual but they work really well. So do fried apples, if you go for dessert apples that hold their shape, such as Russet, Cox's or Ashmead's Kernel. Alternatively, dress your burger with a mild, fruity chutney (nothing too wildly spicy or it'll smother the very lovely seasoning in the burger).

Makes 8

½ teaspoon juniper berries

3 bay leaves

4 sage leaves, chopped

1 teaspoon white peppercorns

5g/1 teaspoon sea salt

750g venison, coarsely minced

250g fatty pork, such as pork belly, minced

1 tablespoon white wine

A little rapeseed or olive oil

To serve:

A knob of butter

2–3 pears, cored and thickly sliced

8 slices of good white bread or rolls, such as sourdough or ciabatta

Put the juniper berries, bay leaves, sage, peppercorns and salt into a coffee or spice grinder and grind to a fine powder (or chop the bay leaves very finely, then pound to a powder with the other ingredients using a pestle and mortar). Place the seasoning mixture in a bowl with the meat, add the wine and mix with your hands until well combined. Leave for an hour for the flavours to develop.

Heat a little oil in a frying pan, break off a small piece of the mixture and fry it until cooked through. Taste and adjust the seasoning if necessary. Don't be tempted to add too much more in the way of spices, as the flavour will develop as the burgers cook – what you're really checking for is saltiness.

Shape the meat into 8 patties about 2cm thick and fry in a lightly oiled, heavy-based frying pan, or barbecue them for 4–5 minutes on each side, until well browned and cooked through. Remove the burgers to a warm plate and rest while you fry the pears.

In the same pan, melt the knob of butter over a medium heat. Once it is foaming, add the pears and cook, turning occasionally, until they start to take on a little colour but still hold their shape.

Serve the burgers on top of thickly sliced bread or inside rolls, topped with the sautéed pears. I like to rub the cut sides of the bread in the pan juices before adding the burger.

Spiced lamb burgers

I do love a spicy lamb burger. Made with good meat, they can be incredibly tender, juicy and flavoursome. Over the years, I've enjoyed seasoning lamb patties with various combinations of herbs and spices. This North African-inspired recipe is my current favourite and an absolute winner when the barbecue's out.

Makes 8

1 teaspoon cumin seeds
1 teaspoon coriander seeds
1 teaspoon fennel seeds
1 teaspoon black peppercorns
½ cinnamon stick, broken up
A pinch of cayenne pepper or chilli powder
3 teaspoons paprika
1 garlic clove, finely crushed
2 teaspoons fine sea salt
1kg minced lamb shoulder
A little rapeseed or olive oil

For the spiced yoghurt:
½ teaspoon cumin seeds
½ teaspoon coriander seeds
200g Greek yoghurt
A tiny scrap of garlic, crushed with a little sea salt
A dozen mint leaves, finely shredded
A pinch of sea salt
1 tablespoon sesame seeds

To serve:
Flatbreads (page 78) or burger buns
A few Cos lettuce leaves
Some cucumber slices
1 small red onion, very finely sliced

In a dry frying pan, toast the cumin, coriander and fennel seeds, peppercorns and cinnamon, until fragrant, for about a minute or so. (You don't have to toast the spices, but it does get the flavours going.) Grind to a fine powder using a pestle and mortar or spice grinder, then combine with the cayenne or chilli powder, paprika, garlic and salt. Add the minced lamb and mix thoroughly with your hands. Leave for at least an hour for the flavours to develop.

Meanwhile, for the spiced yoghurt, toast the cumin and coriander seeds in the pan you used for the burger spices. Grind to a fine powder using a pestle and mortar, then stir into the Greek yoghurt with the garlic, mint and salt. Toast the sesame seeds in the same pan over a medium heat until golden, rattling as you go, for a minute or two. Leave to cool down a bit, then sprinkle over the yoghurt.

Break off a small piece of the spiced lamb, about the size of a walnut, and fry it until well cooked. Taste and adjust the seasonings if necessary.

Shape the rest of the meat into 8 patties about 2cm thick. Lightly brush with oil, then place on a barbecue over a high heat. Or, if you're cooking indoors, use a lightly oiled, heavy-based frying pan set over a medium-high heat. The cooking time will be determined by the thickness of the burger, the heat of the grill and your preference. For a medium-rare burger, you will probably need to grill for 3–4 minutes, then flip it over and cook the other side for a couple of minutes. Leave the burgers to rest for a few minutes while you cook or warm up your flatbreads.

Serve the lamb burgers wrapped in the soft flatbreads with some torn lettuce, cucumber and onion and a dollop of the spiced yoghurt. You probably won't need all of the yoghurt – what's left over makes a great dip.

My herby barbecued chicken

This is a very appealing way to cook chicken, whether you serve it up hot or leave it to cool and make it part of a picnic. There are no hard and fast rules about the herbs – just use what you've got and what you like. Having said that, I think combining one or two 'lighter' herbs, such as parsley and chervil, with a smaller quantity of a stronger leaf, such as thyme, marjoram, oregano or tarragon, is a good way to go.

You can cook the chicken in the oven, but I like it best over a hot barbecue or in a chargrill pan.

Serves 6

3–4 tablespoons rapeseed or olive oil

½ teaspoon English mustard

3 tablespoons chopped mixed herbs, such as parsley and chives, plus a little tarragon or thyme

A little grated lemon zest

A squeeze of lemon juice

1 small garlic clove, very finely chopped

1 chicken, jointed, or about 1.5kg chicken pieces on the bone

Sea salt and freshly ground black pepper

Combine the oil, mustard, herbs, lemon zest and juice, garlic and plenty of pepper (but no salt) in a large bowl. Slash the chicken in a few places so the flavours can penetrate, then toss the pieces in the marinade; they should be coated, but not swimming in oil. Leave in the fridge to marinate for at least an hour and up to 4 hours.

Before cooking, pat off excess oil, then season the chicken with a little salt. You can either roast it in an oven preheated to 190°C/Gas Mark 5 for 40–45 minutes, turning once, or grill on a moderately hot barbecue or a cast-iron griddle pan, turning regularly until the skin is golden brown, and a little charred in places. Check that the juices run clear when the thickest part of the meat is pierced with a knife or skewer. If you are barbecuing, give the breast pieces about 15 minutes on the hotter part; cook the more muscular legs and wings on a cooler part for at least 25 minutes.

Transfer the chicken to a warm dish, sprinkle with a little more seasoning and leave to rest for 5–10 minutes before serving.

VARIATION

Spicy yoghurt marinade for chicken

Mix together 4 tablespoons plain yoghurt, 1 crushed garlic clove, 1 teaspoon lemon juice, 2 rounded teaspoons medium-hot curry powder and 1 rounded teaspoon garam masala. Coat on-the-bone chicken portions in the marinade (as above) and leave to marinate in the fridge for at least 3 hours. Season with a little salt before cooking.

Tupperware Mexican chorizo (meatballs)

I find the mild heat and smoky flavour of chorizo goes with so many things, from eggs to vegetables, fish and shellfish. Making and maturing your own 'real' chorizo (as described in *The River Cottage Cookbook*) is fun but undeniably a commitment, so here's the easy version – very popular in Mexico and also here in East Devon.

It's a highly seasoned mix of coarsely minced pork, which you keep in a tub or plastic container in the fridge and use in a variety of ways. You can shape some into mini meatballs or little patties and fry until browned, then chuck into tomato sauces, bean casseroles, vegetable soups and the like.

Or you can fry a couple of handfuls of the mixture, breaking it up with the edge of a wooden spatula as you go, until you have a pan of coarse, crisp chorizo crumbs to scatter over salads, soups and egg dishes – especially scrambled eggs – or toss with pasta (see page 208) or vegetables, such as purple sprouting broccoli (see page 302).

Makes about 750g

750g pork shoulder, coarsely minced

1 tablespoon sweet smoked paprika

2 teaspoons hot smoked paprika

2 garlic cloves, finely chopped

10g/2 teaspoons fine sea salt

1½ teaspoons fennel seeds

¼ teaspoon cayenne pepper

50ml red wine

Freshly ground black pepper

A little rapeseed or olive oil for frying

Put all the ingredients except the oil into a bowl and mix thoroughly with your hands, squishing the mix through your fingers to distribute the seasonings evenly.

Heat a little oil in a frying pan, break off a small piece of the mixture, shape into a tiny patty and fry for a few minutes on each side, until cooked through. Taste to check the seasoning, remembering that the flavours will develop further as the mixture matures. If you're a heat fiend, you can add more cayenne and black pepper.

Cover the mixture and store in the fridge for at least 24 hours before using; this will allow the flavours time to develop. It will keep for about 2 weeks.

Chorizo carbonara

A bit of a cross-cultural recipe this one, using a classic Spanish sausage in a classic Italian pasta sauce. I'm sure no one will mind. The result is a remarkably delicious – and quick – dish that illustrates why my Mexican Tupperware chorizo has become such a family staple. Combined with a few other everyday ingredients – in this case, pasta, eggs and cream – it is the key to all sorts of satisfying meals.

Serves 2

150g spaghetti, linguine or other long pasta

1 tablespoon rapeseed or olive oil

150–175g Tupperware Mexican chorizo (page 206), crumbled (or bought cooking chorizo, diced quite small)

2 large egg yolks

100ml double cream

Sea salt and freshly ground black pepper

Add the pasta to a large pan of well-salted boiling water and cook until al dente.

Meanwhile, heat the oil in a frying pan. Add the chorizo and fry briskly for about 10 minutes, until crisp and cooked through. If you're using the soft Tupperware chorizo, you can start with a bit of a lump and break it up with a spatula as it fries, so it forms lots of succulent little nuggets and crumbs, thereby maximising the surface area available for crisping.

Beat the egg yolks and cream together and season lightly (since the chorizo is already highly seasoned).

When the pasta is done, drain thoroughly and immediately return it to the hot pan. Tip in the crisp chorizo, followed by the egg mixture. Use 2 forks to mix the eggy cream into the hot pasta. It will cook in the heat of the pasta, coating each strand in a light, creamy sauce. Serve straight away, with a final twist of black pepper on top.

Sticky glazed spare ribs

These sweet, sticky, spicy ribs make an excellent dish to share with friends – no one can stand on ceremony while tucking into them. They're also brilliant children's party food. Make sure you keep a few back for a solitary treat, nibbled cold, once everyone has gone home.

You can roast the ribs as whole racks, which looks great, or, to make serving easier, ask the butcher to chop them into one- or two- rib pieces.

Serves 4–6

1.5kg pork ribs (roughly 2 whole racks' worth)

For the marinade:
6 tablespoons redcurrant, plum, crab apple or other fruit jelly

2 tablespoons runny honey

2 garlic cloves, crushed to a paste

1 tablespoon finely grated fresh ginger

½–1 medium-hot red chilli, finely chopped, or ½ teaspoon dried chilli flakes

2 tablespoons soy sauce

Combine all the marinade ingredients, whisking them together well. Put the ribs in a large ovenproof dish, pour the marinade over them and use your hands or a brush to get them well coated. Cover and leave to marinate in a cool place for at least an hour, several hours if possible, turning them from time to time.

Turn the ribs in their marinade, cover the dish with foil and bake in an oven preheated to 170°C/Gas Mark 3 for 45 minutes. Raise the temperature to 190°C/Gas Mark 5.

Remove the foil and turn the ribs again, basting them with the sauce. Return the dish to the oven, uncovered, and cook for 35–45 minutes, turning and basting the ribs 2 or 3 more times, until they are glossy and dark and coated in the caramelised sauce.

Spoon any remaining sauce from the dish over the ribs. Leave until they are cool enough to pick up with your fingers, then tuck in. Serve with steamed rice and wilted greens.

Leftover pork with fennel and new potatoes

Pork has a great affinity with fennel – the aniseedy note in the vegetable cuts the porky richness beautifully. This is one of those recipes that developed in an impromptu kind of way when I had various leftovers to deal with. It is now a firm favourite. Feel free to make the dish your own by playing fast and loose with the quantities, or adding some different ingredients. It also works well with chicken.

Serves 4

2 large fennel bulbs

3 tablespoons rapeseed or olive oil

About 400g cold cooked new potatoes, cut into chunky pieces

300–400g cold roast pork loin, shoulder or belly, thickly sliced, then cut or torn into strips

Juice of ½ lemon

A few roughly torn mint leaves (optional)

Sea salt and freshly ground black pepper

Trim the top and bottom from the fennel bulbs. Remove the tough outer layers and cut each bulb in half lengthways. Then place each half, cut-side down, on the board and cut into thick wedges, keeping a bit of the rooty base on each wedge if possible, as it will hold the layers together.

Heat the oil in a large frying pan, add the fennel with a pinch of salt and sauté over a medium heat for 6–7 minutes, until tender and golden, or even a little tinged with brown. Add the potatoes to the pan and fry for a few more minutes until they start to turn golden, then add the pork and fry, stirring a few times, until heated through.

Squeeze over the lemon juice, season with salt and pepper to taste and scatter over the mint, if using. Serve straight away.

Chicken and mushroom casserole with cider

Somewhere between a stew and a braise, this rich and warming dish is perfect to serve in autumn, perhaps with mushrooms you've gathered yourself. If you're feeling wild and gamey, you could do this with a whole, jointed wild rabbit instead of the chicken.

Serves 4

1 chicken, jointed into 8 pieces, or 8 skin-on, bone-in chicken pieces (about 1.5kg in total)

2–3 tablespoons plain flour, seasoned with salt and pepper

3–4 tablespoons rapeseed or olive oil

250–400ml dry or medium cider

A knob of butter

350–400g mushrooms (any kind you like, really), cut into large chunks or slices

1 bay leaf

1 large sprig of thyme

5 tablespoons double cream

2 teaspoons English mustard

1 tablespoon chopped parsley

Sea salt and freshly ground black pepper

Dust the chicken pieces with the seasoned flour, shaking off the excess. Heat 2 tablespoons of the oil in a large frying pan over a medium-high heat. Brown the chicken pieces well in the hot frying pan (in two batches if necessary, adding a little more oil for the second batch). Transfer the chicken to a large casserole dish or pan.

Add 250ml cider to the frying pan to deglaze, letting it bubble for a minute or two as you scrape up the bits from the bottom. Pour over the chicken and top up with more cider as necessary, so the liquor comes about halfway up the chicken.

Heat the butter in another pan, add the mushrooms and sweat gently until their juices run. Add them with their juices to the chicken. Tuck the bay leaf and the thyme among the chicken and bring to a simmer. Cook uncovered, or partially covered, very gently over a low heat (or with the lid on in the oven preheated to 140°C/Gas Mark 1) for about 1½ hours, until the chicken is cooked through and tender, turning the pieces halfway through cooking.

Remove the bay leaf and thyme. Pour the juices off into a pan, leaving the chicken and mushrooms in the casserole. Whisk the cream and mustard into the juices and bring to a simmer. Taste and adjust the seasoning, then pour back over the chicken. Bring the whole lot back to a simmer, and it's ready to serve.

Top with a sprinkling of chopped parsley and serve with creamy mash or plain boiled potatoes and some steamed greens.

Sausage and root vegetable stew

A hearty dish to put on the table when it's cold and grey outside. It's very good with sausages, but also works well with pork chops – or even both together. While pretty much a meal in itself, you could serve it with shredded cabbage or leeks with greens (page 300).

Serves 4

2–3 tablespoons rapeseed or olive oil

6 good sausages, cut into large chunks, or 4 pork chops (or 4 of each)

1 glass of dry cider or white wine

2 onions, chopped

1 leek, sliced

2 celery stalks, chopped

¼–½ celeriac, cut into chunky cubes

2 medium floury potatoes, such as King Edward, Maris Piper or Desiree, peeled and cut into chunky cubes

1 large parsnip, cut into chunky cubes

1 bouquet garni (a bay leaf, 2 sprigs of thyme and some parsley stalks, tied together with string)

1 tablespoon chopped parsley (optional)

Sea salt and freshly ground black pepper

Heat 1 tablespoon of the oil in a casserole or large saucepan. Add the sausages (and/or chops) and brown them well over a medium heat – if you're using chops, you might need to do this in 2 batches. Transfer them to a dish.

Pour the cider or wine into the casserole and stir to deglaze, scraping to release any bits of caramelised meat from the base of the pan. Pour the pan juices into the dish with the sausages (and/or chops).

Heat another 1–2 tablespoons of oil in the casserole, add the onions, leek and celery and cook gently for 10 minutes or so, until softened. Then return the sausages (and/or chops) to the casserole with their juices and add the celeriac, potatoes and parsnip. Tuck in the bouquet garni, season with salt and pepper and add enough water to almost cover everything. Bring to a very gentle simmer.

Cook uncovered, or partially covered, very gently over a low heat (or with the lid on in the oven preheated to 140°C/Gas Mark 1) for about 1 hour, until everything is tender.

Take out the bouquet garni and check the seasoning. The potatoes should have started to break down and thicken the liquor a little. If not, just mash some of the vegetables against the side of the dish with a fork. Scatter over some chopped parsley, if you like, and serve.

Rabbit stew with tomato

This is a lovely way to cook rabbit. I've never met anyone who didn't like it and, as a bonus, it also works brilliantly with pheasants, partridges and grey squirrels. You'll need to use two squirrels for this recipe.

You can adapt the recipe slightly to make a flavoursome rabbit ragù, to serve with pasta or soft polenta (see below).

Serves 3 as a main course, 6 as a starter

1 wild rabbit, jointed

2 tablespoons rapeseed or olive oil

4 streaky bacon rashers, chopped, or about 100g home-cured bacon belly (see page 186)

2 carrots, roughly sliced

2 celery stalks, sliced

1 onion, sliced

2 bay leaves

A few sprigs of thyme

A few black peppercorns

2 garlic cloves, chopped

1kg tomatoes, skinned, deseeded and roughly chopped, or 2 x 400g tins of chopped tomatoes

½ glass of white wine

Water or chicken or game stock, to cover

Sea salt and freshly ground black pepper

Season the rabbit pieces well with salt and pepper. Heat 1 tablespoon of oil in a large saucepan or flameproof casserole, add the bacon and brown over a medium-high heat. Then add the rabbit and cook, turning frequently, until browned all over.

Stir in the carrots, celery and onion and let them take a little colour too. Add the bay leaves, thyme, peppercorns, garlic, tomatoes, wine and just enough water or stock to cover everything. Bring to a very low simmer and cook uncovered, or partially covered, very gently (or with the lid on in the oven preheated to 140°C/Gas Mark 1) for about 1½ hours, until the rabbit is very tender.

Take out the thyme and bay leaves. Taste the liquid and adjust the seasoning, then serve, with plenty of fluffy mashed potato and some steamed greens, or leeks with greens (page 300).

VARIATION

Rabbit ragù for pasta

After the long, slow simmer, take the rabbit pieces out of the sauce. Strain the sauce into a clean pan, pushing hard through a sieve, so that plenty of the tender vegetables go through with the tomatoey liquor. It should be rich and flavoursome as it is but, if you want, you can simmer to reduce it further, until really thick and saucey. Adjust the seasoning. Pull all the rabbit meat off the bones, in chunks and shreds, wasting nothing. Return the picked meat to the sauce in the pan. Bring back to a simmer and finish by stirring in a knob of butter.

Serve spooned on top of pappardelle or tagliatelle, or soft polenta if you like, in deep dishes. You can offer Parmesan to grate but there are already plenty of great flavours here, and I like it better without.

Neck of lamb with lemon and barley

This beautifully simple recipe from my Russian friend, Ivan Samarine, is one I've revisited and reworked over the years. This latest incarnation makes an easy one-pot supper of it with the addition of pearl barley or pearled spelt and a few handfuls of shredded greens.

Neck, or scrag end, is one of the cheapest cuts of lamb you can buy. It rewards thrifty, patient cooks for their trouble with loads of flavour and melting tenderness.

Serves 5–6

1kg scrag end or neck of lamb on the bone, cut into chunks about 2cm thick

4 tablespoons rapeseed or olive oil

Juice of 1½ lemons

4–8 sprigs of thyme

Water or stock to cover

120g pearl barley or pearled spelt

About 200g kale, Brussels tops or spring greens, roughly chopped, tough stems removed

Sea salt and freshly ground black pepper

Season the lamb with salt and pepper. Heat the oil in a large, heavy-based flameproof casserole, add the lamb and allow it to sizzle and spit for a few minutes, turning until it is lightly browned all over. Add the lemon juice, thyme and some salt and pepper, then enough water or stock barely to cover the ingredients.

Bring to a gentle simmer, cover and put in an oven preheated to 140°C/Gas Mark 1. Cook for about 2 hours, then add the pearl barley or spelt and cook for a further 30 minutes. Remove the casserole from the oven and place on the hob over a medium heat.

Add the greens and simmer for a couple of minutes, until they are just cooked through. Serve with plenty of good white bread to soak up the juices.

Baked chicken curry

This may not be quite as quick as opening a jar of ready-made curry sauce but it tastes far better. If you want to put a little curry 'banquet' together, you could serve this dish with flatbreads (page 78), lamb and squash curry (page 224) and spring onion bhajis with radish raita (page 256).

Serves 6

2 heaped teaspoons cumin seeds

2 heaped teaspoons coriander seeds

1 heaped teaspoon fennel seeds

2 teaspoons ground turmeric

2 teaspoons ground fenugreek

1 large onion, roughly chopped

3 large garlic cloves, roughly chopped

1 large green chilli, roughly chopped

1 thumb-sized piece of fresh ginger, roughly chopped

3–4 tablespoons sunflower or groundnut oil

1 chicken, jointed into 6 pieces, or 6 skin-on, bone-in chicken pieces weighing about 1.5kg in total

400g tin of tomatoes

400ml tin of coconut milk

Sea salt and freshly ground black pepper

If you've got the time, toast the cumin, coriander and fennel seeds in a dry frying pan for a minute or two, until fragrant. Grind the whole spices (toasted or otherwise) to a rough powder in a spice grinder or with a pestle and mortar, then mix with the turmeric and fenugreek.

Put the onion, garlic, chilli and ginger in a food processor or blender. Blitz to a coarse paste, stopping to scrape down the sides a few times.

Heat 2 tablespoons of the oil in a large frying pan over a medium-high heat. Add half the chicken pieces, season well and brown them all over, making sure you get the skin a good colour. Transfer them to a large roasting dish, skin-side up. Repeat with the remaining chicken pieces.

Reduce the heat under the frying pan, add the spice mix and fry for a minute or two, then add the onion paste. Fry, stirring frequently, for about 5 minutes, until the paste is soft, fragrant and reduced in volume. Add a little more oil if it seems to be sticking.

Tip the tomatoes and coconut milk into the food processor (no need to wash it out first) and blitz to combine. Pour into the frying pan and bring to a simmer, stirring constantly. Add 1 teaspoon of salt and a grinding of pepper, then pour the sauce over the chicken pieces. Make sure they are all coated in the sauce, then push most of the sauce off the top of the chicken – if there's too much sauce sitting on them, the skin won't brown in the oven.

Place in an oven preheated to 180°C/Gas Mark 4. Bake, uncovered, for 1 hour or until the chicken is cooked through and nicely browned on top, turning and basting it a couple of times. Serve with lots of basmati rice to soak up the sauce.

Lamb and squash curry

Slow simmering renders the lamb meltingly tender, while adding
a jar of chutney is a great shortcut to creating real depth of flavour.
Use a good, spicy, fruity chutney – if it's home-made, all the better.

I have no qualms about using a good-quality ready-made curry
powder or masala in a recipe like this, but including some freshly
ground cumin and coriander certainly enhances the flavour.

Serves 6–8

1 teaspoon cumin seeds

1 teaspoon coriander
seeds

1.5kg shoulder (or neck)
of lamb, trimmed of
excess fat and cut into
4cm cubes

3 tablespoons rapeseed
or sunflower oil

1 onion, sliced

2 garlic cloves, chopped

6cm piece of fresh
ginger, grated

3–6 teaspoons medium-
hot curry powder, to
taste

500g jar of chutney

1 bay leaf

Water or stock to cover

About 750g butternut
or Crown Prince squash,
peeled and cut into
3cm cubes

Cayenne pepper
(optional)

A handful of coriander
sprigs (optional)

Sea salt and freshly
ground black pepper

If you have time, lightly toast the cumin and coriander seeds
together in a dry frying pan for a minute or so, until fragrant. Then
grind them finely using a pestle and mortar or spice grinder. Season
the meat with the ground spice mix, a little salt and black pepper.

Heat 2 tablespoons of the oil in a large, heavy-based frying pan, add
the seasoned meat and cook over a medium-high heat until browned
all over. Don't overcrowd the pan – you will probably need to do
this in batches. Transfer the browned meat to a large, heavy-based
saucepan, using a slotted spoon.

Heat the remaining oil in the frying pan and add the onion, garlic,
ginger and curry powder. Sauté for 4–5 minutes, until softened.
Tip the spiced onion mixture into the pan with the meat, then add
the chutney, bay leaf and enough water or stock just to cover. Bring
to the boil, reduce the heat and simmer very gently, uncovered, for
1 hour.

Add the squash and cook for a further 1 hour, until the lamb is
very tender. Adjust the seasoning, if required – if you want a hotter
curry, you could add a good pinch of cayenne. Serve with flatbreads
(page 78) and/or rice, and a scattering of coriander if you like.

Stewed venison with juniper and bay

Juniper's pungent, bracing and rather piney flavour makes it a natural companion to game and other richly flavoured meats, and I particularly like it with venison.

A lot of recipes for venison stew require you to marinate the meat in advance, often in a vast amount of wine, in order to 'tenderise' it. This is senseless, as it only pickles the meat and makes it drier. It is long, slow cooking that will tenderise it, and the fat oozing slowly from the bacon that will help to keep it moist.

Serves 6

2 tablespoons rapeseed or sunflower oil, or dripping

250g home-cured bacon belly (see page 186), or bought pancetta, cut into chunky cubes

1.5kg venison neck and shoulder meat, cut into large chunks

2 onions, finely sliced

2–3 large carrots, cut into big chunks

2 celery stalks, sliced

6–10 juniper berries, bashed slightly

2 bay leaves

A large sprig of thyme

At least 500ml beef, venison, chicken or game stock

150ml red wine

Sea salt and freshly ground black pepper

Heat 1 tablespoon of the oil or dripping in a large, heavy-based frying pan, add the bacon and fry until it is lightly browned and the fat runs. Transfer to a casserole dish. Now brown the venison in the same pan, in batches, transferring it to the casserole as soon as it's well coloured.

Add the remaining oil or dripping to the frying pan, then add the onions and sweat until soft but not coloured. Add the carrots and celery and cook, stirring often, for 5 minutes. Transfer to the casserole and add the juniper berries, bay leaves and thyme.

Pour a little of the stock into the frying pan and stir well for a few minutes to deglaze the pan, then add this to the casserole too. Pour over the remaining stock and the wine, adding a little water too, if you need it – the liquid should cover the meat by a good couple of centimetres. Season with pepper, but no salt, as the bacon will be quite salty.

Bring to a simmer and cook, uncovered, at a very low, tremulous simmer for 2–3 hours, until the meat is completely tender, skimming any scum off the top as you go along. You can also cook it in a low oven, about 120°C/Gas Mark ½, with a lid on.

When the meat is cooked, taste the stew and season. The juice will be thin but well flavoured; if you prefer a thicker sauce, you can strain the liquid off the meat and boil to reduce and thicken it, then return it to the pan. Serve the stew with a dollop of good buttery mash and some steamed cabbage, sprout tops, kale or other greens.

Oxtail stew with cinnamon and star anise

Succulent and tender oxtail, slowly braised with lots of onions and red wine, is always a treat. Cinnamon and star anise give it an extra flavour dimension that cuts the richness a little. This recipe works well with lamb shanks, and shanks or shoulder of veal and venison too, though with these you'll probably want to leave out the chocolate. The stew improves with keeping so, if you can, make it a day or two in advance.

Serves 6–8

2kg oxtail (about 2 tails), cut into slices 4–5cm thick

2 tablespoons sunflower or groundnut oil

3 onions, sliced

1 bottle of red wine

2–3 cinnamon sticks

2 star anise

2 bay leaves

¼ teaspoon black peppercorns

Thinly pared zest of 1 orange

750ml–1 litre beef stock

25g dark chocolate (about 70 per cent cocoa solids), optional

1–2 tablespoons chopped parsley (optional)

Sea salt and freshly ground black pepper

Season the oxtail with salt and pepper. Heat the oil in a large, heavy-based flameproof casserole and fry the meat over a medium-high heat in batches, so as not to overcrowd the pan, until browned on all sides. Remove the browned oxtail with a slotted spoon and set aside.

Reduce the heat to low and gently cook the onions in the casserole for 15–20 minutes, until soft and translucent. Return the meat, raise the heat, then pour in the wine and let it bubble until slightly reduced. Add the cinnamon, star anise, bay leaves, peppercorns, orange zest and enough stock just to cover the meat.

Bring to a slow simmer and cook very gently, partially covered, for about 3 hours, stirring occasionally and adding more stock as necessary to keep the oxtail moist. When it is ready, the meat should be falling off the bone. (You can also cook it in a low oven at 120°C/ Gas Mark ½ with a lid on, if it's more convenient.)

Drain the meat in a colander set over a bowl, to catch the liquid, then pass the liquid through a fine sieve into a clean pan. Boil until slightly thickened and glossy, then skim off most of the fat. If you'd like to take the meat off the bones, do so once it's cooled a bit. Discard the cinnamon, star anise and bay leaves, return the meat to the pan, then stir in the chocolate, if using.

If serving straight away, warm through; otherwise, leave to cool and keep in the fridge for a day or two, then reheat slowly and simmer for a minute or two. Check the seasoning before serving, with creamy mash or noodles and a scattering of chopped parsley if you like.

Shin of beef with ginger and soy

This is based on one of my recipes for spare ribs or pork belly, which turns out to work brilliantly with shin of beef too. Don't be tempted to trim any of the sinewy parts from the meat – they are vital for the final, full-bodied, gelatinous texture.

Serves 4

2 tablespoons sunflower or groundnut oil, or beef fat

About 1.5kg shin of beef, cut into 2cm thick slices, either on or off the bone

6 large garlic cloves, thinly sliced

2 thumb-sized nuggets of fresh ginger, thinly sliced

3 tablespoons tart fruit jam or jelly, such as redcurrant, plum or crab apple

150ml soy sauce

350–500ml apple juice

2 tablespoons cider vinegar

2 medium-hot fresh or dried chillies

Sea salt and freshly ground black pepper

Heat the oil or fat in a wide, heavy-based flameproof casserole. Season the pieces of meat with salt and pepper and brown them in batches, so you don't overcrowd the pan, turning them to colour all over. Remove each batch and set aside while you brown the rest. The meat may curl up a bit as the membranes contract with the heat, especially if the slices are on the bone; snipping the membranes will help release the tension and flatten the meat out again. Once the beef is browned, remove it from the casserole and set aside on a plate.

Reduce the heat to low, add the garlic and ginger to the casserole and cook gently until softened but not coloured. Add the jam or jelly and soy sauce, mix well, then return the meat to the casserole, in a single layer if possible. Pour in enough apple juice barely to cover the meat. Add the vinegar, whole chillies and a few grinds of black pepper, then cover and place in an oven preheated to 120°C/Gas Mark ½. Cook for 2½–3 hours, until the meat is completely tender.

The garlic and ginger should just about hold their shape and should be eaten with the meat. The chillies will have done their job and can be discarded – or nibbled by anyone brave enough. Serve wit' noodles and steamed greens.

Roast chicken with pearl barley or spelt

I don't often stuff a chicken but when I do I like the stuffing to provide a full accompaniment to the meat. And that's why I love this recipe. The pearl barley (or pearled spelt – see page 16) makes a kind of risotto inside the chicken, and takes on a mildly gamey flavour.

It's important to make sure the chicken is at room temperature before it is stuffed, and to put the stuffing inside while it's still hot. This gets the cooking off to a good start and helps to ensure the bird cooks evenly.

Serves 6

1 teaspoon cumin seeds

½ teaspoon caraway seeds

1 tablespoon rapeseed or olive oil

1 onion, finely chopped

1 garlic clove, finely chopped

150g pearl barley or pearled spelt

500ml chicken stock

6–8 dates or dried apricots, chopped

Grated zest and juice of 1 lemon

3 tablespoons finely chopped parsley

A handful of walnuts, toasted and roughly chopped (optional)

1 large chicken (2–2.5kg), at room temperature

40g unsalted butter, softened

Sea salt and freshly ground black pepper

Toast the spice seeds in a small frying pan over a medium heat for a minute or so, until fragrant (this isn't essential, but it does boost the flavour). Grind using a pestle and mortar to a rough powder.

Heat the oil in a large saucepan, add the onion and sauté for about 10 minutes, until soft and translucent. Add the garlic and sauté for a couple of minutes, then add the ground spices, along with the barley or spelt, and stir until well combined. Pour in the stock and bring to the boil. Reduce the heat and simmer, uncovered, stirring occasionally, until the grain is tender and most of the liquid has been absorbed – this will take 20–25 minutes for spelt, a little longer for barley. If the mixture begins to look dry, top it up with boiling water. Remove from the heat and stir in the dates or apricots, lemon zest and juice, parsley and walnuts, if using, plus salt and pepper to taste.

Undo any trussing on the chicken, take out the giblets if they're inside (save them to make stock) and pull the legs away from the body a little to help hot air circulate. Stuff the chicken with about half of the hot barley or spelt mixture – the cavity should be no more than two-thirds full, as the stuffing will expand in the oven. Put the chicken into a roasting dish or chicken brick, smear the butter over the breast and legs and season with salt and pepper.

Pour a glass of hot water into the dish, cover loosely with foil and place in an oven preheated to 200°C/Gas Mark 6. Roast for 30 minutes, then uncover, baste the chicken with the buttery juices and return to the oven. Turn down to 170°C/Gas Mark 3 and cook for a further 45 minutes – 1 hour, upping the heat for the last 10 minutes if you want the skin a little browner and crisper. Check the bird is cooked by piercing the thigh close to the bone with a sharp knife – the juices should run clear. Leave to rest in a warm place for 20 minutes before carving. The rest of the barley or spelt can be reheated gently (or left at room temperature) and served alongside the chicken.

Serve each portion of chicken with a generous spoonful of the stuffing, plus juices from the dish and perhaps some wilted greens or a salad.

Pot-roast pheasant with chorizo, butter beans and parsley

Pheasant has a slight tendency to dryness but pot-roasting it like this, with plenty of rich chorizo to provide a little fat and extra flavour, ensures a very satisfying result. The butter beans are a fine addition: they soak up all the flavours of the meat, wine and herbs and then you can mash them deliciously into the juices on your plate.

If you prefer, you can joint the pheasants and brown the individual pieces rather than the whole birds. This recipe works brilliantly for a couple of jointed rabbits, too.

Serves 4

A knob of butter

3 tablespoons rapeseed or olive oil

2 onions, finely sliced

4 garlic cloves, finely sliced

A few sprigs of thyme

2 bay leaves

2 oven-ready pheasants

300g cooking chorizo, skin removed and cut into 2cm chunks, or use Tupperware Mexican chorizo (page 206), crumbled into small nuggets

400ml white wine

500ml vegetable, chicken or light pheasant stock

400g tin of butter beans, drained and rinsed

A good handful of flat-leaf parsley, chopped

Sea salt and freshly ground black pepper

Place a large flameproof casserole (one that will accommodate both birds) over a medium heat and heat the butter with 1 tablespoon of the oil until foaming. Add the onions, garlic, thyme and bay leaves and cook for 10 minutes, until the onions are soft and slightly golden.

Heat the remaining oil in a large frying pan. Season the pheasants all over with salt and pepper, add to the pan and brown on all sides over a high heat for 3–4 minutes. Transfer to the casserole. Add the chorizo to the frying pan and fry for 3–4 minutes, until browned, then add to the casserole too.

Deglaze the frying pan by pouring in a little of the wine and stirring to scrape up any bits from the base of the pan. Add to the pheasants with the rest of the wine, the stock and the butter beans. The liquid doesn't need to cover the birds but it should come at least halfway up. Bring to a simmer, cover and place in an oven preheated to 140°C/Gas Mark 1. Cook for 2 hours, until the birds are tender.

Remove the pheasants from the casserole and leave to rest in a warm place for 15–20 minutes. If the chorizo has released a lot of fat, skim some off the juices in the pan. Add the parsley to the casserole and season to taste. Cut the birds into halves or quarters and divide between 4 warm plates. Spoon over the chorizo, beans and sauce, and serve with mash or lots of bread.

Slow-roast beef brisket with potatoes and onions

Brisket's open-grained texture and depth of flavour make it perfect for slow cooking. Don't let the butcher trim off too much fat – a certain amount is needed in order to achieve the final, full-bodied result. It makes an easy Sunday lunch – you'll need to put the meat into the oven first thing in the morning, but then you can more or less leave it alone until lunchtime. Use any leftovers for sandwiches during the week.

Serves 6–8

2–2.5kg piece of boned, rolled beef brisket, tied with string

4–5 garlic cloves, coarsely chopped

A good handful of thyme sprigs

2–3 tablespoons rapeseed or olive oil

1–1.2kg potatoes, peeled and cut into 3–4cm chunks

500g small onions or shallots, peeled

Sea salt and freshly ground black pepper

Put the tied brisket in a large roasting tin and tuck the garlic and thyme inside and under it. Massage the oil into the meat, then season well with salt and pepper. Place in an oven preheated to 200°C/Gas Mark 6 and roast for 30 minutes, then take it out of the oven. Turn the temperature down to 140°C/Gas Mark 1, cover the meat with foil and return it to the oven for 4 hours, by which time it should be very tender.

Baste the meat with its fatty juices, add the potatoes and onions to the roasting tin and toss them in the juices too. Turn the oven up to 160°C/Gas Mark 3 and cook, uncovered, for a further hour, until the joint has crisped up and the spuds and onions are cooked through.

Serve the beef in thick slices, with the potatoes and onions. There won't be much in the way of juices, as they will have been absorbed by the veg, but any that remain should be spooned over the meat.

Roast breast of lamb with lemon and apricots

Breast of lamb is inexpensive, yet full of flavour. It is one of those cuts that look a little unpromising, being an odd shape and quite fatty, but get the cooking right and it delivers a great result (as you'll see in the photographs overleaf). Here, the lamb is rolled around a sweet-sharp stuffing that balances its richness. It is then given a long, slow cook to tenderise the meat.

Serves 6

2 breasts of lamb, boned, any skin and surplus fat removed

2–3 fennel bulbs, cut into 6 wedges each

2 large onions, cut into 4 wedges each, or 4 small ones, cut in half

2 lemons (the ones you've zested for the stuffing), cut into quarters

A little white wine or water (optional)

Sea salt and freshly ground black pepper

For the stuffing:
A knob of butter

3 or 4 small shallots, chopped

3 garlic cloves, crushed

125g fresh breadcrumbs

75g dried apricots, chopped

Grated zest of 3 lemons

1 tablespoon thyme leaves

1 medium egg, lightly beaten

First, make the stuffing. Melt the butter in a small pan, add the shallots and garlic and cook gently until soft but not coloured. Mix the breadcrumbs with the apricots, lemon zest, thyme, shallot mix and plenty of seasoning. Stir in enough egg to bind the mixture lightly.

Lay the breasts of lamb flat on a board and season well. Divide the stuffing between them and spread it evenly, leaving a little space at the edges and at each end. Roll the breasts up tightly, starting at a pointed end, and tie each one in 3 or 4 places with string.

Place the two lamb rolls side by side in a roasting dish. Put into an oven preheated to 200°C/Gas Mark 6 and cook for 30 minutes. Remove from the oven and turn the temperature down to 150°C/Gas Mark 2. Lift the lamb rolls out on to a board. Scatter the fennel, onions and lemon wedges in the roasting tin, turn in the oily pan juices and season with salt and pepper.

Place the lamb rolls on top and return to the oven. Cook for about 1½ hours, turning the fennel, onions and lemons occasionally, until both meat and veg are tender. Check from time to time and sprinkle the vegetables with a little white wine or water if they appear a little dry. If everything seems to be browning too quickly, cover the whole dish with foil.

Transfer the lamb to a warm serving plate and leave to rest in a warm place for about 15 minutes. Cut the lamb into thick slices and arrange on warm plates with the roasted vegetables and lemons. Spoon over any juices from the roasting tin (they'll be fatty, but tasty). Serve with rice or couscous.

Slow-roast shoulder of lamb with merguez spices

Lamb shoulder is an underrated cut. Treated to a very long, slow cook with pungent spices, it offers meltingly soft, flavourful meat that you can pull off the bone easily – as well as a pool of rich juices. This recipe works best with larger, more mature lambs, or hogget or mutton. You can also rub the spice paste on the inside of a boned lamb shoulder, then roll and tie it. Give it an initial 30 minutes at a high temperature (as below) then roast at 160°C/Gas Mark 3 for 2½ hours.

Serves 6–10, depending on the size of the joint

1 shoulder of mature lamb, mutton or hogget, on the bone

For the spice paste:
1 teaspoon cumin seeds
1 teaspoon coriander seeds
1 teaspoon fennel seeds
½ cinnamon stick, broken up
1 teaspoon black peppercorns
A pinch of cayenne pepper or chilli powder
2 teaspoons sweet smoked paprika
2 garlic cloves, finely chopped
Leaves from 2 large rosemary sprigs, finely chopped
2 teaspoons sea salt
2 tablespoons olive oil

If you have time, toast the cumin, coriander, fennel seeds, cinnamon and peppercorns in a dry frying pan over a medium heat for a minute or so, until fragrant (this boosts the flavour but isn't essential). Crush to a coarse powder using a pestle and mortar, then combine with the cayenne or chilli powder, paprika, garlic, rosemary, salt and olive oil.

Lightly score the skin of the meat with a sharp knife, making shallow slashes just a few millimetres deep and 1–2cm apart. Rub half the spice paste all over the lamb shoulder, underneath as well as on top, and especially into the cuts. Put into a large roasting tin and place in an oven preheated to 220°C/Gas Mark 7. Roast for 30 minutes.

Remove from the oven and rub the remaining spice paste over the meat using the back of a wooden spoon. Pour a glass of water into the tin (not over the meat), cover with foil and return to the oven. Reduce the heat to 120°C/Gas Mark ½ and cook for 6 hours, or until the meat is very tender and falling off the bone. You can add another glass of water halfway through, to keep the pan juices ticking along.

Transfer the lamb to a warm serving plate. Skim the excess fat off the juices in the tin. Tear the meat into thick shreds and serve with the juices spooned over. Simple accompaniments are all you need: boiled new potatoes (in summer) or some roasted squash (in winter) and a dish of shredded cabbage, greens or kale would be ideal.

Roast thick end of pork belly with coriander and fennel crackling

This cut of pork is fantastically forgiving. It's quite fatty, which means you can keep cooking it until the crackling reaches a point of exquisite crunchiness without fear of the meat drying out. The wonderfully aromatic flavour of the coriander and fennel seeds really enhances the flavour of the pork. If you've got one or other of the spices but not both, that's fine.

Serves 6

3 teaspoons coriander seeds

2 teaspoons fennel seeds

1 piece of thick-end pork belly (the last 6 ribs), skin scored by your butcher if possible

Sea salt and freshly ground black pepper

Put the coriander and fennel seeds in a mortar and bash lightly with the pestle a few times. You don't need to grind them to a powder, just crack them a bit to release the aromas.

If the butcher hasn't already scored the skin of the meat, do it yourself with a sharp knife (a Stanley knife works very well). Rub the skin with salt, pepper and a little more than half the cracked seeds, getting the seasonings right into the cracks.

Scatter the remaining seeds into a roasting tin, put the meat on top and place in an oven preheated to 220°C/Gas Mark 7. Roast for 30 minutes, then turn the temperature down to 180°C/Gas Mark 4 and cook for roughly 1½ hours, until the juices run clear when the meat is pierced with a skewer and the skin has crackled to an irresistible golden brown. If the crackling is reluctant, whack up the heat again, as high as you like, and check every few minutes till it's done. Leave to rest, uncovered, in a warm place for 20 minutes.

Remove the crackling from the pork before carving, then cut the joint into thick slices and break up the crackling into portions. Serve with apple sauce (see page 339), mashed potatoes and steamed greens or cabbage. Leftovers are equally delicious cold, with plenty of home-made fruity chutney.

Slow-roast boned shoulder of pork with chestnut stuffing

Shoulder of pork, sometimes confusingly called the 'spare rib joint', is economical and very tasty. It stands up well to long, slow cooking and is ideal for stuffing. You'll need a sizable joint for this – anything under 2kg really isn't worth stuffing. Go for a 3kg boned shoulder and you can feed a crowd.

Serves 8–10

1 boned shoulder of pork, about 2–3kg (ask your butcher to score the skin for you, if possible)
A few sprigs of thyme
3 tablespoons rapeseed or olive oil
A glass of dry cider
1 teaspoon plain flour
250–350ml chicken or pork stock
Sea salt and freshly ground black pepper

For the chestnut stuffing:
A knob of butter
1 onion, finely chopped
2–3 celery stalks, finely chopped
2 Cox's or other tart eating apples, peeled, cored and finely chopped
250g peeled cooked chestnuts, roughly mashed with a fork
1 tablespoon finely chopped sage, thyme or rosemary
Finely grated zest of 1 lemon
50g fresh white breadcrumbs
1 medium egg, beaten

To make the stuffing, melt the butter in a large pan, add the onion and celery and sweat for 10–15 minutes, until softened. Remove from the heat, add the apples, chestnuts, herbs, lemon zest, breadcrumbs and egg, season well and mix thoroughly. Leave to cool.

Lay out the boned pork shoulder, skin-side up, on a work surface. If the butcher hasn't already done so, score the skin at 1.5cm intervals with a sharp knife (a Stanley knife, set to about 5mm, is the best tool for the job). Turn the meat over and spread the stuffing evenly over the flesh, leaving a margin around the edge. You will have some stuffing left over – this can be packed into a buttered ovenproof dish and put in the oven for the last 30 minutes of the pork's cooking time.

Roll up the meat and tie securely in several places with string. Put it into a smallish roasting tin (this ensures the juices don't reduce and blacken too much) and tuck the thyme underneath it. Trickle the oil over the skin, season well with salt and pepper, then massage the oil and seasoning into the skin with your fingers. Put in an oven preheated to 220°C/Gas Mark 7 for a 30-minute 'sizzle'.

Remove from the oven, pour the cider and a glass of water into the dish and turn the temperature down to 140°C/Gas Mark 1. Cook for another 4–5 hours until the meat is very tender, then raise the heat to 190°C/Gas Mark 5 and roast for another 20–30 minutes to crisp up the crackling. Transfer the pork to a warm dish and leave to rest, uncovered, in a warm place for 20 minutes.

Pour off most of the fat from the roasting juices in the tin. Place the tin over a low heat, sprinkle in the flour and stir it into the juices to form a smooth paste. Add as much stock as you need to form a thin but tasty gravy, bring to a simmer and cook for a few minutes. Taste and adjust the seasoning, then pour into a warm jug.

Cut the crackling from the pork and break it into large pieces. The pork should be tender enough to spoon or tear into thick shreds. Serve with the crackling, gravy, creamy mashed potatoes and sautéed leeks or shredded Savoy cabbage (or both – see page 300).

vegetables galore

The fact that there are way more recipes here

than in any other chapter is no coincidence. Vegetables also play a key role in the Weekday Lunch(box) chapter, and almost every meat or fish recipe in the book contains at least a suggestion of the kind of vegetables it might be nice to serve it up with. So you'd be right to conclude that I'm serious about vegetables. In fact, I'd go as far as to say that vegetables are, quite simply, the most important food there is. I couldn't even contemplate giving them up. Ever. But let's not get too serious. The last thing I want to do is come over all hair-shirted, virtuous and ascetic about vegetables. Frankly, there's no need. Because not only should they give us great goodness but they should – must – give us untold pleasure as well.

As I have long been pointing out, vegetables provide the essential variety that is the spice of life in any well-tended kitchen. The range of tastes, textures and aromas that can be conjured from the roots, shoots, fruits, stems, leaves, seeds and flowers that we call vegetables is almost beyond limit, and certainly beyond the scope of a single lifetime to explore and experience fully. This becomes more obviously the case when you include all the herbs and spices, fresh and dried, whole and ground, that derive from edible plants. But even if you put that lot on one side, as a special case, your ordinary, non-exotic, common or garden, locally grown, seasonally available veg will still do you proud.

There are well over fifty types of vegetable being grown in the UK, by professionals and amateurs, and the subtly differentiating varieties within each type run into the thousands. So if you think you don't like peas, for example, then perhaps you just haven't found the particular pea you like: try baby Kelvedon Wonder – just podded and utterly raw – and you might well change your mind.

The truth is, if ever you are tempted to put the words 'vegetables' and 'boring' into the same sentence, then something must be not quite right, either in your head or in your kitchen (unless, of course, your sentence is 'Vegetables are never boring', to which I would add, 'but sometimes cooks are').

I wouldn't presume to judge you guilty of not doing justice to your vegetables on the odd occasion, because that would make me a hypocrite. We are all guilty of it once in a while. The aim of this chapter is to unburden you of that guilt, by making it a very rare occurrence indeed. In its place, I want you to feel pride and pleasure, and a sense of possibility oozing from every veg-laden corner of your kitchen.

To help make that happen, the guiding principle in the recipes that follow is quite simple: to bring out the very best in each vegetable and make it so irresistibly delicious that you would happily eat it on its own (and perhaps even more happily with something else). Sometimes this means applying to a familiar vegetable a cooking method you may not have tried before: have you ever roasted skin-on wedges of squash as though they were spuds? Or made a well-buttered purée of parsnips? Or barbecued a lettuce? Often it means choosing one or two simple additional flavourings: some garlic with your runner beans, a few capers and a little handful of chopped mint with your lovely sliced, ripe tomatoes, a yoghurty dressing on sliced radishes…

Once this process of mild but purposeful elaboration is under way, you'll soon appreciate the extraordinary versatility of vegetables. It struck me only recently that another way of expressing this commitment to making a bit more of, and going a little bit further with, the many vegetables we're in danger of taking for granted is to embrace the notion that there is no vegetable that can't be made the star of a simple dish. It might take a cunning combination of clever cooking methods plus complementary co-stars, but when you put together a dish of kale with chestnuts and bacon, or purple sprouting broccoli with chorizo and soft-boiled egg, or beetroot with goat's cheese and redcurrants, you'll soon see that the vegetable is in every case the *sine qua non* of the dish in question, and thoroughly deserves its top billing.

This is the thinking that has been applied to all the recipes that follow. Although a fair few of them are principally intended as accompaniments (the three-root mash on page 308 is a killer with roast lamb or game), I'm nevertheless vouching for all of them as stand-alone pleasures (I've served the same mash as a first course, trickled with rapeseed oil and scattered with shavings of hard goat's cheese). Many can be served up as delightful starters or offered, with one or two other dishes, as substantial main courses. One pleasure I hope you'll explore is putting together a simple spread of seasonal vegetable dishes as a kind of mezze, or vegetable banquet. You may want it to be strictly vegetarian, you may not. But it will certainly be the abundance of the season's crop you are celebrating rather than the acquisition of some special piece of meat.

So, before we dive into the recipes and immerse ourselves in the sheer fecundity of what we can take from our soil and use in our kitchens, a few thoughts on where and how you might acquire your vegetables. There are many options open to the modern cook, some quite modern in themselves (ordering vegetables on the internet is a method on the march), but underlying all the best options is one time-honoured principle that can never be cast aside: try to minimise the time and distance between the reaping and the eating, the harvest and the supper.

It could hardly be simpler. Freshly picked seasonal vegetables that haven't travelled far will be sweeter, more flavoursome and better for you. Time isn't always of the essence. Some vegetables – potatoes, carrots and onions, for example – store well, mainly because, if kept in the right environment (cool and dark) they remain alive, capable of reproducing when released from their dormant state. But even for these veg, long-distance travel will never be conducive to fine quality. It will at best be neutral (though, of course, it will never be neutral to the environment).

Obviously, for all the above reasons, vegetables that you grow yourself are the best you can ever hope to cook with. Add the inescapable psychological factor – the immeasurable pleasure of raising your own food from seed to plate – and it's clear that the home harvest is a kind of miracle food for both body and soul. And while I appreciate that not everyone can grow enough to make a significant contribution to the family diet, I do believe that almost everyone can grow something they can eat – even if it's just a few herbs in a window box, a one-crop wonder such as a tomato plant in a grow-bag or a dustbin full of potatoes. Never underestimate the power of such a project, however small, to bring you joy. It will also do something else very useful: it will serve as a benchmark, both real and in principle, for the vegetables you buy.

So where will they come from? With luck, from the nearest purveyor of top-quality, locally grown seasonal fruit and veg. That might be a greengrocer's in the high street of your nearest town or a farm shop a few miles away. Or it may very well be the supermarket. If it is, then you are by no means doomed to second-rate vegetables. The road and air miles supermarkets eat up in transporting fresh produce around the world and around the country are a source of concern, but it is still possible to find good, fresh British vegetables in many of our supermarkets. Such is the speed of their operations that the produce is often in pretty good nick.

The best strategy in a supermarket is to favour what is in season and has not travelled very far. The more shoppers choose this kind of fresh produce over imported out-of-season exotics (especially ones that have travelled by air), the more supermarkets will commit to supporting the British farmers who are ready and willing to supply the vast majority of the vegetables we need.

Having said that, there is another way to get a regular supply of top-quality vegetables. If you're not a customer already, I would heartily recommend giving a veg box scheme a go. We use one at home during the colder months (my bid for self-sufficiency in winter vegetables is improving every year, but I still haven't got it licked). It also brings us local organic milk, and organic and Fairtrade 'exotic essentials' – the bananas, oranges, lemons and avocados that, like most families, we would find it hard to do without.

As a box-scheme veteran, let me offer you a few tips: always tackle the leafy greens and salads within the first few days of your box's arrival. Try to use up everything in the box before the next one arrives. And never despair at the mounting frequency of roots, cabbages and kales as the winter wears on. With the recipes that are coming up, you won't be short of exciting and surprising ways to make them sing for your supper.

Asparagus soldiers with soft-boiled egg hollandaise

This is a quick and rather nifty way to enjoy the combination of tender, fresh asparagus and a buttery, eggy sauce without any of the work that a proper hollandaise requires. And it's an awful lot of fun to eat. As with all asparagus recipes, get the very freshest spears you can.

Serves 2

About 20 asparagus spears

2 large eggs, at room temperature

A knob of unsalted butter

A little cider vinegar

Sea salt and freshly ground black pepper

Prepare the asparagus by snapping off any woody ends (the spears will break naturally where they are tender). You could steam the asparagus spears above the boiling eggs – if very freshly cut, they will take about the same amount of time. Otherwise, simmer or steam the asparagus separately until tender but not too floppy – 8 minutes at the most for the thickest stems. Time them so they are ready just ahead of the eggs.

Meanwhile, bring another pan of water to the boil. Carefully lower in the eggs and simmer for about 4 minutes (the yolk must be quite runny or the hollandaise effect will be hard to achieve).

Drain the asparagus well as soon as it is cooked and divide the spears between 2 warm plates. Transfer the eggs to egg cups and put them on the plates with the asparagus.

To eat, crack the egg and take off enough of the top to expose the runny yolk. Drop a nut of butter, a few drops of cider vinegar and some salt and pepper into the yolk, stir with a bit of asparagus, dip and eat. You can add a little more butter, vinegar and seasoning as you go. Some brown bread and butter won't go amiss.

Spring onion bhajis
with radish raita

Crisp, light and delicate, these are a far cry from the greasy, lumpy bhajis that can turn up with a dodgy take-away. Served with the minted radish raita, they make a truly summery snack or swish starter.

Obviously this is a dish for those who are not shy of the deep-fat fryer. But once you've sliced the spring onions and assembled the ingredients for the batter, it comes together pretty easily.

Serves 4–6

150g spring onions, trimmed

100g chickpea flour (i.e. gram or besan flour)

50g plain flour

½ teaspoon ground coriander

½ teaspoon fine sea salt

A good pinch of cayenne pepper

A good pinch of black onion (nigella or kalonji) seeds

3 tablespoons finely chopped coriander, plus extra to serve if you like

100–130ml beer or water

Sunflower or groundnut oil for deep-frying

For the radish raita:

200g firm radishes, trimmed

100g fresh, soft goat's cheese

300g plain yoghurt

2–3 teaspoons chopped mint

Sea salt and freshly ground black pepper

Make the raita first. Slice the radishes into 1–2mm discs. Place the goat's cheese in a small bowl and mash well with a fork, then mix in the yoghurt a little at a time. The cheese doesn't have to be blended smoothly with the yoghurt – in fact it's nice if there are a few little lumps. Fold in the radishes and mint and season to taste. Set aside.

Finely slice the spring onions on the diagonal and set aside. Sift the flours, ground coriander, salt and cayenne into a bowl. Mix in the black onion seeds and chopped coriander, then gradually pour in the beer or water, stirring as you go, until you have a smooth, thick batter. You may not need all the liquid. Add the sliced spring onions and stir until well coated.

Pour the oil into a deep, heavy-based saucepan (or a deep-fat fryer) to a depth of 8–10cm and place over a medium heat. The oil should be hot but not too hot, to allow the spring onions and flour to cook through without the outside of the bhajis burning. Test the temperature by dropping in a cube of white bread: it should turn crisp and golden in about a minute – no faster.

Drop heaped teaspoonfuls of the batter into the oil and cook for 3–4 minutes, until deep golden brown. Don't overcrowd the pan; cook them in batches of 3 or 4, tops. Drain briefly on kitchen paper and then serve with the radish raita, sprinkling with a little chopped coriander if you like.

Crudités with garlic and anchovy dressing

This punchy anchovy-based dressing – similar to the Italian classic *bagna cauda* – is a year-round favourite of mine and easy to whip up from the sort of ingredients you're likely to have in your store-cupboard and fridge. It's a superb accompaniment to all kinds of veg – raw or cooked. I love it as a dip for crunchy summer crudités, but I also serve it as a dressing for steamed purple sprouting broccoli, calabrese, cauliflower and kale. It will keep happily in a jar in the fridge for at least a couple of weeks. It will probably separate, but can be re-emulsified by shaking or whisking.

Serves 4

For the crudités:

A selection of raw baby vegetables, such as carrots, courgettes, beetroot, lettuce hearts, radishes, fresh young peas in pods and tender celery stems

For the dressing:

50g anchovy fillets, drained

150ml olive oil

2 garlic cloves, peeled

Leaves from a sprig of thyme

A few basil leaves (optional)

½ small red chilli, or a pinch of dried chilli flakes

1 teaspoon Dijon or English mustard

2 teaspoons cider vinegar or wine vinegar

A few twists of black pepper

For the dressing, simply blitz all the ingredients together in a blender until completely smooth. Or, if you are using fresh chilli, you might prefer to chop it very finely by hand, then stir it into the blitzed dressing to give it a little texture.

Leave the dressing for half an hour or so, to allow the flavours to mingle and develop, then transfer to a large bowl.

Prepare the crudités: halve or quarter lengthways the lettuce hearts and larger baby vegetables, such as courgettes and carrots. Leave the smaller ones, such as pea pods and radishes, whole. Arrange them on a platter and serve with the dressing.

Broad beans on toast

This is full of bittersweet and salty flavours, with the lovely, nubbly texture of the beans and bacon lubricated by a little oil and lemon juice... quite the nicest kind of beans on toast.

Serves 2

750g–1kg young broad beans in the pod

1 tablespoon rapeseed or olive oil

100–150g pancetta or streaky bacon, cut into 5mm strips

A small bunch of spring onions, finely sliced

Juice of ½ lemon, or to taste

2 thick slices of bread (ideally sourdough)

Sea salt and freshly ground black pepper

Extra virgin olive or more rapeseed oil, to finish

Pod the broad beans, putting the large ones in one bowl and the smaller ones in another. Bring a large pan of water to the boil. Add the large beans, let the water return to a simmer and cook for 1 minute. Add the small beans and simmer for a further minute, 90 seconds tops. Drain the beans. Pop the large, thick-skinned ones out of their skins. Very small beans don't need to be skinned.

Place a frying pan over a medium-high heat, add 1 tablespoon of oil, then the bacon. Cook until just starting to crisp, then add the spring onions and cook for a minute longer. Tip in the beans and toss to combine with the bacon and onions. Add lemon juice, salt and pepper to taste.

Toast the bread and spoon the broad beans and bacon on top, along with any pan juices. Trickle with a little oil, add a final squeeze of lemon and serve.

VARIATION
Beans with broken sausages on toast

Replace the bacon with a similar quantity of good pork sausage – or try the Tupperware Mexican chorizo on page 206. Remove the skin from the sausage, tear the meat into lumps, then fry it until crisp, breaking it down into nuggets and crumbs as you do so. Add the spring onions and beans and finish as above.

Lemony courgettes on toast

Courgettes are very gluttish – one minute you're wondering if you're ever going to see any peeking out from under the leaves in your veg patch, and the next minute you've got armfuls of them and your friends and neighbours are politely refusing to take any more off your hands. This is one of the ways in which I like to use up my glut. Even if you don't grow your own, you should find an abundance of courgettes in farm shops and veg boxes from mid-summer.

As a quick, straight-from-the-garden lunch, this is hard to beat. The courgettes are wonderful served hot on toast, but they're just as good cold – as an addition to a couscous or bulghur wheat salad (see page 117), or in pitta bread with some soft goat's cheese.

Serves 2

3–4 courgettes, about 500g in total

2 tablespoons rapeseed or olive oil

1 small garlic clove, crushed

¼ teaspoon thyme leaves

Grated zest of ½ lemon and 1½ tablespoons juice

2 thick slices of bread

10 basil leaves, cut into thin strips

Sea salt and freshly ground black pepper

Extra virgin olive or more rapeseed oil, to finish

Slice the courgettes into thin discs. Heat the oil in a largish frying pan, add the courgettes with a large pinch of salt and sauté over a medium-high heat for about 5 minutes, until their moisture evaporates and they are just beginning to brown a little.

Stir in the garlic and thyme and cook for another minute or so, until a little softer and a little more coloured. Stir in the lemon zest and juice. Season with a few grinds of pepper and some more salt.

Toast the bread. Remove the courgettes from the heat and add the basil. Tip the courgette mixture with all its juices over the toast, trickle on a little olive or rapeseed oil and tuck in.

Barbecued Little Gems and spring onions with goat's cheese

I love cooked lettuce – braised in stock, wilted into a risotto, puréed in soups or, as here, subjected to the fierce heat of the grill. The lettuce softens deliciously, but forms a crisp, charred, pleasantly bitter outer surface. Combined with spring onions and some salty cheese, this makes a wonderful summer starter.

If you don't want to use a barbecue, you can achieve very similar results with a ridged griddle pan indoors – just be sure to get it good and hot.

Serves 4

4 Little Gem lettuce hearts, halved

3–4 tablespoons olive or rapeseed oil

12 spring onions, trimmed

60–80g Ticklemore cheese, or other fairly hard, crumbly goat's cheese

Sea salt and freshly ground black pepper

Extra virgin olive or more rapeseed oil, to finish

When your barbecue is ready for cooking, brush the cut side of the lettuces with a little of the oil and place on the hot grill. After a minute or so, turn them over. Put the spring onions, also brushed with oil, on to the barbecue alongside the lettuce. When both are nicely charred and slightly softened, divide them between 4 plates and sprinkle with some salt and pepper.

Use a vegetable peeler to shave over the goat's cheese – or, if it's a very crumbly type, crumble it. Trickle over a little oil and serve.

Ten-minute veg stock

Few things are more useful
in the kitchen than a pot of
good stock, and this simple,
light vegetable broth is
much quicker to make than
a meat, chicken or fish stock.

Makes about 1 litre

1 large onion
1 large carrot
2 celery stalks
1 fat garlic clove
1 tablespoon sunflower
or rapeseed oil
1 bay leaf, finely
shredded

Coarsely grate the vegetables and garlic or chop them roughly in
a food processor.

Heat the oil in a saucepan and add the vegetables, garlic and bay
leaf. Cover and sweat for 5 minutes, until softened, then pour a litre
of boiling water over the vegetables. Bring back to the boil, reduce
the heat and simmer, uncovered, for 5 minutes.

Strain the stock and it's ready to use straight away, or to cool and
refrigerate for a day or two until needed, or freeze.

Seven soups

Soups may be the epitome of thrifty, simple cooking
– undemanding both to make and to eat – but that
doesn't mean they ever have to be humble or dull.
A good soup is a glorious thing, distilling the flavours of
its principal ingredients, and the perfect way to show off
whatever's fresh and in season at any given time of year.
I hope you'll use this clutch of lovely recipes as a guide
and an inspiration, and then experiment to your heart's
content with the vegetables, herbs and spices that get
your juices flowing.

Potato and fennel soup

A lovely, soothing, creamy soup, like a faintly aniseedy vichyssoise. Served
with one of the suggested toppings below, it's posh enough for a dinner party.
If you're serving it on a hot summer's day, it's delicious chilled.

Serves 4

1 tablespoon rapeseed
or olive oil

A knob of unsalted
butter

1 large onion, chopped

1 celery stalk, chopped

1 garlic clove, chopped

3 large fennel bulbs,
trimmed and chopped
(feathery fronds saved,
if they look good)

500g floury potatoes,
such as Maris Piper,
King Edward or Desiree,
peeled and roughly
chopped

About 800ml chicken,
fish or vegetable stock
(pages 192, 162 and 266
respectively)

100ml cream or crème
fraîche (optional)

Sea salt and freshly
ground black pepper

Heat the oil and butter in a large saucepan and add the onion, celery, garlic and fennel, plus a good pinch of salt. Stir well, then cover and sweat for about 15 minutes, stirring occasionally. Add the potatoes and stock, bring to the boil, then reduce the heat and simmer, uncovered, for about 15 minutes, until the potatoes are tender.

Purée the soup in a blender and return to the pan (or use a stick blender in the pan). Add a little more stock or water if it seems too thick. Stir in the cream, if you're using it, then season to taste. Reheat gently before serving.

This is delicious with any of the following toppings:

- The feathery fronds from the fennel, finely snipped and stirred into a little yoghurt.

- Croûtons or coarse breadcrumbs fried in garlicky oil.

- Crumbled fresh goat's cheese.

- Any of the pestos on page 132.

- Flakes of cooked smoked pollack or snippets of smoked salmon.

Pea soup

This soup is the essence of high summer, and an excellent way to use home-grown peas once they've passed the teeny-tiny, supersweet phase and are getting a bit big and 'cannonbally'. Shop-bought peas, fresh or frozen, will work perfectly well too.

Serves 4

A knob of unsalted butter

1 onion, chopped

1 garlic clove, chopped

1 celery stalk, chopped (optional)

A few thyme leaves (optional)

500g fresh or frozen peas or petits pois

750ml chicken or vegetable stock (pages 192 and 266 respectively)

Sea salt and freshly ground black pepper

Melt the butter in a large saucepan. Add the onion and garlic, and the celery and thyme, if using, then cover and sweat gently, stirring often, for about 12 minutes, until soft. Stir in the peas and the stock. Bring to the boil, reduce the heat, then simmer, partially covered, until the peas are soft – this will take 3–8 minutes, depending on the size and mealiness of the peas.

Purée the soup in a blender and return it to the pan (or use a stick blender to blend it in the pan). Add a little more stock or some water if it's too thick for your taste. Season well.

You can either reheat the soup and serve it hot or let it cool and chill it thoroughly to serve cold. Either way, you can, if you like, make it more elegant with one of the following garnishes:

- Fine shreds of mint or lovage (or both), mixed with a little yoghurt or crème fraîche.

- A swirl of cream and a sprinkling of snipped chives.

- Fine slivers of air-dried ham, or crisp-fried bacon.

Five-root soup with bacon

The key to success with this soup is to cut the root vegetables small and keep the pieces all about the same size so they cook evenly. It helps to be in a chopping mood when you set about this one.

If you don't have any Cheddar to hand, or you want to go easy on the cheese, you can finish the soup with a trickle of rapeseed or olive oil instead. You could also leave out the bacon to make a vegetarian version.

Serves 4–6

1 tablespoon rapeseed or olive oil

100g unsmoked streaky bacon or pancetta, cut into small dice

1 large onion, finely chopped

150g carrots, cut into small dice

150g swede, cut into small dice

150g not-too-floury potatoes, such as Wilja, peeled and cut into small dice

150g parsnip, cut into small dice

150g celeriac, cut into small dice

1 litre light vegetable or chicken stock (pages 266 and 192 respectively)

Sea salt and freshly ground black pepper

To serve:

A few chives, snipped

About 100g mature Cheddar cheese, grated

Heat the oil in a large saucepan, add the bacon or pancetta and cook gently until the fat runs and the bacon starts to turn golden. Add the onion and sweat for 10–15 minutes, until soft and golden. Add all the diced root vegetables, cover the pan and let the whole mixture sweat and soften for 10 minutes or so, stirring occasionally.

Pour in the stock and bring to a simmer. Cover and cook for about 15 minutes, until all the vegetables are tender.

Taste the soup and season accordingly. Ladle into warm bowls, scatter over some chives and top with grated cheese. Serve straight away, with some thick pieces of toast.

VARIATION

This soup is also very good whizzed up in a blender until smooth. Then I like to serve it topped with a dash of pesto, such as the parsley and walnut pesto on page 132.

Beetroot and cumin soup with spiced yoghurt

Sweet beetroot and earthy cumin are a very seductive combination (see also beetroot and walnut hummus, page 127).

Served hot or cold, this soup has been known to win over even the most beetroot-phobic guests. Don't use the spiced yoghurt just for the soup, either. It's very good with fried leftover roast chicken or lamb, either with rice or piled into pitta bread with shredded lettuce.

Serves 4–6

750g beetroot, peeled

A knob of unsalted butter

1 tablespoon rapeseed or olive oil

1 large onion, roughly chopped

1 fat garlic clove, chopped

1 teaspoon cumin seeds

800ml vegetable or chicken stock (pages 266 and 192 respectively)

Sea salt and freshly ground black pepper

Chopped flat-leaf parsley, to serve

For the spiced yoghurt:

1 teaspoon cumin seeds

1 teaspoon coriander seeds

A pinch of caraway seeds

½ teaspoon sweet paprika

A pinch of cayenne pepper

4 tablespoons plain yoghurt

1 tablespoon rapeseed or olive oil

Cut the beetroot into small chunks. Heat the butter and oil in a large saucepan until foaming, then add the onion, garlic and cumin. Cook gently for 5–10 minutes, until soft but not coloured. Add the beetroot, toss well with the onion, then pour in the stock. Bring to a simmer, cover and cook for 20–30 minutes, until the beetroot is tender.

Meanwhile, for the spiced yoghurt, toast the cumin, coriander and caraway seeds in a dry frying pan over a medium heat for a minute or so, until fragrant (this stage isn't essential but it does enhance the flavour). Transfer to a spice grinder, coffee mill or pestle and mortar and grind to a powder. Combine with the paprika, cayenne and a pinch of salt. Stir a heaped teaspoon of this mixture into the yoghurt (keep the remaining spice mix for another batch of the spiced yoghurt – it's very good with lamb or chicken). Add the oil and whisk until combined.

Purée the soup in a blender and return it to the pan (or use a stick blender to purée it in the pan). Season to taste. If it seems excessively thick, you can thin it down with a little more stock or water. Serve hot or chilled, with spiced yoghurt swirled or dotted in at the last moment and parsley sprinkled on top.

Celeriac soup

Given its humble ingredients, this soup has a surprisingly sophisticated
flavour. Celeriac's earthy intensity and velvety texture are wonderful
combined with the spicy, salty or sweet finishes I recommend here,
and a swirl of parsley and walnut pesto (see page 132) works very well
too. For a rather splendid starter, you could also top each bowlful with
a fat, juicy oyster – steamed open in a little white wine.

Serves 6

50g unsalted butter

1 large celeriac, about
1kg, peeled and roughly
chopped

About 350g leeks, tough
green parts removed,
sliced

100g potato, peeled and
diced

1 onion, chopped

2 garlic cloves, chopped

1 litre vegetable or
chicken stock (pages 266
and 192 respectively)

100ml double cream
(optional)

Sea salt and freshly
ground black pepper

Melt the butter in a large, heavy-based saucepan. Add the celeriac,
leeks, potato, onion and garlic, season generously, then sweat for
about 10 minutes, until the vegetables are starting to soften.

Add the stock, bring to the boil, then turn down the heat and simmer
for 20–25 minutes, until the celeriac is tender.

Purée the soup in a blender and return it to the pan (or use a stick
blender to purée it in the pan). Reheat gently. If the soup is too thick,
thin it with some water or stock, though remember you may be
adding cream.

Just before serving, check the soup for seasoning and stir in the
cream if you want to enrich it a little.

Garnish with one of the following:

- Diced eating apple, fried gently in butter until golden, then
  spooned on to the soup, buttery juices and all.

- A few crisp shreds of fried smoked bacon or ham.

- A little confit chilli. To make this, deseed and finely slice a few
  hot red chillies. Put them in a small saucepan with a couple of
  peeled garlic cloves and cover with olive oil. Cook slowly over an
  extremely low heat for 45 minutes–1 hour, until the chillies are
  really soft. Spoon a teaspoonful of the confit chilli and its oil on
  to each bowl of soup. Alternatively, just use a trickle of any good,
  chilli-infused olive oil.

Lentil soup with caraway and minted yoghurt

This soup is a brilliant standby if you need to produce a quick meal from store-cupboard ingredients. The humble lentil is elevated to great heights when enhanced with coriander, caraway and garlic. Should you happen to have some confit chilli to hand (see left), it makes an excellent alternative to the minted yoghurt. Any good bread is a suitable accompaniment, but I think this soup goes particularly well with flatbreads (page 78).

Serves 6

2 tablespoons rapeseed or olive oil

2 onions, roughly chopped

1 carrot, roughly chopped

2 teaspoons coriander seeds

1 teaspoon caraway seeds

2 garlic cloves, crushed

350g red lentils

1.5 litres water or vegetable stock (page 266)

Sea salt and freshly ground black pepper

To finish:

5 tablespoons plain yoghurt

2 tablespoons finely chopped mint

Heat the oil in a large saucepan, add the onions and carrot and sweat for about 10 minutes, until soft.

Meanwhile, if you have time, toast the coriander and caraway seeds in a small frying pan over a medium heat for a minute or so, until fragrant (this enhances the flavour, but is not essential). Grind to a fine powder in a spice grinder, coffee grinder or pestle and mortar. Add half the ground spices to the softened vegetables along with the garlic and stir over a medium heat for a minute or two.

Add the lentils and water or stock and bring to the boil, skimming off any scum that comes to the surface. Reduce the heat, then cover and simmer gently for 15 minutes or until the lentils are soft. Purée in a blender or food processor until smooth, adding more water if it is a little thick. Return to the pan and heat through. Adjust the seasoning with salt, pepper and more of the ground spices, if you like.

In a small bowl, whisk together the yoghurt and mint and season well. Serve the soup with a dollop of the minted yoghurt swirled on top of each portion.

Butternut and nut butter soup

This might sound like too clever a joke by half, but it's a really good soup. Peanut (or other nut) butter is a very handy way to add richness and nuttiness to a soup. You can use smooth or crunchy peanut butter, depending on whether you want a silky soup or one with a slightly chunkier texture. To make it easier to whisk the peanut butter into the soup, warm it slightly first to soften it. You can do this by standing the jar in a bowl of hot water or leaving it in a warm place (I put it on top of my wood-burning stove) for 10 minutes or so.

You can use other squash varieties too, or indeed a 50:50 mixture of sweet and regular potatoes, but then you wouldn't have the joke. And let's be fair, it's a good one isn't it?

Serves 6–8

1 butternut squash, about 800g–1kg

A large knob of unsalted butter

1 large onion, chopped

1 small medium-hot chilli, deseeded and chopped, or a pinch of dried chilli flakes

A 3cm piece of fresh ginger, grated

1 small garlic clove, chopped

About 1 litre chicken or vegetable stock (pages 192 and 266 respectively)

227g jar of crunchy or smooth peanut butter (or use home-made, see page 52)

Juice of 1 lime

3 tablespoons finely chopped coriander

Sea salt and freshly ground black pepper

To serve:

Plain yoghurt

Coriander leaves

2 tablespoons toasted pumpkin seeds or chopped toasted peanuts (optional)

A little finely chopped chilli (optional)

Halve and peel the squash, then scoop out the seeds and cut the flesh into 1cm cubes. Melt the butter in a large saucepan, add the onion and sweat until soft and translucent. Add the chilli, ginger and garlic and cook for another couple of minutes. Add the squash, a sprinkling of salt and a few grinds of pepper. Stir well and cook for 5 minutes.

Pour in the stock. Bring to the boil and simmer gently, partially covered, for about 20 minutes, until the squash is soft – you should be able to mash it easily against the side of the pan with the back of a wooden spoon. Whiz in a blender (or use a stick blender to purée it in the pan) until very smooth; you may need to do this in batches.

In a bowl, whisk the peanut butter with a ladleful of the hot soup until well blended. Return this mixture to the soup in the pan, stir well and heat through. Remove from the heat, add the lime juice and coriander, then taste and adjust the seasoning with salt and pepper.

Serve each portion topped with a dollop of yoghurt and a few coriander leaves. Sprinkle toasted pumpkin seeds or peanuts and/or a little finely chopped chilli on top, if you like.

Ten salads

I eat a salad of one kind or another pretty much every day. Often that means just a few lettuce or winter salad leaves tossed with a light vinaigrette to be eaten with or after something more substantial. But sometimes our salads are big, seasonal family affairs that become the main meal. Fresh vegetables – raw or cooked – tossed with a flavoursome dressing, and augmented with nuts, seeds, meat, fish or cheese, make a meal that's wholesome, delicious, easy to eat and beautiful to look at. Add to this the fact that salads are easy to prepare (and to adapt or invent) and you'll understand why I see them as a cornerstone of good everyday cooking.

Warm leek and white bean salad with mustard dressing

This simple little dish works very well as a vegetarian starter, but can also function as a side dish to something robust, such as pork chops or sausages. It's all about the sweetness of the leeks and the creaminess of the beans. Put the extra wholegrain mustard into the dressing if you like real bite.

Serves 4

2 tablespoons rapeseed or olive oil

2 large leeks, trimmed, washed and finely sliced

410g tin of white beans such as cannellini, drained and rinsed

1 heaped tablespoon chopped flat-leaf parsley

Sea salt and freshly ground black pepper

Salad leaves, to serve

For the dressing:

1 tablespoon Dijon mustard

1 teaspoon wholegrain mustard (optional)

3 tablespoons rapeseed or extra virgin olive oil

2 teaspoons cider vinegar

A pinch each of sea salt, freshly ground black pepper and caster sugar

Heat the oil in a large frying pan over a medium heat, then add the leeks and a good pinch of salt. As soon as the leeks begin to soften, turn the heat down fairly low and continue to cook, stirring from time to time for 6–7 minutes, until they are soft; don't let them colour. Add the beans and toss together until heated through. Remove from the heat and stir in the parsley and plenty of black pepper.

For the dressing, whisk all the ingredients together to combine. Add to the pan of warm leeks and beans and stir well.

Divide the salad leaves between 4 plates and spoon the warm bean and leek mixture on top. Serve straight away, accompanied by toasted sourdough bread. Alternatively, forget the leaves and just serve the dressed beans on toast.

Celeriac Waldorf salad

I've used celeriac as well as celery in my take on this classic salad, plus raisins or sultanas plumped in orange juice. Try it with some brown bread and perhaps some cold chicken or pork. If you don't want to make your own mayonnaise, you could simply add a dab of mustard and a squeeze of lemon to your favourite bought version. Or, for a lighter dressing, mix mayonnaise with an equal quantity of yoghurt.

Serves 4

50g raisins or sultanas
Juice of 2 oranges
100g walnuts
150g celeriac, peeled
150g celery
2 crisp eating apples, such as Cox's or Russet
5–6 tablespoons mayonnaise (see below)
Sea salt and freshly ground black pepper

Put the raisins or sultanas in a pan with the orange juice and bring to a simmer. Take off the heat and leave for an hour or so to plump up.

Scatter the walnuts on a baking tray and toast in an oven preheated to 180°C/Gas Mark 4 for 5–7 minutes, until fragrant – check them regularly, as they can burn easily. Leave to cool, then chop roughly.

Cut the celeriac into thick matchsticks. Cut the celery, slightly on the bias, into slices 3–4mm thick. Core the apples, leaving the skin on, and cut into fine slices. Drain the raisins or sultanas (reserve the orange juice and drink it later) and toss them with the celeriac, celery, apples and walnuts. Add enough mayonnaise to coat everything lightly, toss to mix, then check the seasoning and serve.

Mayonnaise

I'm not a total mayo fascist: like most families, we usually have a jar of bought mayo in the fridge. However, I make my own if I have time and I hope you will too, as it will be far superior to standard shop-bought options. Adding a teaspoonful of ready-made mayo to your raw egg yolk at the start reduces the risk of splitting.

Makes about 175ml

¼ garlic clove
¼ teaspoon English mustard
1 medium egg yolk
1 teaspoon wine vinegar or cider vinegar
1 generous teaspoon ready-made mayonnaise (optional)
75ml sunflower oil
75ml rapeseed oil or a mild olive oil
Lemon juice (optional)
Sea salt, freshly ground black pepper and a little caster sugar

Crush the garlic to a paste with a pinch of salt. Transfer it to a bowl, add the mustard, egg yolk, vinegar, ready-made mayo if using, plus a little pepper and a tiny pinch of sugar, then whisk together.

Combine the oils in a jug. Pour a few drops into the yolk mixture and whisk to emulsify. Repeat this once or twice, then start pouring in the oil in a very thin, steady stream, whisking all the time.

When all the oil has been whisked in and you have a thick, glossy mayonnaise, taste it and add more salt, pepper, sugar and some lemon juice if it needs it. If it's too thick, let it down with a little warm water. Refrigerate until needed and use within a week.

Carrot, orange and chervil salad

This is one of those simple combinations of just a few ingredients that complement each other beautifully. The sharp, juicy tang of the oranges; the sweet crunch of the carrot; the nutty texture of the seeds – it just works. It's also very good if you replace the seeds with around 100g crumbled freshly roasted chestnuts.

Serves 2–3

2 oranges

1 large carrot

50–60g mixed pumpkin and sunflower (or other) seeds

A few sprigs of chervil (or tender parsley)

For the dressing:

1 tablespoon lemon juice or cider vinegar

1 tablespoon sunflower oil

2 tablespoons rapeseed or extra virgin olive oil

Sea salt and freshly ground black pepper

Cut the top and bottom off one of the oranges. Place it cut-side down on a chopping board and work around it with a sharp knife, cutting off the peel and pith in strips so that the juicy flesh is exposed. Then, holding the orange in the palm of your hand and working over a bowl to catch the juice, slice down either side of each membrane, as close as you can, to release the segments. Drop the segments into the bowl. Repeat with the other orange.

Peel the carrot and cut into matchsticks using a sharp knife or a mandolin. Add these to the orange segments with the seeds and toss to mix.

To make the dressing, whisk all the ingredients together, along with any juice saved from the oranges.

Add the chervil or parsley to the salad along with the dressing, toss everything together and serve.

Tomato salsa salad with capers and mint

What's the difference between a fresh tomato salsa and a tomato salad? Not much really, but for me, a tomato salsa should always include some kind of raw allium – shallot, onion, spring onion – to give it an edge. And if you chopped the tomatoes more finely for this recipe, you'd have a definite salsa, I'd say – perfect for eating with burgers or spicy chicken. But leave the tomatoes in fat chunks and this is a salad, needing only some torn fresh bread to mop up the juices, and perhaps some buffalo mozzarella or tangy fresh goat's cheese alongside.

Capers are not everyone's favourite thing, so just leave them out if they don't appeal. And if you don't fancy mint, torn basil leaves or roughly chopped parsley are good options, too.

Serves 4

500g ripe, tasty tomatoes

1 shallot or ½ small red onion, very finely chopped

1–2 tablespoons tiny capers, rinsed

A small squeeze of lemon juice

2–3 tablespoons rapeseed or extra virgin olive oil

A tiny pinch of sugar

A few torn mint leaves

Sea salt and freshly ground black pepper

Cut the tomatoes into quarters, then halve each quarter widthways. Place in a bowl and lightly stir in the shallot or onion and capers.

Put the lemon juice and oil in a small jug, season well and add the sugar. Whisk together, then trickle over the tomatoes. Scatter over the torn mint leaves and serve.

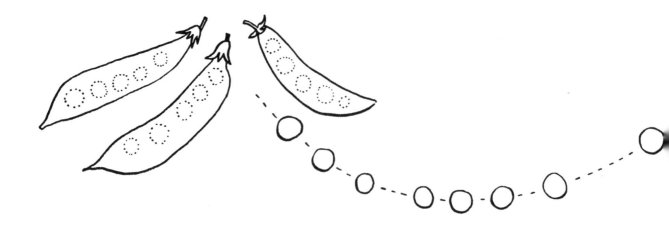

Salad of baby peas, ricotta and spring onions

A stunning, fresh and pretty salad to serve as a starter or light lunch in the summer, when young peas can be popped straight from the pod into the pan.

Serves 4–6

500g very fresh baby peas or frozen petits pois

2 tablespoons rapeseed or olive oil

10–12 spring onions, trimmed and sliced on the diagonal

200g ricotta or other soft, fresh cheese

1 teaspoon chopped thyme (optional)

For the dressing:

1 tablespoon lemon juice

2 tablespoons extra virgin olive or rapeseed oil

Sea salt and freshly ground black pepper

Bring a pan of lightly salted water to the boil, drop in the peas, cook for a maximum of 2 minutes, then drain.

Heat the oil in a frying pan, add the spring onions and cook gently for 4–5 minutes, until soft. Transfer to a bowl and mix in the still-warm peas.

To make the dressing, whisk the lemon juice and oil together in a bowl with plenty of seasoning, or shake the ingredients in a screw-top jar to combine. Trickle this dressing over the spring onions and peas and stir gently until well coated.

Spoon the salad on to plates or dishes. Crumble the cheese over the top, scatter on the thyme if using, and serve immediately.

Roast Jerusalem artichoke, hazelnut and goat's cheese salad

The earthy flavour of roasted artichokes is delicious with toasted hazelnuts. Jerusalem artichokes have a tendency to collapse into fluffiness when roasted, but keeping the skin on stops them breaking up too much when you toss them into the salad.

Serves 4–6

75g hazelnuts

600g Jerusalem artichokes

4 tablespoons rapeseed or olive oil

2 sprigs of thyme

1–2 bay leaves

1 teaspoon hazelnut oil

½ lemon

A couple of handfuls of winter salad leaves (optional)

75g hard goat's cheese, crumbled or shaved into strips with a vegetable peeler, according to texture

Sea salt and freshly ground black pepper

First, toast the hazelnuts. Spread them out on a baking sheet in a single layer and place in an oven preheated to 180°C/Gas Mark 4 for about 5 minutes, until they are lightly coloured and the skins are blistered and cracked. Wrap them in a clean tea towel for a minute and then rub them vigorously with the towel until the skins fall off. Cool and chop very roughly or leave whole.

Turn the oven up to 190°C/Gas Mark 5 and put a large roasting tin in to heat up. Scrub the artichokes well and cut into halves or quarters lengthways, depending on size – you need chunks about 1.5cm thick. Put the artichokes in a bowl and turn over in 3 tablespoons of the rapeseed or olive oil with the thyme, bay and a little salt. Tip into the hot roasting tin and roast for about 35 minutes, until tender and lightly golden, taking the tray out after 15 minutes to turn the artichokes over. Allow to cool slightly.

Whisk the remaining tablespoon of oil with the hazelnut oil, trickle it over the warm artichokes, squeeze on a good spritz of lemon juice and season with salt and a few grinds of black pepper. Turn the artichokes over gently with your hands so that everything is well combined. Add the hazelnuts, and the salad leaves if you're using them, toss gently, then divide between serving plates. Scatter over the crumbled or shaved goat's cheese and serve straight away.

Seedy spinach salad

Obviously this is not seedy in the gutter sense – far from it. Indeed it's full of virtues, being packed with lovely, healthy, lightly toasted seeds. I particularly like eating this using the roll-your-own method (see below), which creates a very satisfying leafy, grainy crunch in the mouth.

The fennel or cumin seeds add an intense, aromatic flavour, which some will love and others may wish to avoid. You can, of course, prepare and keep them separate, as an optional sprinkle.

Serves 4

1–2 tablespoons pumpkin seeds

1–2 tablespoons sesame seeds

1–2 tablespoons hemp seeds, or poppy seeds

1 teaspoon fennel or cumin seeds (optional)

250g young spinach leaves, trimmed

For the dressing:

A good squeeze of lemon juice

A pinch each of sea salt, freshly ground black pepper and caster sugar

3 tablespoons rapeseed oil (or half olive and half sunflower oil)

Combine all the seeds in a dry frying pan over a medium heat. Toast them for a minute or two, tossing frequently so they don't burn, until they are starting to brown and smell really lovely. Tip into a bowl and set aside to cool.

To make the dressing, stir the lemon juice and seasonings together in a bowl and then whisk in the oil, or shake the ingredients together in a screw-top jar to combine.

Put the spinach leaves in a serving bowl, trickle over the dressing and toss together. Scatter over about half the seeds, toss lightly again, then sprinkle the remaining seeds over and serve.

Alternatively, you can turn this into a roll-your-own affair. Put the spinach in a bowl on the table, with the toasted seeds and dressing in separate bowls. Everyone can then help themselves to a leaf, sprinkle a pinch of seeds down the centre and roll it up, like a little leafy pancake (or, let's face it, a roll-up), then dip the 'rollie' into the dressing and eat. If you choose to serve the salad this way, you'll probably get through more seeds, so increase the quantity a touch.

Beetroot, goat's cheese and redcurrant salad

Beetroot is one of my favourite roots and I particularly like it, post-roasting, in various salad combos with salty cheese. This shamelessly pink-tinged dish has a winning combination of sweet, tart and salty flavours. I enjoy it most when made with a blue goat's cheese, such as Harbourne Blue (see page 19), but any crumbly goat's cheese will do.

**Serves 4 as a starter,
2 as a main course**

About 400g small beetroot

1 garlic clove, finely chopped

A large sprig of thyme (optional)

2 tablespoons rapeseed or olive oil

3–4 handfuls of seasonal salad leaves

175–200g crumbly goat's cheese

50–100g redcurrants

Sea salt and freshly ground black pepper

For the dressing:

1 tablespoon cider vinegar or lemon juice

3 tablespoons rapeseed or olive oil

A pinch each of sea salt, freshly ground black pepper and caster sugar

Scrub the beetroot well, but leave them whole, then place on a large piece of foil. Scatter with the garlic, the leaves from the thyme, if you're using it, and some salt and pepper, then trickle over the oil. Scrunch up the foil to make a baggy but tightly sealed parcel, place it on a baking tray and put it in an oven preheated to 200°C/Gas Mark 6. Roast until tender – about an hour, though it could take longer. The beetroot are cooked when a knife slips easily into the flesh. Leave to cool, then top and tail them and remove the skin. Cut into wedges and place in a large bowl.

Whisk together all the dressing ingredients. Arrange the salad leaves on serving plates and trickle on a little of the dressing. Roughly crumble the cheese over the beetroot, add the remaining dressing and toss together loosely with your hands. Arrange on top of the leaves, scatter over the redcurrants and serve.

VARIATIONS

Feta, beetroot and parsley salad

Prepare the beetroot as above, then place it in a large bowl with 200g feta cheese, crumbled into small chunks, 75g flat-leaf parsley leaves and, if you like, 50g lightly toasted walnuts. Mix the dressing as above, pour on to the salad and toss lightly with your hands. Serve straight away, with brown bread on the side.

Roast squash salads

You can replace the beetroot in either of the above recipes with a similar quantity of squash, such as butternut or Crown Prince. Deseed the squash and cut into chunks with the skin still on. Roast with the garlic, thyme and oil – in an open tray rather than a foil parcel – for about 40 minutes, turning once or twice, until tender and lightly browned. Leave to cool, then assemble the salad with the roast squash chunks replacing the beetroot.

Fried halloumi salad

A delicious summer starter or light lunch. I love the Mediterranean tradition of using herbs as a main ingredient. Rather than being relegated to the understudy role of seasoning, big handfuls of mint and parsley are the stars in this salad, adding freshness, flavour and colour. The sweet-sour dressing brings it all together and counterbalances the salty halloumi cheese.

Made from sheep's milk, halloumi is a traditional Cypriot ingredient, but I've been making this salad lately with an organic halloumi from High Weald Dairy in Sussex (available online from www.highwealddairy.co.uk), with excellent results. Along with cucumber, tomatoes and herbs from the River Cottage garden, this very Mediterranean-feeling dish can actually be surprisingly home-grown (and our head gardener, Mark Diacono, tells me his Devon-grown olives are just around the corner).

Serves 4

1 small red onion, very finely sliced

150g cucumber, cut into chunks

200g cherry tomatoes, halved

50g Kalamata or other black olives, stoned

A large handful of mint leaves, roughly shredded

A large handful of flat-leaf parsley leaves

50g plain flour

A large pinch of smoked paprika

250g halloumi cheese, cut into 8 slices

2 tablespoons rapeseed or olive oil

Sea salt and freshly ground black pepper

For the dressing:
1 teaspoon honey

Juice of ½ lemon

1 small garlic clove, crushed

A pinch of dried chilli flakes

A pinch of sea salt

3 tablespoons rapeseed or olive oil

First, make the dressing. Stir together the honey, lemon juice, garlic, chilli flakes and salt until well combined, then whisk in the oil.

In a large bowl, toss together the onion, cucumber, tomatoes, olives, mint and parsley.

In a small bowl, whisk together the flour, paprika and some salt and pepper. Moisten the halloumi slices slightly with water, if necessary, then press them into the seasoned flour and shake off any excess.

Heat the oil in a large frying pan and fry the halloumi slices over a medium heat for about 2 minutes on each side, until golden and slightly soft inside.

Toss the salad vegetables with the dressing, turning them over with your hands to make sure everything is lightly coated.

Divide the salad between 4 plates, put 2 pieces of the hot halloumi on each one and serve immediately.

Hot new potato and sorrel salad

A firmly established River Cottage favourite, I couldn't resist sneaking this recipe back in here. The lemony tang of sorrel is wonderful with the best sweet, creamy, earthy spuds of early summer, and this merits being served as a dish in its own right. But it's also just a lovely way of dressing new potatoes for a side dish – perhaps to serve with fish.

Later in the season, you can use the waxy, knobbly Pink Fir Apple maincrop potato for this dish.

Serves 4

500g Jersey Royals, Charlotte, Ratte or other small new potatoes, mainly whole, the large ones cut in half

2–3 handfuls of sorrel, cultivated or wild

50g unsalted butter

1 tablespoon extra virgin olive or rapeseed oil

Fine sea salt and freshly ground black pepper

Scrub or scrape the new potatoes. Put them in a pan, cover with cold water and salt well. Bring to the boil and cook until just tender. Small, freshly dug new potatoes cook much faster than you think, so be vigilant and taste a small one after just 5 minutes or so; Jersey Royals in particular lose some of their charm if over-boiled.

While the potatoes are cooking, strip the central veins out of the sorrel. Wash the leaves well and shred into ribbons, about 1cm wide.

As soon as the potatoes are ready, drain and put them into a bowl with the butter and oil. Throw the shredded sorrel into the bowl and toss well. Leave for a minute, so the heat of the potatoes wilts the sorrel, then toss again. Rest for another minute, then season with salt and pepper and serve at once.

If you do happen to slightly overcook the spuds, don't despair, just stir them vigorously with the sorrel and butter so they break up a little and get a bit 'mashy'. Pretend it was quite deliberate – your 'bashed' new potatoes will still be delicious.

VARIATION

Parsley potatoes

Garnishing just-boiled new potatoes with a little chopped parsley and some butter is always nice, but here I'm talking about loads of parsley – and quite a lot of butter too. Use a couple of bunches of flat-leaf parsley, stripped of their coarse stalks and washed well. Chop the leaves fairly fine (but not to dust), and proceed as above, with the finely chopped parsley going in instead of the sorrel. The lightly 'bashed' version of this (see above) is especially scrumptious.

Three greens

I've never had much trouble eating my greens and I hope these recipes will ensure you don't either. The golden rule with almost any brassica or beet leaf, whether it's the leaf or stem, or unformed flower (as with broccoli and caulis) is to keep the cooking time short. Stick to this, and pair your lightly done greens with a smidgeon of something rich and lubricating, and/or textured and savoury – most obviously a knob of butter (garlicky, if you like), but also a little crisp bacon, a just-cooked egg, a few toasted seeds… you get the idea.

Leeks with greens

Soft, buttery, wilted leeks bring a lovely sweetness to any kind of lightly cooked cabbage or greens. This simple preparation is one I turn to frequently, both at home and when cooking at River Cottage: it's so easy to throw together, can be made with different seasonal greens throughout most of the year and works as a side dish to everything from a bit of grilled fish to a full-on Sunday roast.

Serves 4

About 500g leeks

A knob of unsalted butter

1 Savoy or other green cabbage, 2 heads of spring greens, or a few bunches of curly kale

Sea salt and freshly ground black pepper

Trim the leeks, slice them finely (maximum 5mm) and give them a good rinse to get rid of any grit. Heat the butter in a large frying pan or wide saucepan and add the leeks with a pinch of salt. Let them cook gently for 5–6 minutes, stirring or shaking the pan occasionally, until wilted and tender.

Meanwhile, trim and coarsely shred the cabbage, greens or kale. Cook lightly – in either a steamer or a large saucepan of salted water – for 3–4 minutes, until wilted and tender but not too soft. Remove from the heat immediately, drain well and let the excess moisture steam off for a minute or so. Then add to the pan of buttery leeks, along with some more seasoning, and stir over a low heat for about a minute until thoroughly combined. Serve straight away.

In theory you can use any leftovers for bubble and squeak… but in practice there rarely are any.

PSB with chorizo and soft-hard-boiled eggs

I love purple sprouting broccoli and eat it at least twice a week when it's in season (roughly February to May), often just with a little melted butter. It's also excellent in substantial salads like this one, which is equally good as a starter or light meal. If you have to hand some Tupperware chorizo, use it here. Otherwise, good cooking chorizo (i.e. the softer, lightly cured one) or a spicy butcher's sausage will do just as well.

Serves 4

200g cooking chorizo or Tupperware Mexican chorizo (page 206)

1 tablespoon rapeseed or olive oil

4 medium eggs, at room temperature

About 500g purple sprouting broccoli, trimmed

Sea salt and freshly ground black pepper

If you're using bought chorizo, skin and cut into chunks; if using home-made, shape into walnut-sized balls. Heat the oil in a frying pan, add the chorizo and fry over a medium heat, turning regularly, for about 10 minutes, until starting to crisp up.

Meanwhile, cook the eggs: put them in a pan of hand-hot water, cover and bring quickly to the boil. Boil for exactly 4 minutes – 5 if they are extra large. Then run them under the cold tap and peel them as soon as they are cool enough to handle.

At the same time, cook the broccoli in a large saucepan of boiling salted water for 3–4 minutes, until just tender. Drain well.

Add the warm broccoli to the chorizo pan and toss it in the hot, spicy fat until well coated. Divide the broccoli and chorizo between 4 warm plates and add a boiled egg, cut in half, to each. Season with salt and pepper and serve straight away, with some bread.

Kale with bacon and chestnuts

This is a perfect Christmas-dinner side dish, especially for sprout dodgers. It also makes an excellent accompaniment to roast partridge or pheasant, or can be served with a fried egg for supper.

Serves 6 as a side dish, 2–3 as a main course

600–700g curly kale (or cavolo nero, or Savoy or other winter cabbage)

2 tablespoons rapeseed or olive oil

200g streaky bacon, finely chopped

200g cooked peeled chestnuts, roughly chopped

A knob of butter

Sea salt and freshly ground black pepper

Remove the tough stalks from the kale or other greens and roughly shred the leaves. Cook the kale in a large saucepan of boiling salted water for 3–4 minutes, until tender, then drain well and leave to steam off excess moisture.

Meanwhile, heat a large frying pan, add the oil, then the bacon, and fry over a medium heat until it is just starting to become crisp. Toss the chestnuts into the pan, stirring well so they absorb the hot bacon fat. Add the kale, along with the butter and some seasoning. Toss well and serve straight away.

Three green beans

Runner and French beans grow abundantly in
this country and can be had for a song – or for
free, of course, if you grow them yourself – during
their summer and early autumn season. Since
they are also delicious, it pays the prudent cook
to have a few nifty bean recipes up their sleeve.
Here are three of my absolute favourites.

Runner beans stewed with garlic

This recipe is from my friend Sarah Raven. It's a very simple but amazingly good
way to cook runner beans – and a change from the usual procedure of steaming
them for a few minutes and serving them simply tossed with a nut of butter. The
relatively long cooking time renders them very tender. It can also mean that they
lose a little of their colour, but don't let that worry you. They taste heavenly.

Serves 4

500g runner beans
2 garlic cloves, finely
chopped
A knob of butter
1 tablespoon rapeseed
or olive oil
Sea salt and freshly
ground black pepper

Use a potato peeler to remove the strings from the edges of the
beans, then chop them into small pieces, on the diagonal. Put them
in a large pan with the garlic, butter, oil and 3 or 4 tablespoons of
water. Heat until steaming, stirring to distribute the melting butter
and the garlic over the beans.

Cover the pan, leaving a slight gap, put it over a very low heat and
stew gently for about 30 minutes, until the beans are completely
tender. Stir every now and then and add a splash more water if the
beans look as if they are going to catch on the bottom. Remove
the lid and let most of the water evaporate for the last 5–10 minutes
of cooking. Season well and serve hot or warm, with all the buttery,
garlicky juices.

French beans with tomatoes

I always enjoy this combination of tender green beans and garlicky tomatoes during the summer and autumn. It can be served as part of an al fresco spread, or with the meats at a barbecue, but even on its own with a good hunk of bread it's a lovely supper dish.

Serves 4

1 tablespoon rapeseed or olive oil

1 onion, finely chopped

2 garlic cloves, finely chopped

400g tin of chopped tomatoes, or 1kg fresh tomatoes, blanched, skinned, deseeded and roughly chopped

500g French beans, topped, tailed and cut into 4–5cm lengths

Sea salt and freshly ground black pepper

Heat the oil in a large saucepan or frying pan, add the onion and sweat for at least 10 minutes, until soft but not coloured. Add the garlic and cook gently for another minute or two, then add the tomatoes and stir well. Stir in the beans, bring the mixture to a gentle simmer and season well. Turn down the heat, partly cover the pan and cook very gently, stirring frequently, for about 30 minutes, until the beans are fully tender. If the mixture seems to be in danger of sticking, add a splash of water or stock. Serve warm or cold.

VARIATION

You can make this with runner beans, too. String and slice them lengthways through one of those clever little 'zip' cutters, or string and slice diagonally before proceeding as above.

French beans with seeds and almonds

Dressing French beans with a crunchy, spicy topping is a great way to serve them and you can customise the recipe to suit your own nut-and-seed preferences.

Serves 4

300g French beans

A handful of blanched almonds

½ tablespoon cumin seeds

1 tablespoon coriander seeds

2 tablespoons sesame seeds

1 tablespoon poppy seeds

2 tablespoons rapeseed or olive oil

1 small garlic clove, grated or finely chopped

Sea salt

Cook the beans in a saucepan of boiling salted water for 4–5 minutes, until tender but still with a bit of crunch. Drain well.

Meanwhile, roughly chop the almonds and place in a dry frying pan with all of the seeds. Toast gently over a medium heat for a few minutes, until the seeds start to smell fragrant and the almonds are taking on a little colour. Remove from the heat, add the oil and garlic to the hot pan and stir well. Leave for a minute or so, then stir again, so the residual heat in the pan just takes the edge off the garlic. Season with a little salt.

Put the warm beans on to a serving plate and scatter the seedy mixture over the top. Serve straight away.

Mixed mashes

Mashed potato is hard to beat, but it would be a shame to overlook the mashing potential of other vegetables. Two or three roots combined, seasoned well and made silky with a little cream, butter and/or oil, can be a revelation served up with stews, grills and roasts. In all cases, go for floury potatoes, such as King Edward, Desiree or Maris Piper, and don't be tempted to cut corners at the mashing stage: potatoes need to be mashed by hand or with a potato ricer, as they'll go gluey if put in a food processor. Other roots, however, need processing to achieve a lovely, silky texture. Below are some of my favourite rooty combos.

Three-root mash

Of course, you don't have to stick to three roots: you could use two, four or as many as suits you. Do always include potatoes, however, to give the mash body and to stop it getting too sweet.

Serves 6

500g carrots, peeled and cut into chunks

500g parsnips, peeled and cut into chunks

500g floury potatoes, peeled and cut into chunks

50g unsalted butter or 50ml rapeseed oil

100ml milk (or half milk and half double cream)

Freshly grated nutmeg (optional)

Sea salt and freshly ground black pepper

Cook the carrots and parsnips in a pan of boiling salted water until tender. Cook the potatoes in a separate pan. Drain the vegetables and let them steam dry for a minute or two. Put the carrots and parsnips in a food processor, with half the butter or oil, and blend to a creamy purée. Heat the milk and the remaining butter or oil in the pan in which the potatoes were cooked, then add the potatoes and mash until smooth. Combine the mashed vegetables, adding plenty of seasoning, including nutmeg if you like, to make a creamy, golden mash. Serve steaming hot, with sausages or roast lamb or venison.

VARIATIONS

Celeriac and potato mash

Use 750g each celeriac and potatoes. Peel both, cut into large chunks and cook separately in lightly salted boiling water until tender. Drain and leave to steam dry for a few minutes. Heat the butter or oil and milk in one of the pans, seasoning with salt, pepper and nutmeg. Add the potatoes and mash until smooth. Rub the celeriac through a sieve, or purée it in a food processor, then add to the potatoes and beat well until combined, adding more hot milk and butter or oil if needed. Check the seasoning. Perfect with roast chicken, steak or baked fish.

Swede and potato mash

Use 750g each swede and potatoes and prepare exactly as for celeriac and potato mash. Excellent with roast game and haggis.

Mushy squash

I call this buttery purée mushy squash because it's a kind of cold-weather alternative to mushy peas – and I quite often serve it with battered or breadcrumbed fish in autumn and winter. It is also excellent with scallops (see page 156), or boiled ham or slow-cooked pork belly. A lovely alternative to roasted vegetables or mashed potato.

Serves 4

1 tablespoon rapeseed or olive oil

50g unsalted butter

About 600g butternut or Crown Prince squash, peeled, deseeded and cut into small cubes (roughly 2cm)

1 garlic clove, finely chopped

3–4 sage leaves, finely chopped

Sea salt and freshly ground black pepper

Heat the oil and half the butter in a small frying pan, add the squash and fry gently for a few minutes, until it begins to take on a hint of colour. Add the garlic and sage, season with salt and pepper and sizzle gently until the garlic just begins to colour. Immediately add 2–3 tablespoons of water to stop the garlic browning any more. Partly cover the pan with a lid and let the squash finish cooking in the steam from the water; it should be completely tender within about 10 minutes. Add a little more water if the pan becomes dry.

Tip the squash and any liquid into a blender or food processor, along with the rest of the butter, and blend until smooth. If it doesn't quite come together, add a dash of hot water to give a thick, creamy purée. Taste and adjust the seasoning, then serve straight away.

Thyme and caramelised onion mash

This is delicious – there is nothing better to go with sausages, chops or roast lamb. It's also great with grilled or roasted fillets of robustly flavoured fish, such as mackerel, bream or gurnard.

Serves 6

2 tablespoons rapeseed or olive oil

1 large onion or 4–5 shallots, finely chopped

2 teaspoons chopped thyme

1.5kg floury potatoes, peeled and cut into chunks

50g butter or 50ml rapeseed oil

100ml milk (or half milk and half double cream), warmed

Sea salt and freshly ground black pepper

Heat 2 tablespoons of oil in a large saucepan over a medium heat. Add the onion or shallots and a good sprinkling of salt and pepper, stir well as the onion starts to sizzle, then turn the heat right down and cook gently for about 20 minutes, until soft and golden. Add the chopped thyme and cook for another 5 minutes or so. Taste – the onion should be very sweet. If not, cook for a little longer. It needs to take on a good golden colour, but don't let it start to go crisp and brown. Taste for seasoning at this point, too.

Meanwhile, cook the potatoes in a pan of boiling salted water until tender, then drain and leave to steam dry for a few minutes. Heat the butter or oil and milk in the pan in which the potatoes were cooked, then add the potatoes and plenty of seasoning and mash until smooth. Mix in the caramelised onion, check the seasoning and serve.

Six roasted veg

Roasted vegetables – root veg and winter squashes in particular – are rarely less than delicious. The roasting process intensifies flavour, brings out sweetness and adds a rich, caramelised exterior. It's forgiving to the cook (you can be relaxed about timings, and serve your veg hot, warm or cold) and versatile too. The following recipes make fantastic accompaniments, but can also be the main focus of a meal, with just a little something else on the side. Leftover roasted roots can be tossed into salads or puréed in soups, or just nibbled cold as an extra something in your lunchbox. So you can see why this is a method I return to time and again.

Roast squash with chilli, garlic and rosemary

Butternut squash is delicious roasted in this way, but do try some alternative squashes and pumpkins if you get the chance. The fluffy, slightly chestnutty Crown Prince is outstanding, as is the smaller, sweet, yellow-fleshed acorn squash.

This makes an excellent side dish for sausages, chops, roast chicken or robust fish such as gurnard or bream. Since it is creamy and starchy, I tend to serve roast squash instead of, rather than as well as, any kind of spuds. On the other hand, dished up with a good pile of plain boiled rice and some steamed greens or a green salad, this makes a lovely vegetarian main course.

Serves 4

1 large butternut squash, about 1kg, or the equivalent weight of Crown Prince, acorn or other squash or pumpkin

6–8 fat garlic cloves, skin on, lightly squashed

A few sprigs of rosemary

1 fairly hot red chilli, deseeded and finely chopped

4–5 tablespoons rapeseed or olive oil

40g pine nuts or walnuts (optional)

Juice of ½ lemon

Sea salt and freshly ground black pepper

Slice the squash into quarters and deseed it, scooping out the seeds with a spoon (you can dry the seeds in an airing cupboard and use them to grow your own squashes). I leave the skin on most squashes when I'm roasting them, but you can peel it off if you prefer. Cut the squash into wedges or chunks and put them in a small roasting tin. Add the garlic and rosemary, the chopped chilli and lots of salt and pepper. Trickle over 2–3 tablespoons of oil and toss the lot together. Roast in an oven preheated to 190°C/Gas Mark 5 for 40–55 minutes, stirring halfway through, until the squash is completely soft and starting to caramelise.

Meanwhile, if using nuts, toast them in a dry frying pan over a medium heat for a few minutes, until golden brown, then scatter over the roasted squash. Add a squeeze of lemon juice and another good trickle of oil, then serve.

Roasted red onions with port and bay

This is a lovely, simple and rather beautiful side dish that works very well with most meats – it would make a superb accompaniment to your Christmas roast, whatever that may be. You can serve it hot, warm or cold, and the rich fragrance that wafts from the oven as it cooks is quite delectable.

Serves 4–6

2 tablespoons rapeseed or olive oil

750g small red onions

About 12 bay leaves

10–12 juniper berries, lightly squashed

200ml port

Sea salt and freshly ground black pepper

Pour the oil into a roasting dish and tilt the dish so that the oil more or less covers the base. Peel the onions, keeping the root ends intact, and slice into 8 thick wedges from root to tip. The root end should hold the layers of each wedge together.

Put the onions in the roasting dish, tuck the bay leaves in amongst them, scatter over the juniper berries and a good seasoning of salt and pepper, then trickle the port over everything. Cover with foil and roast in an oven preheated to 160°C/Gas Mark 3 for 45 minutes.

Take off the foil, give the onions a gentle stir and cook, uncovered, for 30 minutes. At the end of cooking, the onions should be very soft and starting to caramelise, and the liquid in the pan should have reduced to a few spoonfuls of intense, aromatic juice. Serve hot, warm or cold, with roast meats or as a relish for cheese.

Roast beetroot with balsamic, rosemary and garlic

Sweet, sticky, garlic-scented roast beetroot makes an ideal side dish for oily fish such as mackerel, or for barbecued chicken or pork. But let it go cold and you could add some soft goat's cheese and salad leaves and eat it as a dish in its own right. I like to use English apple balsamic vinegar, but any good traditional balsamic would work.

Serves 4

About 1kg beetroot

1 large rosemary stem, broken into little sprigs

1 head of garlic, broken into cloves, skin left on, each lightly squashed

3 tablespoons rapeseed or olive oil

2 tablespoons balsamic vinegar

Sea salt and freshly ground black pepper

Peel the beetroot, cut them into thick wedges and place in a roasting dish. Add the sprigs of rosemary and squashed garlic cloves, trickle on the oil and season generously. Toss everything together, cover the dish with foil and roast in an oven preheated to 190°C/Gas Mark 5 for 40 minutes, or until the beetroot is almost tender.

Remove the foil, trickle over the vinegar, give everything a good stir and return to the oven. Cook uncovered, stirring again once, for another 30–40 minutes or until the beetroot is starting to caramelise. Serve straight away or leave to cool.

Roast potatoes with lemon, rosemary and thyme

It's not just floury maincrop potatoes that roast well. An olive-oil-roasted new potato, with salty skin and caramelised edges, is a fine thing too. I like to serve this flavour-packed dish alongside a summer roast chicken or barbecued meat or fish. In fact, you can roast a whole fish or two, such as mackerel, red mullet or small sea bass, right in the middle of the roasting spuds (see page 149 for more on roast fish and potatoes).

The lemons, including the peels, add a bitter note that goes particularly well with fish, but you can leave them out and stick with just the herbs and garlic, if you prefer.

Serves 5–6

1.5kg new potatoes
2 lemons, plus an extra lemon half
7–8 garlic cloves, skin on, lightly squashed
Several sprigs of rosemary
Several sprigs of thyme
Olive or rapeseed oil
Sea salt and freshly ground black pepper

Wash the potatoes to remove the dirt but try not to remove the skins. Up to, say, golf-ball size, they can be roasted whole, but any larger than that and they should be cut into halves or quarters. Parboil the potatoes in a pan of salted water for 5 minutes, then drain and leave to dry for a minute or two.

Cut the 2 lemons into thick slices. Put the potatoes in a roasting dish and scatter over the lemon slices, garlic, rosemary and thyme. Trickle oil generously over everything and toss the whole lot together with your hands, making sure each potato is covered in oil. Season well with salt and pepper. Bake in an oven preheated to 200°C/Gas Mark 6 for 35–40 minutes, turning everything at least once, until the lemons are starting to caramelise and the potatoes look irresistibly golden brown.

Squeeze on the juice from the extra lemon half, sprinkle with a little more salt and serve immediately.

Roast carrots with butter, cumin and orange

This is particularly lovely made with young summer carrots, freshly pulled and no more than thumb-thick. Don't peel them unless you really have to – just scrub them before slicing in half down the middle. Or, if they're really slender, leave them whole. If you're using big old winter carrots instead – and there's no reason why not – peel them and slice thickly.

This is very good served with roast lamb, chicken or pork.

Serves 4–6

1 tablespoon rapeseed
or olive oil

A large knob of unsalted
butter

750g carrots, small ones
scrubbed and halved
lengthways, large ones
peeled and cut into thick
batons

2 teaspoons cumin seeds

Finely grated zest of
1 orange, plus some juice

Sea salt and freshly
ground black pepper

Put the oil and butter into a large roasting dish and leave in an oven preheated to 180°C/Gas Mark 4 for a couple of minutes, until the butter melts. Remove from the oven and add the carrots, cumin and plenty of seasoning. Toss together, cover with foil and return to the oven for 30–40 minutes, until the carrots are tender.

Remove from the oven, take off the foil and give everything a good stir. Then return to the oven, uncovered, for about 20–30 minutes, so the carrots start to caramelise.

When you take the dish from the oven, stir in the orange zest and a good squeeze or two of the juice. Serve at once.

Roasted roots with mustard, rosemary and honey

The earthy character of root vegetables is wonderfully enhanced by the addition of hot, sweet and aromatic flavours. This warming winter side dish goes well with most meats, but I particularly like it with sausages. You could also dish it up with a plate of beans or lentils as a vegetarian main course.

Serves 4–6

About 1.5 kg mixed root
vegetables, such as
parsnip, celeriac, carrot,
salsify, swede and turnip

3 generous tablespoons
wholegrain mustard

2–3 tablespoons runny
honey

100ml rapeseed or olive
oil

2–3 large sprigs of
rosemary

Sea salt and freshly
ground black pepper

Peel the root vegetables and cut into bite-sized chunks. Combine the mustard, honey and oil in a large bowl. Add plenty of seasoning and the rosemary sprigs, then tip in the prepared root vegetables. Mix the whole lot together well with your hands, then transfer to a roasting dish that is big enough to hold the vegetables in a single layer, fairly snugly packed.

Cover the dish with foil and place in an oven preheated to 180°C/Gas Mark 4. Cook for 30 minutes, then uncover, give everything a good stir and turn the heat up to 200°C/Gas Mark 6. Continue to roast for another 30–40 minutes, until the vegetables are tender in the middle, a bit crispy here and nicely caramelised there. Sprinkle with salt and a few grinds of pepper and serve.

Jerusalem artichoke and nettle gratin

This is the lovely creation of our resident River Cottage baker, Dan – hence the stale bread topping. We've made very successful variations using a combination of celeriac and potatoes instead of artichokes. It goes down a storm as a vegetarian starter or main course.

Serves 4

1 tablespoon sunflower oil

A knob of butter

2 onions, finely sliced

3 garlic cloves, sliced

500g Jerusalem artichokes, peeled and cut into 3mm thick rounds

1 teaspoon chopped thyme

200ml double cream

100ml vegetable stock or water (page 266)

100g fresh nettle tops or spinach, roughly chopped

Sea salt and freshly ground black pepper

For the topping:

A handful of porridge oats

3 thick slices of stale bread, torn into little pieces or whizzed to coarse crumbs in a food processor

½ handful of hazelnuts or walnuts, toasted, skinned and bashed into rough pieces (optional)

25g butter, melted

30g Cheddar cheese or hard goat's cheese, grated

Heat the oil and butter in a frying pan, add the onions and garlic and cook gently until soft and starting to take on a little colour. Add the artichokes and thyme, then season well with salt and pepper. Cook, tossing occasionally, for 5 minutes.

Pour over the cream and water or stock and simmer gently until the liquid has reduced by half. Stir in the nettles or spinach, then transfer everything to a greased gratin dish, levelling it out as you go.

Mix all the topping ingredients together. Sprinkle over the artichoke mixture and bake in an oven preheated to 190°C/Gas Mark 5 for 25–30 minutes, until golden and bubbling.

Cauliflower cheese

One of the all-time classics. You can make broccoli cheese in the same way, or try my chardy cheese variation. For macaroni cheese: make a double quantity of sauce, cook 300g macaroni and combine the two. Put in an oven dish, top with breadcrumbs, more grated cheese and a trickle of oil and bake until golden.

Serves 3 as a main course, 5–6 as a side dish

1 large cauliflower (about 1kg untrimmed), trimmed and cut into large florets

For the sauce:
300ml whole milk
½ onion, cut in two
1 bay leaf, twisted
A few black peppercorns
20g unsalted butter
20g plain flour
100g strong, mature Cheddar cheese, grated
25g Parmesan or mature hard goat's cheese, grated (optional)
¼ teaspoon English mustard
Sea salt and freshly ground black pepper

For the sauce, put the milk into a saucepan with the onion, bay and peppercorns. Bring to just below simmering point, then turn off the heat. Leave to infuse for at least 30 minutes, an hour or two if possible.

Meanwhile, cook the cauliflower in a pan of boiling salted water for 3–4 minutes until almost tender but still a bit al dente. Drain well, allowing it to steam off for a minute or so, then keep warm.

If the milk has cooled completely, warm it gently before straining it into a jug. Melt the butter in a medium saucepan over a fairly low heat, then stir in the flour to form a smooth paste (a roux). Cook gently, stirring frequently, for 1–2 minutes. Remove from the heat and add a third of the warm milk. Stir vigorously with a wooden spoon, or a whisk, until you have a thick, smooth paste. Add the rest of the milk in one or two lots. Return the sauce to the heat and bring to the boil, stirring. Let it bubble for 2 minutes, stirring occasionally, to 'cook out' any raw taste of flour. Turn the heat right down.

Set aside about 25g of the Cheddar and add the rest to the hot sauce, along with the Parmesan, if using, and mustard. Stir gently until the cheese has melted into the sauce; don't let it boil again. Season.

Combine the cauliflower with the hot cheese sauce, gently folding the florets into the sauce until well coated. Transfer to a greased ovenproof dish, scatter the remaining cheese over the top and bake at 190°C/Gas Mark 5 for about 20 minutes, until golden and bubbling. Serve as a main course, with bread, or as a side dish.

VARIATION

Chardy cheese

In place of the cauliflower, use 750g Swiss, ruby or rainbow chard. Separate the stalks from the leaves. Blanch the leaves in a pan of boiling salted water for a minute or two until just wilted. Remove with tongs, drain, squeeze out excess water and chop roughly. Cut the stalks into 1.5cm thick slices and blanch for 3–4 minutes, until just tender. Drain well and toss with a knob of butter and some seasoning. Put the stalks in a greased ovenproof dish. Stir the chopped leaves into the hot cheese sauce and pour this over the stalks. Scatter with coarse breadcrumbs and a trickle of oil and bake as above.

Stuffed butternut squash

This is one of my favourite autumn main courses, another great vegetable idea that I've borrowed from my friend, Sarah Raven. It's easy to adapt and alter the stuffing for the squash, according what you have and what you fancy. You can even alter the squash too, for that matter – I've made it very successfully with acorn and small Crown Prince squashes.

Serves 4

1 large butternut squash (about 1.5kg) or 2 small ones

1 garlic clove, finely chopped

About 50g unsalted butter

A little rapeseed or olive oil

75g walnuts, lightly toasted and very coarsely chopped

200g blue cheese, such as Dorset Blue Vinny or Harbourne Blue, crumbled into small lumps (or use a crumbly goat's cheese)

2 teaspoons chopped thyme

1 scant tablespoon runny honey

Sea salt and freshly ground black pepper

Make sure the outside of the squash is scrubbed clean. Cut the squash in half lengthways and scoop out the seeds and soft fibres. Put in a roasting dish, add the chopped garlic and a nut of butter to each cavity, then brush with a little oil and season well. Place in an oven preheated to 190°C/Gas Mark 5 and bake for ¾–1 hour, until the flesh feels very tender when pierced with the tip of a knife.

Scoop the soft flesh and all the buttery, garlicky juices out into a bowl, leaving a 1cm thick layer of flesh still attached to the skin, so the squash holds its shape. Roughly mash the flesh. Keep back a few pieces of walnut and a little of the cheese, then fold the remaining walnuts and cheese into the soft squash, along with the thyme and some more salt and pepper.

Spoon the filling back into the empty squash halves and scatter on the reserved cheese and walnuts. Finish with the merest trickle of honey, then return the squash to the oven and bake for 15 minutes, or until the cheese is bubbling. Serve with a crisp green salad.

VARIATIONS

Crispy bacon-stuffed squash

Chop 4 rashers of smoked streaky bacon and fry for a minute or two until crisp and golden. Stir these into the soft squash flesh, along with about 50g finely grated Gruyère cheese, a tablespoon of chopped chives and plenty of black pepper. Top with a little more grated Gruyère before returning to the oven.

Crème fraîche and herb-stuffed squash

Add 1 teaspoon each of finely chopped basil, thyme and oregano to the mashed squash, stir in 3–4 tablespoons of crème fraîche and season very well before returning to the oven.

Mixed mushroom tart

This is a simple little tart that works well with regular cultivated mushrooms, but will be extra special if you include a few wild mushrooms that you've gathered yourself. Serve it as a starter or light lunch.

Lemony courgettes (page 263) are a good summery alternative for topping this tart, so long as you let them cook long enough for most of the juices to evaporate. Tear a little mozzarella over the top before you put it in the oven.

Serves 2

25g unsalted butter

About 200g mixed mushrooms, sliced

1 garlic clove, finely chopped

25g fresh white breadcrumbs

Finely grated zest of 1 lemon

1 tablespoon finely chopped parsley

200g bought puff pastry or rough puff pastry (see page 110)

1 medium egg, lightly beaten

1 heaped tablespoon grated Parmesan, or matured hard goat's cheese or Cheddar

Sea salt and freshly ground black pepper

Heat the butter in a large frying pan, add the mushrooms and a pinch of salt and cook fairly briskly until they start to soften. Stir in the garlic and cook, stirring often, until the mushrooms are tender and all the liquid they release has evaporated. Remove the pan from the heat and stir in the breadcrumbs, lemon zest, parsley and a few grinds of black pepper.

Roll out the pastry on a lightly floured surface to no more than 5mm thick. Using a plate or cake tin as a guide, cut out a 20cm circle and place it on a lightly oiled baking tray. Then, with a small, sharp knife, score a circle 1–2cm in from the edge of the pastry, without going right through to the base. This will create a puffed-up golden rim to the tart.

Brush the pastry border with beaten egg. Spread the mushroom mixture over the pastry, leaving the border clear, and sprinkle the cheese on top. Place in an oven preheated to 200°C/Gas Mark 6 and bake for about 20 minutes, until the pastry is puffed up and golden. Serve hot or cold.

Gill's poached leek and Dorset Blue Vinny tart

This recipe of Gill's has become a River Cottage
classic, and a particular favourite during
the colder months. If you have time,
make double the quantity of pastry,
bake two pastry cases blind
and freeze one. This means
that next time you want
to make a savoury
tart, you will have
already done
half the
work.

Serves 4–6

2 large or 3 medium
leeks (about 500g),
trimmed of tough green
leaves, washed and
sliced into 1cm rounds
A knob of unsalted
butter
100g Dorset Blue Vinny
or other good blue
cheese, grated
2 medium eggs
2 medium egg yolks
350ml double cream
Sea salt and freshly
ground black pepper

For the shortcrust pastry:
250g plain flour
125g unsalted butter
A pinch of sea salt
1 medium egg yolk
25–50ml cold milk

First make the pastry. Put the flour, butter and salt in a food processor
and pulse until the mixture looks like breadcrumbs. Add the egg
yolk, then pour in the milk in a gradual stream. Watch carefully and
stop adding the milk as soon as the dough starts to come together.
Turn out and knead lightly a couple of times, then wrap in cling film.
Chill for half an hour.

On a lightly floured surface, roll the pastry out quite thinly and use
to line a 25cm loose-based tart tin, letting the excess pastry hang
over the edges. Line the pastry case with greaseproof paper, fill with
baking beans and place in an oven preheated to 170°C/Gas Mark 3.
Bake blind for 20 minutes, then take the tart out of the oven, remove
the paper and beans, lightly prick the base all over with a fork and
return to the oven for 5 minutes, until the base is dry but not too
coloured. Carefully trim off the excess pastry with a small, sharp
knife. Turn the oven temperature up to 180°C/Gas Mark 4.

To make the filling, put the leeks into a saucepan with 100ml water,
the butter and some salt and pepper. Bring to a low simmer, then
cover and cook gently, stirring once or twice, for about 10 minutes,
until just tender. Drain well, reserving the cooking liquor. Spread the
cooked leeks in the tart case and cover with the grated cheese.

Put the eggs and egg yolks, cream and leek liquor in a bowl and
beat until smooth. Season to taste, then pour this custard over the
cheese and leeks. Put the tart back into the oven and bake for about
30 minutes – the custard should be just set when you gently shake
the tin. Serve warm or cold.

the whole fruit

If we only ever ate one kind of food, it would have to be fruit. Why?

Because fruit is just about the only food we have that was absolutely unambiguously designed to be eaten. Not by us, of course, but by a force whose power to shape things that are fit for purpose is second to none. Evolution has offered us fruit as the perfect food: visually irresistible, cleverly packaged for convenience, full of good things that benefit the eater and, most importantly, delicious. It's all part of a cunning ploy to keep us coming back for more. And by us, I mean not only humans, but our primate cousins and more distant mammalian relatives – and let's not forget the birds.

It's a symbiotic deal, of course. Fruit eaters do a massive favour for the plants that bear the fruit they eat. They habitually remove the seed some distance from the parent plant and, having devoured the fleshy casing around it, deposit that seed in a new place where it might just have a chance to grow. Sometimes, if they've actually swallowed the seed whole, they'll deposit it with a nice little pile of manure to give it the optimum chance of success.

It's all fiendishly clever, and it looks uncannily as if fruit has the animal kingdom in its thrall. But it hasn't all been one way. We haven't exactly been slouches in our relationship with fruit. A few thousand years ago we learned to nurture and cultivate the fruits we loved best, to make them fatter, riper, juicier and more delicious than ever before. And a few hundred years ago we worked out how to breed them selectively, effectively 'inventing' new varieties with specific characteristics. The sole purpose of such practices was to create fruits that delight us even more.

You could conclude that, having been manipulated by fruit for many millions of years, we have now turned the tables and become the arch manipulators ourselves, 'in charge' of the kingdom of fruit. But that would be to underestimate the evolutionary forces at work. One consequence of our incessant dabbling is that certain fruit species are now among the most 'successful' living organisms. The apple tree and the grape vine, for example, are the two most prolific fruit-bearing plants on the planet (no coincidence that both lend themselves rather well to conversion into alcohol). We reap a massive harvest of plenty from them. At the same time, you could say they've got us eating out of the palm of their hand…

This preamble serves to support a view of mine that might otherwise come across as unsupported hyperbolic prejudice. It is my passionate belief that fruit is the most miraculous of foods, a natural wonder, and that to shun it is an act of the deepest human folly that can lead only to despair. Whereas to cultivate a consuming relationship with the best fruits of your region (wherever you are in the world), understanding their seasonality so that you get to enjoy them at their best, is one of the fundamentals of a happy life with food – or even, dare I say, a happy life, full stop.

That's what I've tried to do, over the years, in the way that I have bought fruit, eaten fruit, cooked with fruit and, for a decade or so now, grown fruit in my own garden. Of course, it's the business of cultivation that really puts you in tune with issues of seasonality and ripeness, and you can become deeply involved, obsessing over varieties, fertilisers and the limitless possibilities of training and pruning trees and bushes to suit your garden space and maximise productivity. I'm heading that way myself at the moment, having just planted about thirty more fruit trees and ten grapevines at home. I'm about to start training my first espalier of pears. Will they come when I whistle? Roll over when I raise my hand? Only time will tell…

However, it's equally possible to grow some fruit in a pretty casual and non-interventionist way. Stick an apple tree or two at the bottom of your garden and let them get on with it. Plant a blackcurrant bush – or a blueberry, a redcurrant or a gooseberry – in a good-sized pot on your terrace and, as long as you water it in a dry spell, it will reward you amply. Often the town gardener with a small plot or even just a back yard can find themselves at a surprising advantage. A sun-trapping corner or wall in a sheltered spot can offer you a chance to grow fruit that will be the envy of those with windswept acres at their disposal. You can ripen figs, apricots, greengages or cherries to the peak of sun-drenched perfection. Don't expect to get many in the kitchen, though. You'll eat most of them straight from the tree, the warm juices pouring into you like intravenous sunshine.

Much as I love fruit as a cooking ingredient, I think it's entirely right that you should eat more of it raw and unadulterated than you do cooked or fussed into some kind of dish. Some years I have my fill of strawberries yet barely get round to strawberries and cream, let alone pavlova or jam. But at the same time, it doesn't take much to transform a pile of good fruit into a deeply indulgent pud. When you look at the recipes that follow, you'll see that the way I like to cook and eat fruit is really by ringing the changes with a few well-chosen companions, thrown together with the fruit of the moment. Cream appears often enough: whipped into an Eton mess, stirred into a cranachan, served as a topping for a fruit-filled sponge or set into a panna cotta with a tart compote on the side. A good custard goes hot on a crumble, cold in a trifle or spooned into a bowl with lightly cooked fruit to make a deconstructed fool. Meringues are just aerated sugar crying out for some fruit and cream to make them a touch less reckless. A sponge is just a sponge, but swamped with raspberries and cream it's almost too good to be true.

If growing fruit in any quantity is wholly impractical for you, then you'll have to take steps to make sure you don't miss out on the seasonal bonanzas. Pick-your-own is the next best thing to grow-your-own – some would say better, since others have done all the hard work. It's a lovely way to spend a few hours with the kids on a sunny afternoon, especially since you come back groaning under a weight of fruity goodies. The real fun starts when you set about transforming your glut into a summer's worth of ice cream and a winter's worth of jam.

Otherwise, farm shops, farmers' markets and greengrocer's that are genuinely plugged into the local supply chain should all be well stocked with the best seasonal fruits. If you're lucky, your nearest farmers' market might have a fruit grower as a stallholder. If so, they are likely to be offering exciting varieties that you'll struggle to find in any supermarket. My friends Robin and June Small, for instance, of Charlton Orchards in Somerset, delight the shoppers at Taunton farmers' market from September through to January with baskets of Ashmead's Kernel and Orleans Reinette (apples), Doyenne du Comice and Beurre Hardy (pears). This is a great way to find a favourite variety – and perhaps you'll be inspired to seek out and plant a tree so you can have your own ready supply.

Having said that, the supermarkets are beginning to sharpen up their act in the way they stock and present seasonal British fruits. They'll still offer you American strawberries in December, but when the real-deal English ones start arriving in May, there's a lot more flag waving than there used to be. And the three-way stranglehold of Golden Delicious, Granny Smith and Cox's on the supermarket apple supply is finally being loosened. If ever you see an apple in a supermarket that isn't one of these and is UK grown, then vote for it by sticking a few in your shopping basket. The big retailers are also cottoning on to the fact that increasing numbers of their customers would like their fruit pesticide free, so look out for labels that make this pledge.

If you really want to maximise the pleasure available from our own seasonal fruits, you'll need to seek out the less obvious ones. Blackcurrants and gooseberries, for example, tend to be cheaper than strawberries and raspberries. Unless they are unusually well ripened by a spectacular summer, they tend to need cooking, but a cooked, sweetened compote of either – sieved, if you like, to give you a smooth, tart 'coulis' – is a fantastically versatile resource, or indeed sauce. The usual suspects of cream, ice cream, sponge and meringue can all be made into the guiltiest of puddings with just a trickle of these intense elixirs.

You'll have gleaned that my overriding passion is for the fruits we can grow in this topsy-turvy but roughly rhythmic climate of ours, and the focus of my recipes is very much on this produce. But I would never be such a killjoy as to suggest you should boycott fruit from overseas. We get through kilos of citrus fruit and bananas at home, particularly in the winter months, and I always keep an eye out for a box of lovely Italian cherries or Turkish apricots in the market even as I try to grow my own at home. I don't suppose I'll ever grow my own mangoes, but I'll pounce on any I see that seem to have achieved genuine ripeness, though there's a lot of rock-hard disappointments out there. The best mangoes, guavas, papayas, pineapples etc are to be found in the ethnic markets of our big cities, where discerning shoppers who know what's right will brook no substandard specimens.

In choosing my exotics, I will generally opt for organic, Fairtrade or both. That's not a kneejerk approach. I've seen and heard enough, some of it at first hand, about the economic and social conditions for agricultural workers in the Third World to believe that these choices make a real difference to real people's lives. The way much fruit is grown for the mass European market is both socially and environmentally unsustainable. Organic and Fairtrade labels offer traceability and transparency, and these are genuine and valuable reassurances.

The recipes that follow are hardly elaborate. In most cases a competent cook could read the recipe once, then put the book back on the shelf and get on with it. If you go that route, you'll quickly start adding your own touches, fixing things your way, and that's how it should be. I'd like to think that, after years of tinkering, my crumble recipe is now pretty much perfect. But I'd also be disappointed if you didn't immediately take that as provocation to prove me wrong.

Macerated strawberries

A little touch of vinegar and black pepper can do wonders for the blowsy sweetness of ripe strawberries. The sweet-sour dressing brings out all their delicious juices and rounds out the flavour to something like a complex wine. I like to serve this with a delicate biscuit or two on the side, such as caraway shortbread (page 390). It also goes well with a plain sponge cake or the honey wholemeal cake (page 386) – or, of course, with ice cream. Or, for breakfast, with eggy bread or drop scones. You don't have to limit yourself to strawberries – raspberries, blueberries and red- or white currants can all be given the maceration treatment.

Serves 3–4

2 tablespoons caster sugar

1 tablespoon apple balsamic vinegar or lemon juice

½ teaspoon freshly ground black pepper

500g strawberries, hulled and halved, bigger ones cut into 3 or 4 thick slices (or use a mixture of other summer berries)

Scatter the sugar over the prepared strawberries, toss lightly and leave for 5–10 minutes to set the juices running. Then add the vinegar or lemon juice and pepper, and toss again. Leave to macerate for at least an hour – ideally 3–4 hours – to draw out the juices from the fruit. Stir again, then serve the strawberries at room temperature with the syrupy juices.

VARIATIONS

Strawberries with mint

Replace the apple balsamic vinegar with cider vinegar or lemon juice, leave out the black pepper and add 2 tablespoons of finely chopped mint.

Strawberries with raspberry sauce

In a blender, blitz about 100g raspberries with 2 tablespoons of caster sugar and 1 tablespoon of balsamic vinegar or lemon juice. Strain to remove the seeds, then pour the purée over your sliced, hulled strawberries. Particularly good with meringues and yoghurt or cream.

Bramley apple compote

We have a tradition of dividing our apples into two groups: cookers and eaters (actually, there is a third – cider apples). Cooking apples (Bramleys being the most widely available) contain lots of malic acid, which gives them a sharp, tangy taste. It also ensures the flesh collapses into a fluffy mush when cooked – perfect for pies and crumbles, and a host of other dishes.

This is the basic way to proceed with cooking apples, to gently transform them into a lovely compote which, sweetened to your taste, can be used in all sorts of ways and not just for pud. I often have a bowlful for breakfast, with some yoghurt and a scattering of muesli (page 34), granola or wheat flakes.

Makes about 800g

2kg Bramley or other cooking apples

2–8 tablespoons caster sugar

Peel, core and finely slice the apples – be thorough, as any little bits of fibre left from the core or peel will catch in your teeth and spoil the pleasure of the otherwise silky compote.

Put the apples in a large pan and add a good tablespoon of sugar and 2–3 tablespoons of water – just to stop them catching on the bottom of the pan. Cook, covered, over a gentle heat, stirring often, until the apple pieces have completely dissolved and you have a thick, slightly translucent purée. It should take about half an hour.

Add more caster sugar to taste – enough to achieve a purée that is still erring on the tart side but not unpleasantly so. You can always add sugar when you serve it up, and in fact the slight graininess of just-sprinkled caster sugar on the compote is a pleasure in itself.

Leave to cool completely, then store in the fridge in a jar or Tupperware container. It will keep for a couple of weeks.

VARIATIONS

Apple fool

Keep the compote tart. Whip up an equal quantity of double or whipping cream and sweeten with a little icing or caster sugar. Lightly swirl the cream into the compote, keeping it rippled. Pile into glasses and chill before serving, with a sweet, crumbly biscuit, such as shortbread (page 390) or digestives (page 88).

Apple sauce

The classic accompaniment to roast pork and goose, and rightly so, as the tart fruit cuts the richness of the meat. Keep the compote tart and try adding the finely grated zest of an orange before you heat it through to serve.

Two dried fruit compotes

These sweet, gently spiced concoctions are very easy to make and will keep happily in the fridge for at least a week. They're delicious with yoghurt or ice cream, but I often find myself snaffling a spoonful or two throughout the day when hunger strikes.

Spiced fig compote

 fig 1. fig 2. fig 3.

Serves 6–8

500g dried figs
25g light brown sugar
2 tablespoons runny honey
2 cardamom pods, lightly squashed
1 star anise
1 cinnamon stick
A finely pared strip of orange zest

Separate the dried figs if they are stuck together and give them a quick rinse in cold water to remove any rice flour if necessary. Put them in a heatproof bowl and pour over just enough boiling water to cover. Cover the bowl with a plate and leave to soak for 4–5 hours.

Strain the water from the soaked figs into a saucepan and add the sugar, honey, spices and orange zest. Stir over a low heat to dissolve the sugar, then bring to a gentle simmer.

Add the figs and poach very gently until completely tender. The timing will depend on how moist your figs were to start with – plump, ready-to-eat figs need 10–15 minutes, but drier fruit will take longer. If the syrup gets too thick, add a little warm water. Cool, then store the figs in their syrup in an airtight container in the fridge until needed.

Serve as a pud with yoghurt, cream, cold custard or ice cream, or with a scattering of my independent crumble (see page 358). Alternatively, try it for breakfast with yoghurt and muesli or other cereal.

Apricot and prune compote

Serves 4–6

100g dried apricots
100g prunes
50g sultanas (optional)
300ml freshly squeezed orange juice (or water)
50ml lemon juice
A few finely pared strips of orange and lemon zest
½ vanilla pod (optional)

Put everything in a saucepan and bring to the barest of simmers. Remove from the heat, place a lid on the pan and allow to cool slowly over an hour or two (i.e. don't put it in a chilly place straight away). The fruit will plump up in the warm juice. Transfer to an airtight container and store in the fridge.

Serve in any of the ways suggested for spiced fig compote, above.

VARIATION

Use 250g dried apricots and forget the prunes and sultanas.

Elderflower panna cotta with gooseberry compote

A delicately wobbly, creamy panna cotta is such a simple but sophisticated dish. Infused with the scent of elderflowers and partnered with a sharp gooseberry compote, it makes a stunning summer pudding. You can use fresh elderflowers during their short season in May, but otherwise elderflower cordial works fine. Leave out the elderflower altogether and this is a great recipe for a plain panna cotta, with a little tang from the yoghurt.

Serves 4

100ml whole milk
250ml double cream
40g caster sugar (or 20g if you're using elderflower cordial)
3–4 large heads of elderflower, or 2 tablespoons elderflower cordial
2 gelatine leaves
150ml plain yoghurt

For the gooseberry compote:
500g gooseberries, topped and tailed
75g caster sugar
A few sprigs of elderflower (optional)

Combine the milk, cream and sugar in a saucepan. Tie up the elderflower heads in a piece of muslin and add to the pan, or stir in the elderflower cordial. Scald the liquid – bring just to the boil, but don't let it bubble. If you're using elderflower heads, leave for half an hour to infuse, then remove the elderflower.

Soak the gelatine in cold water for 5–10 minutes, until soft and floppy, then squeeze out excess water. If you left the cream mixture to infuse for half an hour, reheat it almost to boiling point – if you have used cordial, the cream should still be hot enough. Add the gelatine to the hot cream mixture and stir until dissolved. Leave to cool to room temperature, stirring from time to time.

Once cooled, stir in the yoghurt until thoroughly combined. Pour the mixture into four 125ml moulds, such as ramekins, and chill in the fridge for at least 4 hours, until set.

Meanwhile, make the compote. Put the gooseberries in a pan with the sugar and 50ml water. Tie up the elderflower sprigs, if using, in a piece of muslin and add to the pan. Bring to a simmer and cook gently for about 10 minutes, until the gooseberries are soft. Leave to cool completely, then remove the elderflower sprigs and chill the compote.

To turn out the panna cottas, dip each mould very briefly in hot water – literally just a few seconds – then turn upside down on to a serving plate and give it a shake; if necessary, run a knife around the edge. Serve with the gooseberry compote.

Rhubarb and orange yoghurt fool

A classic fool combines a fruit compote or purée, cream and custard to delicious effect. This is a sort of deconstructed version, with the cream replaced by yoghurt to give the whole thing a lighter feel. You could mix all three elements together, of course, but I enjoy the look of them unmingled in the dish, and the pleasure of choosing exactly how much of each to put on my spoon.

Serves 6

1 quantity of custard
(see page 351)
500ml thick, rich yoghurt

For the rhubarb compote:
1kg rhubarb, cut into
4–5cm lengths
Juice of 1 large orange
125g caster sugar

To make the compote, put the rhubarb, orange juice and sugar in a saucepan and bring to a gentle simmer, stirring occasionally. Cook for about 5 minutes, until the rhubarb breaks down into a purée. You can stop it when some of the rhubarb is still just holding its shape, but make sure it's quite tender and not at all crunchy. Use a sieve to strain off a little of the syrupy juice, so you get a slightly denser rhubarb mixture and some good, tart rhubarb syrup. (You could trickle this syrup on pancakes, or top up with chilled fizzy wine to make a rhubarb bellini.) Cool the rhubarb and then chill.

For each serving, put a couple of tablespoons of the rhubarb into a slightly tilted bowl, turn the tilted bowl slightly, spoon a couple of tablespoons of custard alongside the compote, tilt, and do the same with the thick yoghurt. The idea is that the three elements stay roughly separate in the bowl. It's the eater's prerogative to dip and mix, a little, a lot, or not all, sampling different proportions of the three elements, as they wish.

VARIATIONS

This winning threesome of tart fruit purée, sweet custard and creamy yoghurt can be adapted using any fruit that makes a good, tangy compote – the most obvious being plums, apricots, gooseberries and Bramley or other cooking apples. Or replace cooked fruit with a pile of fresh raspberries, lightly crushed and sweetened with a few pinches of caster sugar. In all cases, you can sprinkle over some independent crumble (see page 358), if you like.

Two seasonal cranachans

Cranachan is a traditional Scottish pudding, a sublime mixture of toasted oats, honey, cream, fruit and whisky. Beautifully simple and quick to make, it's ripe for a bit of seasonal variation. I love a classic raspberry version in the summer, laced with some pungent heather honey. But from January to June, when rhubarb is available (first the indoor-grown, 'forced' variety, then the sturdier outdoor crop), I find that makes a stunning, pink-rippled cranachan, too.

Raspberry and honey cranachan

Serves 4

50g rolled oats
2 tablespoons whisky
250ml double cream
2 tablespoons heather honey (or other favourite honey)
250g raspberries

Warm a smallish frying pan over a medium-low heat. Add the rolled oats and stir until they are golden and toasted – keep a close eye on them, as they can burn easily. Transfer to a plate to cool.

Stir the whisky and cream together in a bowl and then whisk until the cream holds soft peaks. Lightly crush a few of the raspberries, so the juices run. Loosely fold the honey, oats and raspberries into the cream, spoon into glasses and serve straight away.

Rhubarb and Cointreau cranachan

Serves 4

500g rhubarb, cut into 5cm lengths
Finely grated zest and juice of 1 orange
1 tablespoon caster sugar
1 vanilla pod, slit open lengthways and cut in half
50g rolled oats
1 tablespoon Cointreau
250ml double cream
3 tablespoons honey

Put the rhubarb, orange zest and juice, sugar and vanilla pod into a roasting tin and stir to combine. Cover with foil and bake in an oven preheated to 170°C/Gas Mark 3 for 30 minutes or so, until soft. Let the rhubarb cool completely. Remove the vanilla pod, then transfer the rhubarb and any juices to a bowl.

Warm a smallish frying pan over a medium-low heat. Add the rolled oats and stir until they are golden and toasted – keep a close eye on them, as they can burn easily. Transfer to a plate to cool.

Stir the Cointreau and cream together in a bowl and then whisk until the cream holds soft peaks. Loosely fold in the honey, oats and rhubarb with its juices, spoon into glasses and serve straight away.

Raspberry and strawberry Eton mess

Though sadly unheard of at Eton in my day, this delicious pudding is now a British classic. It's really just a fool sweetened with broken meringue instead of sugar – but that extra element of texture makes so much difference. I love it with the traditional strawberries alone, but including raspberries adds a whole new dimension to it. Tart fruit such as gooseberries and rhubarb work well, too. Just fold a cooled, cooked compote into the cream and meringues.

Serves 6

250g strawberries
250g raspberries
35g caster sugar
350ml double cream,
lightly whipped

For the meringue:
2 medium egg whites
100g caster sugar

Start with the meringue: put the egg whites into a spotlessly clean bowl and whisk until they hold soft peaks. Now add half the sugar and whisk to blend well with the egg white. Add the remaining sugar and whisk again until the mixture is thick and shiny and holds stiff peaks. You should be able to turn the bowl upside down without anything sliding out.

Line a baking sheet with baking parchment. Dollop dessertspoonfuls of meringue on the sheet and place in an oven preheated to 120°C/ Gas Mark ½. Leave for 2 hours, until the meringues are completely dry and crisp on the outside (they will still be a bit squidgy in the middle) and can be lifted off the paper easily. Remove and leave to cool completely.

Meanwhile, halve the strawberries, thickly slicing any whoppers. Put in a large bowl with the raspberries and sugar. Roughly crush and squeeze a few of the berries with your hands so the juices start to run. Cover and leave to macerate in the fridge for an hour or two.

To assemble the mess, break the meringues into rough pieces, then fold into the whipped cream. Now lightly fold in the chilled fruit, so everything is rippled together rather than thoroughly blended. Pile into glasses and serve. You can make it an hour or so in advance, but not more, or the meringue will go weepy in the cream.

VARIATIONS

Gooseberry Eton mess
Replace the strawberries and raspberries with gooseberry compote (page 342).

Bramley Eton mess
Replace the berries with Bramley apple compote (page 339), and use 250ml (rather than 350ml) cream.

Blackcurrant trifle

This simple trifle is faithful to the classic combination of booze-soaked sponge, fruit, custard and cream. It tastes amazing and looks dramatic served in tallish glasses. You can make it throughout the year, using all manner of seasonal fruits (see variations).

Serves 6

For the blackcurrant purée:

500g blackcurrants, stripped from their stalks

100g icing sugar (or possibly more)

For the custard:

250ml double cream

250ml whole milk

1 vanilla pod, slit open lengthways

4 large medium egg yolks

100g caster sugar

1 heaped teaspoon cornflour

To assemble:

1 medium egg white, lightly beaten until frothy

A little caster sugar

100g plain sponge cake, such as Genoese sponge page 372), cut into 2cm cubes

4 tablespoons crème de cassis

250ml double cream, lightly whipped

Start with the blackcurrant purée. Set aside about 20 fine, plump blackcurrants. Put the rest into a saucepan with 100ml water, bring to a simmer and cook gently for about 10 minutes, stirring and crushing the fruit, until soft and pulpy. Rub the blackcurrant pulp through a sieve and discard the skins and seeds. Whisk the icing sugar into the warm purée, then taste and add more sugar if necessary. It needs to remain on the tart side, as the custard will be very sweet. Leave to cool.

Next make the custard. Put the cream, milk and vanilla pod in a saucepan and bring to just below boiling point, then set aside to infuse. Put the egg yolks in a bowl, add the sugar and cornflour and beat together until smooth. Remove the vanilla pod from the hot cream. Gradually pour the hot cream on to the egg yolk mixture, whisking all the time. Pour into a clean pan and heat gently, stirring constantly with a wooden spoon, until the mixture is thick enough to coat the back of the spoon; don't let it boil or it will curdle. Strain the thickened custard through a sieve, leave to cool, then chill.

Roll the reserved blackcurrants in the egg white, let the excess drain off, then roll them in a little caster sugar so they take on a 'frosty' coating. Set aside in the fridge.

To assemble, divide the sponge cubes between 6 large glasses and trickle over the crème de cassis. Now layer the blackcurrant purée and custard in the glasses. Finish each with a big spoonful of whipped cream and a few frosted blackcurrants. Serve lightly chilled.

VARIATIONS

Replace the blackcurrant purée with one of the following fruit/booze combinations, keeping the fruit quite tart to counteract the sweet custard. If you don't have the suggested alcohol, use a medium sherry.

- Rhubarb compote (page 344) with Grand Marnier or Cointreau.

- Gooseberry compote (page 342); no alcohol needed for this one.

- Raspberries, roughly crushed, lightly sugared and macerated with a trickle of framboise or crème de cassis.

- Blackberries, cooked, sieved and sweetened as for blackcurrants above, with a little Calvados, or cider brandy.

Roast vanilla plums on toast

This makes a very simple pudding or a rather luxurious breakfast, though for brekkie you might want to forego the ice cream or clotted cream and try some yoghurt instead. Or you might not.

Serves 4

75g unsalted butter, softened

2 large or 4 small thick slices of crusty white bread

About 10 plums, halved and stoned

1 vanilla pod

50g caster sugar

Lightly grease a medium baking dish with a little of the butter, then spread a little more of it on both sides of the bread. Cut the bread in half if large. Lay the pieces in the dish and arrange the plums on top, cut-side up.

Slit the vanilla pod open lengthways and scrape out the seeds with the tip of a knife. Combine the seeds with the remaining butter and dot it over the plums. Sprinkle the sugar on top, then cut the empty vanilla pod lengthways into shreds and scatter these over the plums too. Bake in an oven preheated to 190°C/Gas Mark 5 for 20–30 minutes, until the plums are tender and the bread is caramelised around the edges, yet soggy and syrupy under the plums.

Serve straight away, with clotted cream, ice cream, or thick yoghurt.

Two seasonal clafoutis

This classic French pudding is traditionally made with cherries, but it's so simple to throw together that it seems a shame not to make it with other seasonal fruit too. I've suggested a rhubarb version here, but it also works well with plums, damsons, pears and even prunes.

Cherry clafoutis

Serves 6

500g cherries
50g plain flour
A pinch of sea salt
100g caster sugar
3 medium eggs, lightly beaten
250ml whole milk
Icing sugar for dusting (optional)

Lightly butter a 25cm round baking dish or tin, or a 25 x 20cm rectangular one. Remove the stalks from the cherries but do not stone them; you don't want any of the juices – or flavour – to escape until the moment you bite into your first cherry. Spread them out in a single layer in the dish.

Sift the flour and salt into a bowl and stir in the sugar. Make a well in the centre and add the beaten eggs. Gradually draw in the flour from the sides, mixing well, then beat in the milk, a little at a time, to form a smooth batter.

Pour the batter over the cherries and bake in an oven preheated to 180°C/Gas Mark 4 for 35–40 minutes, until golden and puffed up. Clafoutis is best eaten warm, but it's not bad cold either. Dust with icing sugar, if you like, just before serving, on its own or with cream.

Rhubarb clafoutis

Serves 6

500g rhubarb
A little ground cinnamon (optional)
Grated zest of ½ orange and the juice of the whole fruit
125g caster sugar
50g plain flour
A pinch of sea salt
3 medium eggs, lightly beaten
250ml whole milk
Icing sugar for dusting (optional)

Cut the rhubarb into 5cm lengths and put in a baking tin with a good pinch of cinnamon, if using, the orange juice and 2 tablespoons of the sugar. Toss well and roast in an oven preheated to 200°C/Gas Mark 6 for 10–15 minutes, or until tender and just beginning to caramelise around the edges. Leave to cool completely and then drain in a sieve.

Turn the oven temperature down to 180°C/Gas Mark 4. Lightly butter a 25cm round baking dish or tin, or a 25 x 20cm rectangular one. Make the batter as for the cherry clafoutis (above), stirring in the orange zest and a pinch of cinnamon, if you like, with the sugar.

Arrange the drained rhubarb in the buttered dish and assemble and bake as for the cherry clafoutis. When you are just about to serve, mix together about ½ teaspoon of icing sugar and ½ teaspoon of ground cinnamon, if you like, then sift a light dusting over the top of the clafoutis. Serve with or without cream.

Baked apples

A perfect baked apple is one of the true great puds. It's all about choosing the right variety of apple, and not stinting on the butter and booze that go in the cavity with the dried fruit. Eating apples, such as early Cox's, Egremont Russets, James Grieve and, later in the season, Ashmead's Kernel or Orleans Reinette, work better than giant cookers such as Bramleys, which have a tendency to collapse into a fluffy mush. Cider brandy lends a special flavour here. It is available from the Somerset Cider Brandy Company (www.ciderbrandy.co.uk).

Serve your baked apples piping hot with a scoop of ice cream on the side. Rum and raisin is pretty good, or one flavoured with cinnamon or cardamom, but a good-quality vanilla goes well, too.

Serves 6

100g dried fruit, such as sultanas, raisins and chopped prunes

50ml cider brandy

100g unsalted butter, softened

2 tablespoons light muscovado sugar

Finely grated zest of 1 lemon

½ teaspoon ground cinnamon (optional)

6 fairly large eating apples

Put the dried fruit in a small bowl and pour over the cider brandy. Leave to macerate for at least an hour, ideally overnight.

Beat the soaked fruit into the softened butter, along with the sugar, lemon zest and cinnamon, if using. Core the apples and cut a sliver off the base of each one if you think they won't stand up straight in the tin. It's a good idea to score them around their circumference with a sharp knife too, to stop them bursting. Stuff the cavities with the spiced fruit butter, then arrange the apples in an ovenproof dish, smearing any extra butter over the top.

Cover with foil and place in an oven preheated to 150°C/Gas Mark 2. Bake for 50–60 minutes, until soft but not collapsing, removing the foil about two-thirds of the way through cooking and basting with the buttery juices. Serve the apples with the juices spooned over them and a scoop of ice cream on the side.

VARIATION

Christmas baked apples

If you have any leftover mincemeat at Christmas, you can use this instead of the brandy-soaked dried fruit. Zip it up a bit with some lemon zest and a slosh of cider brandy, stuff it into the cavities and put a knob of butter on top of each one before baking.

Apple and walnut crumble

The nubbly crunch of toasted walnuts adds a new dimension to a classic crumble; pecans are equally good. This basic crumble topping can be used on all sorts of other fruits, from winter rhubarb, through summer gooseberries or plums, to autumnal blackberries, pears or quince. You can also bake it separately to create my 'independent crumble' (see below).

Serves 8

100g walnuts
1.25kg cooking apples, peeled, cored and finely sliced
50–100g caster sugar
1 teaspoon ground cinnamon (optional)

For the crumble:
225g plain flour
A pinch of sea salt
200g cold unsalted butter, cut into cubes
150g caster, granulated or soft light brown sugar
75g medium oatmeal
75g ground almonds (optional)

Scatter the walnuts on a baking sheet and toast in an oven preheated to 180°C/Gas Mark 4 for 5–7 minutes, giving them a shake halfway through, until just beginning to colour and develop aroma. Leave to cool, then chop very roughly.

To prepare the crumble, sift the flour and salt into a bowl (or food processor). Add the butter and rub in with your fingers (or pulse briefly in the processor) until the mixture resembles coarse crumbs. Stir in the sugar, oatmeal and ground almonds, if using. Squeeze a few handfuls of crumble in your fist to make lumps – I reckon it's nice to have a 'rocky' crumble rather than a fine, even-textured one.

Put the apples in a large bowl, sprinkle over the sugar (you'll need to estimate the amount according to the tartness of the apples). Add the walnuts and the cinnamon, if using, and mix roughly. Spread in a pie dish or other ovenproof dish, getting the fruit as compact as you can.

Scatter the crumble over the apples in a fairly even layer and bake for 40–45 minutes, until browned on top. Serve hot, with cream, custard or ice cream. Eat leftovers cold for breakfast, with thick, rich yoghurt.

VARIATION

Independent crumble

Make the crumble as above, squishing a few handfuls of it to make some larger lumps. Spread the mixture out in a baking tin and bake in an oven preheated to 190°C/Gas Mark 5 for 20–25 minutes, until golden brown and crumbly, taking it out a couple of times to give it a good stir. Leave to cool completely, then store in an airtight container in the fridge, or in a cool larder; it will keep for a couple of weeks.

This ready-to-go topping can be scattered thickly over gooseberry compote (page 342) or rhubarb compote (page 344) in a pie dish and baked at 180°C/Gas Mark 4 for 20 minutes to make a quick crumble.

It is also delicious cold, with any tart fruit compote (pages 339–44) or sprinkled over lightly macerated or crushed summer berries. Serve with yoghurt or cream, or even ice cream.

Roast plum sorbet with chocolate brownies

This combination of sweet-tart, icy plums and warm chocolate brownies is deep indulgence, producing pleasing contrasts on so many levels: warm–cold, sweet–sharp, choc–fruit. Whenever I serve it, my friends go all gooey, like the brownies.

Serves 6–8

1kg plums, halved and stoned

2 vanilla pods

100g caster sugar (or more, depending on the tartness of the plums)

1 batch of plain chocolate brownies (see page 397)

Make the sorbet at least 12 hours before you want to serve it. Put the plums in a roasting tin. Slit the vanilla pods open lengthways, chop them into a few pieces and add to the tin, along with the sugar and 250ml water. Roast in an oven preheated to 200°C/Gas Mark 6 for about 30 minutes, until the plums are really soft and slightly blistered around the edges. Rub the plums and all the juices from the tin through a sieve into a bowl. Taste the purée and add more sugar if you think it needs it, then leave to cool.

Churn the purée in an ice-cream machine until very thick, then transfer to the freezer to set solid. Alternatively, put the purée in a shallow container and place in the freezer. Take it out every hour or so and beat it to distribute the ice crystals throughout the mixture and make a soft, sorbet texture. Three interventions should do the trick; two will do if you're pushed.

Serve the plum sorbet accompanied by brownies, still a little warm from the oven.

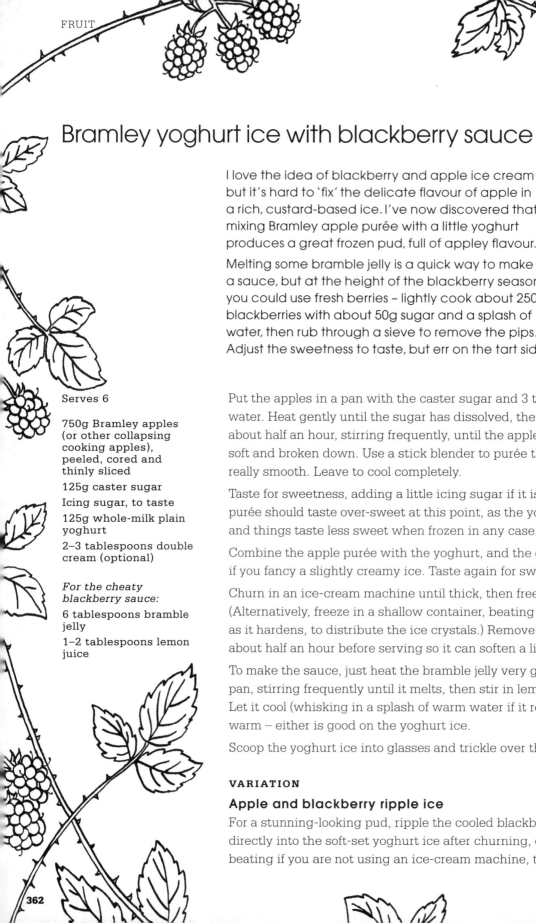

Bramley yoghurt ice with blackberry sauce

I love the idea of blackberry and apple ice cream but it's hard to 'fix' the delicate flavour of apple in a rich, custard-based ice. I've now discovered that mixing Bramley apple purée with a little yoghurt produces a great frozen pud, full of appley flavour.

Melting some bramble jelly is a quick way to make a sauce, but at the height of the blackberry season, you could use fresh berries – lightly cook about 250g blackberries with about 50g sugar and a splash of water, then rub through a sieve to remove the pips. Adjust the sweetness to taste, but err on the tart side.

Serves 6

750g Bramley apples (or other collapsing cooking apples), peeled, cored and thinly sliced

125g caster sugar

Icing sugar, to taste

125g whole-milk plain yoghurt

2–3 tablespoons double cream (optional)

For the cheaty blackberry sauce:

6 tablespoons bramble jelly

1–2 tablespoons lemon juice

Put the apples in a pan with the caster sugar and 3 tablespoons of water. Heat gently until the sugar has dissolved, then simmer for about half an hour, stirring frequently, until the apples are completely soft and broken down. Use a stick blender to purée the apples until really smooth. Leave to cool completely.

Taste for sweetness, adding a little icing sugar if it is needed – the purée should taste over-sweet at this point, as the yoghurt is sharp, and things taste less sweet when frozen in any case.

Combine the apple purée with the yoghurt, and the double cream if you fancy a slightly creamy ice. Taste again for sweetness.

Churn in an ice-cream machine until thick, then freeze until set solid. (Alternatively, freeze in a shallow container, beating several times as it hardens, to distribute the ice crystals.) Remove from the freezer about half an hour before serving so it can soften a little.

To make the sauce, just heat the bramble jelly very gently in a small pan, stirring frequently until it melts, then stir in lemon juice to taste. Let it cool (whisking in a splash of warm water if it re-sets) or keep it warm – either is good on the yoghurt ice.

Scoop the yoghurt ice into glasses and trickle over the sauce.

VARIATION

Apple and blackberry ripple ice
For a stunning-looking pud, ripple the cooled blackberry sauce directly into the soft-set yoghurt ice after churning, or after the final beating if you are not using an ice-cream machine, then freeze.

Quince and Bramley apple sorbet

The fragrant, honey-coloured quince is a jewel among fruit, and greatly under-explored. It appears most frequently in hot dishes, such as pies, cobblers and crumbles, or with roast meats. But it can also be very striking served cold. Combined with tart Bramley apples, which soften its powerful, perfumed flavour, it makes a superb sorbet.

Serves 8

350g caster sugar

600g quince, peeled, cored and chopped

400g Bramley apples, peeled, cored and chopped

Lemon juice, to taste

Put the sugar in a large saucepan with 500ml water and heat gently, stirring to dissolve the sugar. Add the quince, bring to a simmer and cook at a gentle bubble for 20 minutes, stirring occasionally.

Add the apples and cook for a further 10 minutes, or until all the fruit is very soft. Blend to a purée using a stick blender in the pan or in a jug, then add lemon juice to taste – about 2 tablespoons should do. Pass the purée through a fine sieve and leave to cool.

Churn the mixture in an ice-cream machine until semi-frozen and creamy, then transfer to the freezer. Alternatively, put it in a shallow container in the freezer and beat every hour or so, until you have a soft, fluffy sorbet. Return to the freezer until frozen firm.

Allow the sorbet to soften at room temperature for 20–30 minutes before serving, in small dishes, with honey brandy snaps (page 394) or other crisp biscuits.

Blackcurrant granita

A granita is one of the easiest of all iced puds. All you're really doing is freezing a fruit purée/syrup, then semi-roughing it up with a fork to create an elegant pile of rough, sparkling, fruity ice crystals. It's not exactly hard work, but the result is very stylish. Once you've got the hang of it, you can easily invent your own, using all manner of summer and autumn fruits. The tart ones, such as raspberries, gooseberries, plums and rhubarb, are the best.

Serves 8

1kg blackcurrants
At least 250g icing sugar

Put the blackcurrants in a saucepan with 250ml water, bring to a simmer and cook gently for 5–10 minutes, until the fruit is completely soft. Push it through a sieve to remove the pips and skins. Sift in 250g icing sugar and whisk well. Taste the mixture and add more sugar if you think it's needed (bear in mind that, once frozen, it will taste less sweet).

Tip the mixture into a large, shallow container (if the purée is in a layer no more than 5cm deep it will speed up the freezing process). Freeze until rock solid.

Remove the granita from the freezer about 20 minutes before you want to serve it, to allow it to soften slightly. Just before serving, use a fork to scrape and scratch the mixture into crystals and shards. Pile into glasses and serve at once.

VARIATIONS

Gooseberry granita
Replace the blackcurrants with 1kg gooseberries.

Snow-capped granita
Try trickling a little double cream on the granita in each glass just before you serve it (as illustrated). It will half-freeze in a thin layer on the icy fruit crystals. Both creamy cap and frosty crystals will melt and combine in the warmth of your mouth. Nice.

treats

This chapter is pure indulgence. And why not? Despite my passion

for home-reared meat, fresh local fish and seasonal garden vegetables, and the unceasing pleasure I get from using such ingredients, I have to admit that the following collection of recipes takes me to a different level of excitement – one in which I rub my hands together, waggle my eyebrows and break out into a big, broad grin of eager anticipation.

That's not simply because these are my favourite glee-inducing, sweet treat recipes. It's also because they bring my lifelong culinary adventure full circle, taking me right back to my childhood. There is absolutely no doubt that it was my sweet tooth that led me into the kitchen in the first place. It started with me standing on a chair, aged five, mixing icing sugar, egg whites, food colouring and peppermint essence. This sickly green putty was technically destined to become peppermint creams. And sometimes it actually did. It also proved to be an irresistible 'eat me' concoction that got me hooked on cooking, and rapidly transported me to the wonderland of baking cakes and biscuits, and mixing up indulgent puddings and sticky sweets.

For the first three years or so of my fledgling amateur cooking career, I don't think I made a single thing you would call savoury. Instead I built up a repertoire of cakes, sweets and puds from the classic cookbooks on my mother's kitchen shelf, mainly the two domestic goddesses of the 1960s and 1970s respectively, Constance Spry and Katie Stewart. By the age of eight, I was cooking most of the puddings for my Mum's dinner parties – a rotating agenda of profiteroles, pavlova, chocolate rum gâteau and Genoese sponge filled with whipped cream and strawberries or raspberries from the garden. Versions of all these – in my own words, but often not too far from the originals – appear in the pages that follow (or in The Whole Fruit chapter).

I've never lost my sweet tooth, though to my great relief, I managed to find a savoury incisor or two as my cooking adventure progressed – and it's still a great thrill for me to discover a new recipe to add to the 'sugar lounge' collection. Places on this exclusive list are hard won, but having made the grade they invariably do good service for many years. On reviewing the list, it's interesting to note that at least half the recipes go back a decade or more (and quite soon it will be forty years since I first made fudge and profiteroles). It was Gill Meller, our head chef at River Cottage, who introduced me to the honey wholemeal cake (page 386) a year or so ago. Now it's become a big favourite at home, as well as with our guests at the cookery school, and I'm sure I'll still be baking it in five years time. The same goes for the lemon trickle cake on page 378 (a great way to show kids that chocolate is not the only treat) and the chunky fig, apricot and prune cake on page 383, which is my latest solution to the challenge of cramming dried fruit into a cake without it becoming austere, sickly or overtly Christmassy.

So what follows is pretty much my current 'sweet-indulgence top twenty' (though a fair few recipes in the fruit chapter could probably also compete for a place in that chart). At home, these recipes get regular outings on all kinds of occasions – and not only 'special' ones. Although the easy rich chocolate cake on page 384 is a rock-solid (metaphorically speaking, not literally), dependable birthday cake for chocolate lovers, it's also pressed into service frequently when friends drop by for tea, since it's simple to make and delivers its dose of dense, choccy deliciousness without the need for icing. Personally I think it's an important principle of treat cooking that it should not be restricted to hallowed celebrations, or even the arrival of guests. The fact that it's raining outside, or that it 'seems like ages since we made cookies', is reason enough in our household to get out the weighing scales, the sugar, the butter and the big, greedy eyes.

Talking of weighing scales, it's often said that savoury cooking is an art, whereas baking is an exact science – one implication being that you shouldn't meddle with the precise quantities and techniques that have been laid down in print and proven in practice. I concur, but only up to a point. If you meddle with the recipes that follow, they may well not turn out as intended (or as photographed), but stick within the realms of general cakery and all-round puddingness and you won't go too far wrong. Even your worst mishaps are likely to get devoured with gusto (or a good dollop of cream).

I say that not only because I insist on your freedom to adapt my recipes as a matter of principle but also because in this book many successes have been the result of testing hunches and indulging experimental whims. That includes one of my favourite tweaks in this chapter – the frangipane version of the muffins on page 388. They were the result of a 'what if?' conversation of the kind that often occurs when I chat to friends and colleagues: 'What if we replaced some of the flour with ground almonds… would we get a greedier, more gooey muffin that would almost do as a grown-up pud?' Well, I know what I think, but it's a question you can answer only if you give them a whirl…

Genoese sponge cake

This is a
very useful recipe to
have in your repertoire. The light but
firm sponge is delicious filled with fresh
fruit and cream, but is also ideal for a trifle.
You do need to whisk the eggs and sugar
together for about 10 minutes, but this
is easy if you have a hand-held
electric beater.

Serves 10–12

60g unsalted butter
125g plain flour
A pinch of sea salt
4 medium eggs
125g caster sugar

To serve:
200ml double cream,
lightly whipped
250g raspberries or
strawberries
Vanilla sugar or plain
caster sugar

Melt the butter gently and leave to cool slightly. Use a little of it to grease 2 round 18cm cake tins. Dust the sides generously with flour, tip out any excess, then line the bases with baking parchment.

Sift the flour and salt together; set aside. Put the eggs and sugar in a large heatproof bowl that will sit snugly over the top of a saucepan. Pour boiling water into the saucepan and sit the bowl on top. The hot water must not actually touch the bowl; it is the steam that is needed to heat it up, which helps the sugar to dissolve and thickens the mixture slightly. Using a hand-held electric beater, whisk the eggs and sugar for about 10 minutes, until very pale, thick, moussey and at least trebled in bulk. The mixture should hold its shape on the surface for a few seconds if you let a little fall from the beaters.

Sift half the flour into the egg and sugar mixture and gently fold it in with a large metal spoon. Repeat with the remaining flour. Carefully pour in the melted butter and fold this in too, until just incorporated.

Pour the mixture into the tins and bake in an oven preheated to 180°C/Gas Mark 4 for 25 minutes, until golden brown and firm to the touch. Leave to cool in the tins for a few minutes and then, running a small, sharp knife around the edge of the cakes if necessary to help release them, turn them out on to a wire rack to cool completely.

Serve topped with, or sandwiched together with, lashings of lightly whipped double cream and fresh raspberries or strawberries. Finish with a sprinkling of vanilla sugar or plain sugar.

VARIATION
Trifle sponges
Bake the mixture in a large Swiss roll tin instead. Once cooled, slice the cake into fingers or cubes to use for a trifle such as my blackcurrant trifle (page 351).

Apple and almond pudding cake

This is called a pudding cake because you can serve it warm with lots of cream, custard or yoghurt. However, it tastes just as good cold, in thick slices, with a cup of tea or coffee. You need fairly sweet, firm dessert apples that will hold their shape when cooked (generally speaking, the more acidic the apple, the more it will break down on cooking). Try Cox's, Orleans Reinette, Egremont Russet or Ribston Pippin.

Serves 8

150g unsalted butter, softened

125g caster sugar

2 medium eggs

1 teaspoon almond extract (optional – if you like that extra almondy, frangipane taste)

75g white or wholemeal self-raising flour

75g blanched almonds, whizzed in a food processor until finely ground (or use ready-ground almonds)

For the apples:

4 dessert apples

25g unsalted butter

1 heaped tablespoon granulated sugar

¼ teaspoon ground cinnamon (optional)

Grease a 20cm springform cake tin and line the base with baking parchment.

Peel the apples, quarter them and cut out the cores, then cut each quarter into about 3 wedges. Melt the 25g butter in a frying pan and let it start to sizzle gently. Add the granulated sugar and stir until the mixture bubbles. Add the apples, sprinkle over the cinnamon, if using, and cook over a medium heat for about 5 minutes, turning occasionally, until the apples are just tender and very lightly caramelised. Remove from the heat and leave to cool.

Put the butter and caster sugar in a large bowl and beat together with a hand-held electric beater, or using a freestanding electric mixer, until light and fluffy. Break in an egg and beat well, then beat in the second egg, along with the almond extract, if using, and a spoonful of flour (this helps to prevent the mixture curdling). Add the ground almonds, sift in the remaining flour and fold in gently with a large metal spoon.

Scrape the mixture into the prepared tin and gently smooth the surface with a palette knife, then arrange the apples on top. Trickle over any buttery juices from the pan. Place in an oven preheated to 170°C/Gas Mark 3 and bake for 45–50 minutes, until a skewer inserted in the centre comes out clean.

Stand on a wire rack to cool for a few minutes before releasing the tin. Serve warm with cream, custard or Greek yoghurt, or cold for tea.

Carrot cake

This wonderful creation, soaked with honey, manages to be both sumptuous and earthy at the same time. It really doesn't need icing – but, if you're a carrot cake traditionalist, you can always whip up a tart, cream-cheese based topping, perhaps laced with a little orange zest.

Serves 12–14

4 medium eggs

150g caster sugar

300ml rapeseed oil, or 150ml each rapeseed and sunflower oil for a slightly lighter flavour

300g wholemeal self-raising flour

½ teaspoon sea salt

½ teaspoon bicarbonate of soda

3–4 large carrots, about 350g in total, peeled and finely grated

About 150g runny honey

Grease a 23cm springform cake tin and line the base with baking parchment.

Put the eggs and sugar in a large bowl and beat together with a hand-held electric beater, or using a freestanding mixer, for about 10 minutes, until pale, foamy and slightly thickened. Add the oil and beat for another minute or two.

Sift the flour, salt and bicarbonate of soda together into the mixture. Tip in any bran left in the sieve, too. Fold in gently. Finally, fold in the grated carrot. Spoon the mixture into the prepared tin and bake in an oven preheated to 180°C/Gas Mark 4 for 45–50 minutes, or until a skewer inserted in the centre comes out clean. Remove from the oven and stand the tin on a wire rack.

Put the honey into a small saucepan over a low heat and heat gently until it is liquid. Pierce the surface of the hot cake all over with a small knife, or a skewer. Slowly pour on the hot honey so it soaks into the cake. Leave to cool slightly in the tin before turning out. Serve warm or cold.

Lemon trickle cake

This is really a Victoria sponge flavoured with lemon zest and drenched, after baking, in a very lemony liquid icing that soaks through the cake and also forms a glaze. The intense lemony tang saves it from being too sweet.

Serves 10

175g unsalted butter, softened

175g caster sugar

Finely grated zest of 3 lemons

3 medium eggs

175g self-raising flour

A pinch of sea salt

A splash of milk (optional)

200g icing sugar

75ml lemon juice

Grease a large loaf tin, 1 litre capacity, and line the base and sides with baking parchment.

Put the butter and sugar in a large bowl and beat together with a hand-held electric beater, or using a freestanding electric mixer, until very pale and fluffy – at least 5 minutes; up to 10 if you can manage it. This makes all the difference to the lightness of the finished cake. Add the grated lemon zest and then beat in the eggs, one at a time, adding a spoonful of flour with each (to help prevent the mixture curdling).

Sift the remaining flour and salt into the mixture and fold in lightly using a large metal spoon. Add a little milk, if necessary, to achieve a good dropping consistency – i.e. the mixture should drop fairly easily off a spoon when you tap it on the side of the bowl.

Spoon the mixture into the prepared tin, smooth the top gently and place in an oven preheated to 170°C/Gas Mark 3. Bake for 45–50 minutes, until a skewer inserted in the centre comes out clean.

Put the icing sugar in a bowl, add the lemon juice and stir together until smooth. Leaving the hot cake in its tin, use a fine skewer to make lots of holes all over the top of the cake, going quite deep, but not right through to the bottom. Spoon the lemon icing slowly over the cake so that it all soaks in. Leave in the tin until cool, then turn out and serve in slices.

VARIATION

Victoria sponge cake

This recipe can be adapted to make a classic Victoria sponge. Omit the lemon zest. Increase the butter, sugar and flour quantities to 250g each and use 4 medium eggs. Bake the mixture in two greased and base-lined round, shallow 20cm cake tins at 180°C/Gas Mark 4 for 25 minutes. When cool, sandwich the cakes together with raspberry or strawberry jam and dust with caster sugar. Alternatively, fill with lightly whipped cream and gooseberry compote (see page 342) or crushed fresh raspberries, sweetened with a little caster sugar.

Sticky Jamaican-style ginger cake

Black treacle, rum and stem ginger give this cake a deep and sophisticated flavour. It's not for the faint-hearted, but it is incredibly more-ish – especially if you spread it with butter and serve it for tea.

Serves 14–16

75g unsalted butter

125g dark muscovado sugar

150g black treacle

150g golden syrup

75ml dark rum

2 medium eggs, lightly beaten

225g self-raising flour

1 teaspoon ground allspice

1 teaspoon ground ginger

A pinch of sea salt

75g preserved stem ginger, finely chopped, plus a little of its syrup

Grease a large loaf tin, at least 1 litre in capacity, and line the base and sides with baking parchment.

Put the butter, sugar, treacle and syrup into a saucepan and heat gently until melted and combined. Leave to cool a little, then mix in the rum, followed by the beaten eggs.

Sift the flour, allspice, ginger and salt into a large bowl and make a well in the centre. Add the melted mixture from the pan and stir until smooth. Finally stir in the chopped ginger.

Pour the mixture into the prepared tin and bake in an oven preheated to 180°C/Gas Mark 4 for about 50 minutes, until a skewer inserted in the centre comes out clean. If the cake appears to be browning too much, cover it with foil. Leave to cool in the tin (don't worry if it sinks a bit in the middle).

Once the cake is cold, you can brush some of the syrup from the ginger over the top for extra stickiness. This cake improves after a couple of days and will keep in an airtight container for up to a week.

Chunky fig, apricot and prune cake

This moist, lightly spiced, fruit-packed cake, devised by my friend, Nikki Duffy, is a bit different from your average fruit cake, with its citrussy aromatics and slightly chunkier dried fruit. I absolutely love it. A thick slice is fantastic with morning tea or coffee, and a wedge wrapped in greaseproof paper is perfect in a lunchbox. It will keep well in a tin for a week or more. Should you find, as can be the case with fruit cakes, that your fruit sinks, it probably means the cake batter isn't stiff enough. Make sure you stick to the quantities in the recipe, and fold the fruit in as lightly as you can. But don't worry too much – a fruit-on-the-bottom cake is no great tragedy.

Serves 12

225g light wholemeal cake flour or spelt flour

1 teaspoon baking powder

A pinch of sea salt

1 rounded teaspoon ground mixed spice

150g dried figs

150g stoned prunes

150g dried apricots

85g orange marmalade

Finely grated zest of 1 lemon

Finely grated zest of 1 orange

200g unsalted butter, softened

200g light muscovado sugar

4 medium eggs

Lightly grease a 20cm springform cake tin and line with baking parchment. Put the flour, baking powder, salt and spice into a bowl and whisk lightly to aerate and combine.

Use kitchen scissors to cut the dried fruit into chunky pieces – cut each fig into about 6, removing the hard stalk, and each prune and apricot into 2 or 3. Combine them in a bowl. Beat the marmalade with a fork to loosen it, then stir in the lemon and orange zest. Combine the marmalade with the dried fruit.

Put the butter and sugar into a large bowl and beat well until very light and fluffy. Beat in the eggs, one at a time, adding a spoonful of the flour/spice mix with each. Fold in the remaining flour with a large metal spoon, then fold in the marmalade and dried fruit as lightly as you can. Try not to overmix it; everything should be just combined.

Spoon into the prepared tin and place in an oven preheated to 160°C/Gas Mark 3. Bake for 1½ hours, or until a skewer inserted in the centre comes out clean. Leave to cool completely in the tin.

VARIATION

Hot fruit cake with vanilla ice cream

You can make a very lovely pud with this, or any other fruit-laden cake, by gently frying thick slices of the cake in a little butter for a couple of minutes on each side, until thoroughly warmed through. Dish up each slice with a scoop of the best vanilla ice cream.

Easy rich chocolate cake

Everyone should have a little black cake in their culinary wardrobe and this is mine. It is an intensely rich, moist confection. Use the best chocolate you can find and combine it with the other ingredients – with the lightest possible touch to ensure a velvety texture.

Serves 10

250g dark chocolate (around 70 per cent cocoa solids), broken into chunks

250g unsalted butter, cut into cubes

4 medium eggs, separated

200g caster sugar (or 100g caster mixed with 100g soft light brown sugar)

50g plain flour

50g ground almonds

Grease a 23cm springform cake tin and line the base with baking parchment.

Put the chocolate and butter in a heatproof bowl and place it over a pan of barely simmering water, making sure the water doesn't touch the base of the bowl. Stir occasionally until the butter and chocolate have melted.

Meanwhile, whisk the egg yolks and sugar together in a large bowl until well combined. (If you use the caster and muscovado mix, the cake will have a lovely hint of caramel, but caster sugar on its own is absolutely fine.) Stir the melted chocolate and butter into the egg and sugar mixture. Combine the flour and almonds and fold these in, too.

In a separate bowl, whisk the egg whites until they hold firm peaks. Stir a large spoonful of egg white into the chocolate mixture to loosen it, then carefully fold in the rest of the egg whites with a large metal spoon or spatula, trying to keep in as much air as possible.

Pour the mixture into the prepared tin. Place in an oven preheated to 170°C/Gas Mark 3 and bake for about 30 minutes, until only just set. It should still wobble slightly in the centre – this means the cake will have a divinely sticky, fudgy texture once it's cooled down. Leave to cool for 10–15 minutes before releasing the tin.

Serve warm or cold, on its own or with a dollop of thick cream, crème fraîche or Greek yoghurt. For a more adult version, you could stir a slug of whisky into whipped cream sweetened with a little icing sugar and serve it spooned over each slice of cake.

Honey wholemeal cake

This soft, moist, dense, almondy cake is always a big hit. It can be served cold for tea, or warm for pudding with lashings of cream and some fresh berries or poached fruit, or a big scoop of roast plum sorbet (see page 360).

If you can't find wholemeal self-raising flour, use ordinary fine wholemeal flour and increase the baking powder to 2 teaspoons.

Serves 10

300g unsalted butter, softened

250g golden caster sugar

4 medium eggs

150g wholemeal self-raising flour

150g ground almonds

1 teaspoon baking powder

50g flaked almonds

4 tablespoons runny honey

Grease a 23cm springform cake tin and line the base with baking parchment. Place the tin on a baking sheet, as some butter may seep out during cooking.

Put the butter and sugar in a large bowl and beat thoroughly until very light and fluffy. Beat in the eggs, one at a time, adding a spoonful of flour with each. Fold in the ground almonds with a large metal spoon, then sift over the remaining flour and baking powder and fold in gently.

Scrape the mixture into the prepared tin, smooth gently and scatter the flaked almonds over the surface. Place in an oven preheated to 170°C/Gas Mark 3 and bake for about 45 minutes, until a skewer inserted in the centre comes out clean.

Remove from the oven and, while the cake is still hot, evenly trickle over the honey. It will tend to trickle towards the middle, which will end up more moist and honeyed than the edges, but that's fine. Place the tin on a wire rack and leave to cool a little before turning out. Serve warm or cold.

Lemon curd marble muffins

These are indulgent and delicious, but also very quick and easy to make. I sometimes replace 100g of the flour with 125g ground almonds, and add a few drops of almond extract to the mix, to create lemony frangipane muffins – these are lovely served warm, with cream, as a pudding. If lemon curd isn't your thing, try one of the variations below – the chocolate muffins are always popular with kids.

Makes about 12

225g plain flour
2 teaspoons baking powder
A good pinch of sea salt
100g caster sugar
1 medium egg
125g plain yoghurt
125ml whole milk
75g unsalted butter, melted and slightly cooled
150g lemon curd

Put 12 large paper cases into a muffin tray. Put the flour, baking powder, salt and caster sugar in a large bowl and whisk lightly to aerate and combine.

Mix the egg, yoghurt, milk and melted butter together in a jug. Pour them into the dry ingredients and mix lightly, stopping as soon as everything is combined – it's essential not to over-mix or you'll get dense, cakey muffins.

Add the lemon curd in 6 or 7 dollops and quickly 'marble' it lightly through the mixture (a couple of light stirs is really all that's needed). If your lemon curd is a bit stiff, just add it in little blobs.

Spoon the mixture into the paper cases, to three-quarters fill them. Bake in an oven preheated to 180°C/Gas Mark 4 for about 30 minutes until golden brown. Transfer to a wire rack to cool. Eat on the day you bake them, ideally while still slightly warm.

VARIATIONS

Jammy muffins

Replace the lemon curd with your favourite jam, first beating it lightly to soften slightly. Thick, fruity jams work best – a strawberry jam containing whole strawberries is perfect.

Chocolate marble muffins

Replace the lemon curd with 150g chocolate hazelnut spread (warm it gently first, so it's easier to marble).

Fruity muffins

Replace the lemon curd with 1 large, or 2 small ripe bananas, thoroughly mashed; or 75g blueberries; or 75g stoned and halved cherries; or 75g raisins or other dried fruit, such as chopped dried apricots. Stir the fruit into the mixture lightly and quickly, just before piling into the cases.

Caraway shortbread

These little biscuits are great on their own or as an accompaniment to ice cream or syllabub. Don't work the dough any more than you need in order to combine the ingredients or your biscuits won't be quite so meltingly delicious. Feel free to leave out the caraway for a classic, very light and crumbly shortbread.

Makes about 14 biscuits

150g unsalted butter, cut into small chunks and softened

75g caster sugar, plus 2 tablespoons for sprinkling

1 teaspoon caraway seeds

150g plain flour

75g cornflour

Beat the butter and sugar together until pale and creamy, then stir in the caraway seeds. Sift in the flour and cornflour and use a fork to just bring the mix together into a smooth dough. Place between 2 sheets of baking parchment lightly dusted with flour and roll out to about 4–5mm thick. Transfer to the fridge and chill for an hour.

Use a 6cm plain cutter dipped in flour to cut the dough into rounds, then lift them on to a non-stick baking sheet. You can re-roll the offcuts and chill again to get more biscuits but the resulting biscuits will be a little less light.

Place in an oven preheated to 170°C/Gas Mark 3 and bake for about 20 minutes, until very lightly coloured and just firm to the touch. Remove from the oven, sprinkle with caster sugar, and leave to cool and firm up for a couple of minutes before transferring them to a wire rack to cool completely.

VARIATION

Zesty shortbread

For a lovely, citrus-scented biscuit that's great with rich fools and ice creams, add the grated zests of ½ orange and 1 lemon, omitting the caraway seeds.

Ten-minute chocolate chip cookies

This recipe appears in *The River Cottage Family Cookbook* but I couldn't resist including it again here because these chewy, vanilla-rich treats are easy-peasy, taking no more than 10 minutes to make, and 10 to bake. Ideal when people turn up unexpectedly for tea, they are also a mainstay of rainy afternoon cooking sessions with the kids. No batch has ever been known to last till the next day.

Makes 14–16

125g unsalted butter
100g caster sugar
75g soft light brown sugar
1 medium egg, lightly beaten
2 teaspoons vanilla extract
150g plain flour
½ teaspoon baking powder
A pinch of sea salt
100g dark chocolate, chopped into smallish chunks (or use milk chocolate, if you prefer)

Gently melt the butter in a small saucepan. Put both sugars into a mixing bowl, pour in the melted butter and beat well with a wooden spoon. Beat in the egg and vanilla. Sift the flour, baking powder and salt into the bowl and stir them in, then add the chocolate. You should have a pretty sloppy sort of mixture.

Dot heaped dessertspoonfuls of the mixture on to 2 baking sheets lined with baking parchment, leaving a good 4cm in between each one as they really spread out. Place in an oven preheated to 190°C/ Gas Mark 5 and bake for 8–10 minutes, until the cookies are turning pale golden brown.

Remove from the oven and leave on the baking sheets for a couple of minutes to firm up. Then carefully lift the baking parchment on to a wire rack and leave to cool completely. Inevitably they will be eaten as soon as they are cool enough not to burn fingers.

VARIATION

Oat and raisin cookies

Leave out the chocolate and the vanilla extract. Add 2 tablespoons of honey to the butter before melting. Add ½ teaspoon of ground cinnamon to the flour, then add 50g jumbo oats, 100g raisins and 75g chopped, roasted hazelnuts to the batter before baking as above.

Honey brandy snaps

In the 1970s my Mum often used to make brandy snaps for her dinner parties and I always admired them hugely. They seemed so grown up and sophisticated, and learning to make them myself was a kind of coming of age.

They are excellent served with ice cream, panna cotta, mousses or fools, but don't underestimate the classic '70s approach of filling cigar-shaped tubes of brandy snap with whipped cream. Mum used to serve these treats alongside a simple fruit salad of sliced oranges or a compote of stewed rhubarb. Wonderful.

Makes about 15

50g unsalted butter, diced

50g caster sugar

50g honey

50g plain flour

1 teaspoon cider brandy (optional)

A good pinch of ground ginger (optional)

Gently heat the butter, sugar and honey in a saucepan, stirring occasionally, until the sugar has dissolved. Remove from the heat. Stir in the flour, mix until smooth, then add the brandy and/or ginger, if using.

Place heaped teaspoonfuls of the mixture on 2 baking sheets lined with baking parchment, spacing them about 10cm apart. Place in an oven preheated to 180°C/Gas Mark 4 and bake for 7–8 minutes, until brown and lacy. Remove from the oven and leave to cool for a minute or two.

Lift the brandy snaps off the baking sheet with a palette knife while still warm. To make a traditional cigar-tube shape, wrap each one loosely around the handle of a wooden spoon. To create an attractively curled, tuile-shaped biscuit, drape them over a rolling pin. Either way, leave to cool and set for a minute or so before removing. If they become too brittle to shape, simply put the baking sheet back in the oven for a minute or two to soften them up, then have another go.

Serve plain, with creamy desserts. Or fill with whipped cream, as in the picture, and they *are* your dessert.

Chocolate and beetroot brownies

The international success of the carrot cake has surely paved the way for experimenting with root vegetables in other cake recipes. Well, this is my contribution to the genre. It's a corker – rich and velvety, and a tad lighter than a traditional, fudgy brownie. Warm from the oven, it makes a good pudding brownie to serve with vanilla ice cream.

Makes about 20

250g unsalted butter, cut into cubes

250g dark chocolate (about 70 per cent cocoa solids), broken into pieces

3 medium eggs

250g caster sugar

A pinch of sea salt

150g self-raising flour (I use wholemeal, but white works well too)

250g beetroot, boiled until tender, cooled, peeled and grated

Grease a shallow baking tin, approximately 20 x 25cm, and line the base with baking parchment.

Put the butter and chocolate in a heatproof bowl. Set the oven at 180°C/Gas Mark 4 and put the bowl in it for a few minutes until the chocolate and butter start to melt. Stir, then put back into the oven for a few more minutes to melt completely. Of course, you could melt them together in the traditional way, over a pan of hot water, but it seems a shame not to exploit the warming oven.

Whisk the eggs and sugar together in a large bowl until combined, then beat in the melted chocolate and butter until smooth. Combine the salt with the flour, sift them over the chocolate mixture, then gently fold in with a large metal spoon. Fold in the grated beetroot – be careful not to over-mix or it will make the brownies tough.

Pour the mixture into the prepared tin and smooth the top with a spatula. Bake for 20–25 minutes; when the brownies are done, a knife or skewer inserted in the centre should come out with a few moist crumbs clinging to it. Don't be tempted to overcook them or they will be dry. Remove the tin from the oven and leave on a wire rack to cool before cutting into squares.

VARIATION

Plain chocolate brownies

With a little more sugar and a little less flour than the beetroot version, these are dense and fudgy – a classic brownie. They're very good served warm as a pud (see roast plum sorbet with chocolate brownies, page 360), but also excellent cold.

Follow the main recipe but increase the caster sugar to 275g, reduce the flour to 125g and add 1 teaspoon of vanilla extract to the egg and sugar mixture. Omit the beetroot.

Foolproof crème brûlée

This is an all-time classic, and deservedly so. My version – baked in ramekins in a bain marie – is guaranteed to avoid the potential pitfalls of custard that won't set or sugar that somehow scorches before it melts. Using soft brown sugar for the caramel top may not be authentic, but it has a lower melting point than caster sugar and behaves more predictably under the hot grill (or cook's blowtorch). You do need to make the custards well in advance, as chilling them thoroughly in the fridge before the final sugar melting is vital.

In summer and autumn I like to serve crème brûlée with a small bowl of fresh raspberries on the side. These can be eaten as 'sharpeners' between mouthfuls of creamy, sugary brûlée – or dropped right into the custard once the burned sugar top has been cracked.

Serves 6

500ml double cream
1 vanilla pod
100g caster sugar
6 medium egg yolks
About 3 tablespoons soft brown sugar

Pour the cream into a saucepan. Slit the vanilla pod open lengthways and scrape out the seeds into the cream with the tip of a sharp knife, then add the pod to the pan too. Scald the cream by bringing to just below boiling point, then taking off the heat. Leave for a few minutes to infuse with the vanilla.

Whisk the caster sugar and egg yolks together in a bowl, then slowly whisk in the hot, vanilla-infused cream. Strain through a fine sieve into a jug. Pour the custard into six 125ml ramekins or custard cups.

Stand the dishes in a roasting dish and surround with enough hand-hot water to come halfway up their sides. Place in an oven preheated to 150°C/Gas Mark 2 and bake for about 30 minutes until the custards are just set; they should still wobble a bit if you shake the dish gently. Lift out of the roasting dish and leave to cool, then chill thoroughly.

Sprinkle a very thin, even layer of soft brown sugar over each custard and put them under a very hot grill until the sugar melts and bubbles (or use a cook's blowtorch, if you have one). Leave to cool, return the ramekins to the fridge until the sugar is hard – just 15 minutes or so should do it – then serve.

VARIATION

Bramley or rhubarb crème brûlée

I sometimes put a little Bramley apple compote (page 339) or rhubarb compote (see page 344) in the ramekins before filling them with the custard. The compote should be tart, to cut the richness of the brûlée, and not too runny. Fill the ramekins between a quarter and a third of the way up with the compote, then pour in the custard to within 1–2mm of the top. Bake and finish as above.

Lemon sponge pudding

This is a simple, warming pudding for cold days. I love the way the lemon and sugar mixture forms a sweet but tangy goo at the bottom, which then becomes the top of the pud. Fridge-cold double cream is a must – in my house at least.

Serves 4–6

Finely grated zest and juice of 2 lemons
25g light muscovado or soft brown sugar
100g unsalted butter, softened
100g caster sugar
2 medium eggs
100g self-raising flour, sifted

Generously butter an 850ml pudding basin. Stir together the juice of 1 lemon and the brown sugar until the sugar dissolves, then tip it into the basin.

Cream together the butter, lemon zest and caster sugar until very light and fluffy. Beat in one egg at a time, adding a spoonful of flour with each, then fold in the remaining flour. Finally stir in the rest of the lemon juice. Spoon the mixture into the basin. The lemon juice and sugar mixture will rise up the side of the basin – don't worry about this, and don't attempt to stir it in with the batter.

Tie a double layer of buttered foil or baking parchment, buttered side down, over the top of the basin. Put a trivet, rack or upturned small heatproof plate in a large saucepan and stand the pudding on it. Pour in boiling water to come about halfway up the side of the basin, then cover the pan and bring to a very gentle simmer. Steam for 2 hours, topping up the boiling water a couple of times along the way.

Remove the foil and loosen the edges of the pudding with a knife. Place a plate on top, then invert the plate and basin and unmould the pudding. Enjoy the moment as the sauce trickles down the sponge like hot lava, and let your guests admire it, too. Then slice or divvy up with a large spoon and serve piping hot, with chilled double cream.

Eggy bready pudding

This is really a bread and butter pudding made with crumbs instead of slices of bread. It's easier to make – indeed, if you've ever struggled to get neat triangles of buttered bread to stay in serried ranks as you cover them in custard, then this is the recipe for you. What's more, I think it is even better than a traditional bread and butter pud. You can serve it, like rice pudding, with jam (tart fridge jams like the ones on page 50 are ideal) or with stewed/roasted rhubarb or plums.

Serves 4–6

50g unsalted butter
250ml whole milk
150ml double cream
2 medium eggs
2 medium egg yolks
75g caster sugar
125g coarse, slightly
stale white breadcrumbs

Generously grease a small ovenproof dish with some of the butter. Combine the milk and cream in a saucepan, bring to just below simmering point, then remove from the heat.

Whisk the eggs, egg yolks and all but 1 tablespoon of the sugar together in a bowl, then gradually whisk the hot milk and cream into the egg mixture to form a custard. Stir about 75g of the breadcrumbs into the custard and leave to soak for half an hour so the crumbs plump up.

Spoon the mixture into the buttered dish. Melt the rest of the butter and combine it with the remaining breadcrumbs and sugar. Scatter this mixture over the pudding.

Place in an oven preheated to 180°C/Gas Mark 4 and bake for 30 minutes or until golden and just set, but with a bit of wobble left in the middle. Serve hot with jam or stewed fruit.

VARIATIONS

Boozy fruity eggy bready pudding

For a richer pud, soak 75g raisins in 4 tablespoons of rum or cider brandy for several hours or overnight, then stir them into the breadcrumb custard before transferring to the baking dish.

Lemon curd eggy bready pudding

Lightly marble a few blobs of good lemon curd into the breadcrumb custard once it's in the dish, before you add the breadcrumb topping.

Fudge

Buttery, crumbly home-made fudge, dissolving on the tongue in a rush of creamy sweetness, is a wonderful indulgence. It's also very quick to knock up a batch, so this is a brilliant recipe for a rainy afternoon. You do, however, need a sugar thermometer – available from any good kitchen shop and not expensive. A box of fudge is, of course, a lovely home-made present, but I also like to serve tiny squares with coffee after a meal.

Makes 35–40 small squares

300g caster sugar
1 tablespoon golden syrup
100g unsalted butter, cut into chunks
100ml double cream
1 teaspoon vanilla extract

Using a few drops of sunflower oil on a piece of kitchen paper, lightly oil a 15 x 22cm baking dish, or small dish with similar dimensions.

Put the sugar, syrup, butter and cream in a heavy-based saucepan, making sure it is not more than a third full, as the mixture will bubble up when it boils. Heat gently, stirring all the time, until the sugar has completely dissolved – tip the pan to make sure there are no crystals still visible on the base.

Stop stirring, put a sugar thermometer in the pan and turn up the heat. Let the mixture boil hard until it reaches 116°C (soft-ball stage). This may happen quite fast, or take 15 minutes or more, depending on the heat of your hob and the conductivity of your pan – so keep a sharp eye on the thermometer. Take the pan off the heat and leave to stand for 10 minutes.

Add the vanilla and beat vigorously until the mixture thickens, becomes slightly grainy and starts to come away from the base of the pan. This can take up to 10 minutes, so you might want to use an electric whisk. Tip it into the prepared dish, smooth the top with a metal spoon and leave to cool.

Mark it into squares with a small, sharp knife while it's still slightly soft, then leave for 3 or 4 hours to firm up completely. Remove from the dish and store in an airtight container.

VARIATIONS

Salted pecan fudge
Omit the vanilla. Add 100g lightly toasted, roughly chopped pecans (or walnuts) and 1 level teaspoon of best-quality flaky sea salt before beating the fudge.

Chocolate fudge
Replace the vanilla with 50g sifted cocoa powder.

Chocolate ginger fudge
Omit the vanilla and add 2 finely chopped knobs of preserved stem ginger along with 50g sifted cocoa powder before beating the fudge.

index

acknowledgements

I've really enjoyed writing this book, not least because of the fantastic support and input of so many talented people.

This is a volume that celebrates the joys of good family food, and I am forever deeply grateful that I have such a lovely family to cook for. Thank you Marie, to whom this book is dedicated, and Chloe, Oscar and Freddie, not only for your tireless work as tasters-in-chief, but for the inspiration you give me, every day. I love cooking for you, and with you. And I love it when you cook for me!

Very special thanks to my sister Sophy and her family, Nick, Max and Guy. Sophy tested many of the recipes in these pages and her/their careful critiques and excellent suggestions have made this a much better book. My Mum and Dad have helped no less, if more subliminally, by encouraging me for as long as I can remember to enjoy my cooking, and theirs.

This would simply not be a River Cottage book without Simon Wheeler's stunning photography. He makes it look easy – but I know it's not. I'm absolutely thrilled with the way the book looks, for which I must also thank Lawrence Morton, for his gorgeous, elegant design work, and Mariko Jesse, for her lovely, witty graffiti.

I've worked with my publisher Richard Atkinson for a decade now, and I could not wish for a more supportive, collaborative or conscientious editor. The team at Bloomsbury have worked so hard and given so much to the book: Penny Edwards, in Production, and Natalie Hunt, in Editorial, have made complicated tasks invisible and seamless.

Jane Middleton has, as ever, provided faultless copy-editing, recipe testing and many inspired suggestions for changes and improvements. And project editor Janet Illsley has calmly and skilfully brought the whole thing together, guiding us through the tricky final stages. Thank you all.

My huge appreciation and thanks also go to Debora Robertson, for her knowledge, enthusiasm and effort in editing and testing so many of the recipes. And to Nikki Duffy, my right hand foodie and first call sounding board, thank you once again. You're brilliant, and it's a total joy working with you.

My team at River Cottage has, of course, played a crucial part in the creation of this book. Immeasurable thanks to Jess Upton, my marvellous PA, who has organised everything with her trademark efficiency, good-humour and élan. Thank you to my chefs Gill Meller, Daniel Stevens, Nonie Dwyer and Tim Maddams for their incredible hard work, ideas and inspiration. Thanks to Mark Diacono, Victoria Moorey and the River Cottage garden team for supplying wonderful produce and ideas too; to Steven Lamb and Ellie Geraghty for looking after River Cottage, body and soul; to Pam 'the jam' Corbin for a number of invaluable tips; and to Cat Streatfeild for ensuring our many photoshoots ran smoothly. To Andrew Palmer and Zam Baring, Stephen Leigh and Jacky Sloane, and the team at Keo Films, thank you all for your hard work, support and patience. And thank you, Rob Love, for your passion and commitment to all things River Cottage.

And finally, thanks to Antony Topping, the best agent I (or anyone else) could possibly have.

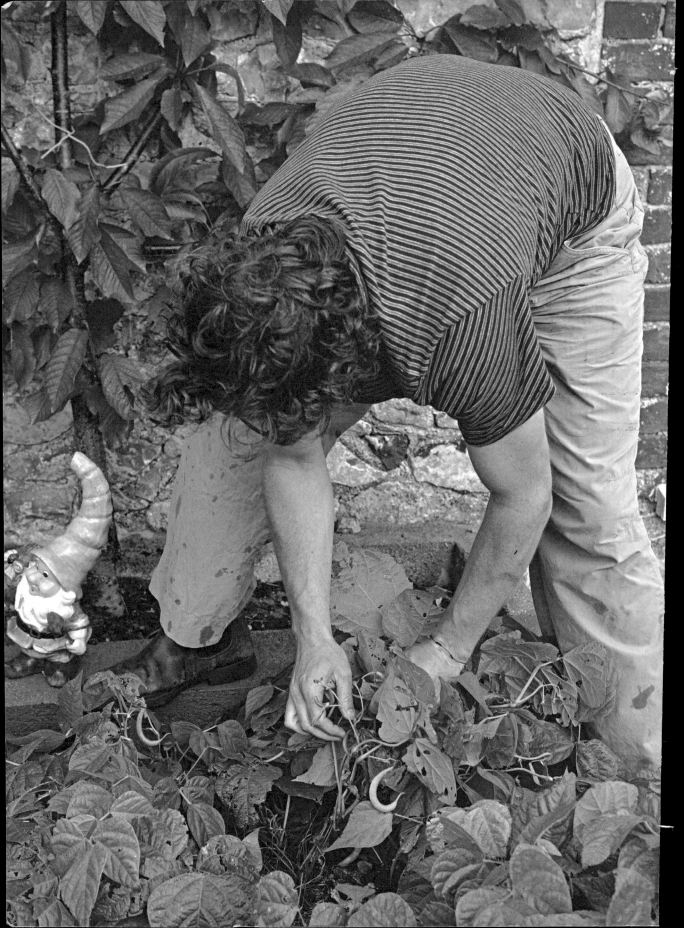